The Challenge of Teaching Social Studies in the Elementary School

The Challenge of Teaching Social Studies in the Elementary School

Second Edition

Dorothy J. Skeel
Indiana University

with assistance from
Ronald E. Sterling

GOODYEAR PUBLISHING COMPANY, INC.
Pacific Palisades, California

Library of Congress Cataloging in Publication Data

Skeel, Dorothy J
    The challenge of teaching social studies in the elementary school,
second edition.

    (Goodyear education series)
    Includes bibliographical references.
    1. Social sciences—Study and teaching (Elementary)
I.   Sterling, Ronald E.   II. Title.
LB1584.S52 1974   372.8′3′044   73-90610
ISBN 0-87620-174-5

Copyright © 1974 by
GOODYEAR PUBLISHING COMPANY, INC.
Pacific Palisades, California

Y-1745-2

ISBN: 0-87620-174-2

Library of Congress Catalog Card Number: 73-90610

Current printing (last digit)
10 9 8 7 6 5 4 3 2

Printed in the United States of America

TO JEFF, SHELLY, AND JILL—

*May they view their changing world
as an exciting stimulating place to live.*

Contents

Preface xi

PART I Introduction 1

CHAPTER 1 What Is Social Studies? 3

Objectives of the Social Studies 4

Developing Objectives 6

Contributions of the Social Sciences 13

Summary 19

CHAPTER 2 Social Studies Curriculum Development 23

Local 26

State 35

National 40

Summary 49

PART II Methodology 53

CHAPTER 3 Problem Solving Through Inquiry 55

Questioning 57

Classroom Conditions 60

Role of the Teacher 60

Objectives 62

Problem Selection 64

Problem-Solving Activities 67

Advantages and Disadvantages of
Problem Solving Through Inquiry 79

CHAPTER **4**   Unit Development 83

Objectives 84

Unit Selection 87

Directing Children's Interests 89

Development of a Unit 90

Teacher/Pupil Planning for the Unit 93

Individual and Group Activities 96

Integrating Activities 97

Culminating Activities 98

Bibliography 99

Evaluation 99

A Sample Resource Unit 100

Advantages and Disadvantages of Unit Teaching 104

CHAPTER **5**   Structure (Conceptual Framework)
As A Method Of Teaching 107

Definition of Concept and Structure 107

Philosophy of the Approach 113

Multidisciplinary Program   105

Interdisciplinary Program 116

Advantages and Disadvantages 121

CHAPTER **6**   Teaching The Disadvantaged 123

Objectives 126

Selection of Content 130

Special Instructional Considerations 134

Role of the Disadvantaged Child in the Classroom '142

PART III Selected Content For Emphasis 147

CHAPTER 7 Teaching Current Affairs—Social, Economic, Political, And Environmental 149

When To Start 150
Suggested Activities 152
Controversial Issues:
Social, Economic, Political, and Environmental 157
Social 158
Economic 160
Political 161
Environmental 162

CHAPTER 8 International Understanding 167

Rationale for Spaceship Earth 167
Guidelines for Selecting Cultures for Study 171
When to Start 172
Atmosphere of the Classroom 176
Activities Toward International Understanding 178

PART IV Skill Development 187

CHAPTER 9 The Skills Of Valuing 191

Rationale 191
Teaching Strategies for Valuing 194

CHAPTER 10 Working In Committees 203

What Is To Be Gained 203
Intellectual Skills 206
Written Reports 213
Graphic Reports 214
Social Skills 214

CHAPTER **11**   Map And Globe Skills   217

  Skills by Grade Levels 218
  Other Suggested Activities 221
  Problems to Determine the Extent
  of Children's Skills 223
  Using Interest Centers To Increase skills 226
  Urban Map Skills 226
  Maps and Globes 227

PART **V**   Utilization Of Materials 233

CHAPTER**12**   Utilization Of Materials
        In The Social Studies 234

  Children's Trade Books 234
  Simulations and Games 237
  Programmed Material 239
  Cartoons 240
  Graphs and Charts 242
  Pictures 246
  Textbooks 246
  Multimedia Kits 249
  Films and Filmstrips 249
  Free and Inexpensive Materials 250

PART **VI**   Evaluation 253

CHAPTER **13**   Evaluation of Social Studies Instruction 255

  In the Classroom 255
  Methods of Evaluation 257
  Local 271
  National 273

Notes 276
Index 285

Preface

Teaching social studies in the elementary school presents a challenge to any teacher, new or experienced. This challenge results from the unique content of the social studies and its contribution to the child's understanding of his world. The content of the social studies is derived from the social sciences, which investigate the actions of human beings. In teaching social studies, teachers attempt to help children to understand the actions of human beings (from the earliest times to the present) so that they can enter society with the knowledge and skills that will enable them to operate effectively within it. Our democratic form of government requires that its citizens be knowledgeable about democracy as well as about other ideologies. The responsibility of imparting this knowledge rests heavily with the social studies.

These challenges would be sufficient without the added concern of selecting appropriate content, teaching methods, and materials to successfully achieve the goals of social studies in the elementary school. The wide divergence in current social studies curricula, the many suggested methods of teaching, and an overabundance of available materials confounds the teacher's task. This text is designed to aid social studies teachers by presenting the current thinking in all these areas.

The text first discusses the importance of social studies in preparing children to enter the mainstream of society. Second, the text delineates social studies programs that have been prepared at the local state, and national level—discussing their rationale, content, method, and materials. Next, several methods of teaching social studies are indicated—including problem solving through inquiry, unit development, a method from the structure (conceptual framework) of the social science disciplines, and a method for teaching the disadvantaged.

The second half of the text presents activities for practical application of the theories in teaching current affairs—including social, economic, political, and environmental—international understanding, skill development in valuing, committee work, and map and globe skills. Also included is a discussion of the selection and utilization of materials and of the important aspect of evaluation of instruction at the classroom, local, state, and national levels.

One of the difficult but pleasurable tasks of an author is to in some way acknowledge the individuals who have assisted in the preparation of the manuscript. Dr. John D. McAulay, a faithful advisor and friend, is acknowledged as the person who stimulated my interest in social studies. Without that thoughtful stimulation, the original work and this revision would not have occurred.

My parents, Mr. and Mrs. Kenneth S. Skeel, surely must not be forgotten for they so frequently have provided the encouragement needed for me to continue my task of learning.

Those individuals who have made this revision possible are Ronald E. Sterling, who contributed chapter 8 on International Understanding and provided many helpful ideas; James P. Levy and David Grady of Goodyear Publishing, who had faith in my writing; Dr. Joseph Howard, Eastern Kentucky University, who diligently reviewed the writing; and Mrs. Margaret Taylor, who typed the manuscript from indistinguishable notes.

Dorothy J. Skeel

The Challenge of Teaching Social Studies in the Elementary School

PART *I*

Introduction

What is social studies? What purpose does this subject serve in the elementary school curriculum? Teachers often ask these questions when they are planning a program of learning experiences for children. Many teachers are bewildered by the complicated problem of combining the proper mixture of reading, writing, arithmetic, science, art, music, health and physical education, as well as numerous other suggested activities. They wonder how social studies can be included in an already crowded schedule, and even more relevant, if the subject is really that important.

Part one attempts to answer these questions by discussing the meaning of social studies as it relates to the child's world. The development of objectives for the social studies is discussed in behavioral or performance terms. This section also outlines social studies programs that have been established at local, state, and national levels and delineates the rationale, objectives, sample content, and activities of each program.

CHAPTER 1

What Is
Social Studies?

Many authors have tangled with the problem of defining the social studies. To some, it means interpreting the social sciences in order to make them understandable to children. To some, it's decision making and value clarification; while others define it as problem solving. To this author, social studies is the area of the curriculum where the child learns about human actions: how to understand himself, other people, and his environment and how these elements interact with one another. In the process of learning about human actions, the child uses the knowledge of the social sciences; he learns to make decisions and to clarify his values as he comes to understand himself, and he acquires the skill of problem solving as he lives and works with others.

If our children are to live effective, productive lives, they must know something about themselves as humans—their feelings, their worth as individuals. They must know something about other peoples: how they are different, why they have different values, why they live differently, as well as understand the common characteristics that make all peoples alike. They must know something about their world: why it operates the way it does, where it's going and why.

In a country of rapid technological changes (men on the moon), whose basic institutions have been challenged (democracy on the defensive), that has encountered such violent acts of man against man (war, hijacking, terrorism), and endangered its own existence by its pollution, the importance of studying social studies cannot be minimized. Unless children early in their schooling acquire an understanding of and skills to cope with these problems, and even more importantly, an attitude that reflects concern for their world, it is doubtful that later attempts will prove fruitful.

If social studies is defined as the study of human actions and is a crucial area of the curriculum, how does one teach it? How do children learn to understand themselves and others? How do they develop good self-concepts? How do they acquire knowledge and understanding of their own environment and other cultures? How do children acquire skills in communicating, cooperating, problem solving, inquiring, decision making, and valuing?

Should the teacher present a hierarchy of the concepts from the social sciences? Should he use the method of unit organization or inquiry through problem solving? What considerations should be made for children who are culturally different? What is the best method of teaching social studies in the elementary school? Is one method more effective than another, or should a combination of methods be used? This text presents the philosophy and procedures of several current methods and suggests that teachers try them and select the method that proves most effective for them and their children.

OBJECTIVES OF THE SOCIAL STUDIES

The objectives specified for a social studies curriculum will vary in accordance with the teacher's viewpoint concerning the major purpose of social studies. A teacher may consider this major purpose to be the development of skill in understanding human relationships, the acquiring of the skills of the social scientists, the development of skill in solving problems, or a combination of these. Whatever purpose the teacher selects, his choice will determine the objectives of his program. If he sees the main purpose of the social studies as a responsibility to help children develop skill in and an understanding of human relationships, his broad objectives necessarily would be:

To develop the student's understanding of himself.

To develop the student's ability to work cooperatively in a group toward the completion of a task.

To increase the student's understanding of the varying abilities of individuals and of the worth of each individual.

To encourage the student's understanding of his own culture and of the cultures of the world and to develop his appreciation for the contributions of each culture to our heritage.

To develop the student's skill in the art of communicating with others through verbal and nonverbal means.

However, if the teacher views the purpose of social study as Clements, Fielder, and Tabachnick to be

the process of learning about variety and change in the actions of people as they arrange to live together in groups. This learning goes on through the gathering of social data, as well as through critical examination of the conclusions and generalizations of social scientists.[1]

his goals might be:

To develop in children the ability to evaluate interpretation, i.e., to use evidence to test ideas.

To provide children with the opportunity to write about how they think and feel about the world in which they live.

To lead individuals to examine the circumstances of their lives, to question the values they have been taught, to become to some extent responsible for their own views.

To develop the ability to use primary documents, a variety of interpretations of past and present events, records, and artifacts that relate what has been and is going on in the world.[2]

If the main purpose of social studies is thought to be the presentation of the concepts of a social science, such as the anthropology project of the Education Development Center, the objectives are stated thus:

To confront children with a number of opportunities to observe and ponder about the lives of other animals to help them think concretely about what it means to be human.

To furnish children with a vocabulary and a frame of reference for thinking about human behavior.

To explore the intriguing fact that survival is a common concern for all living organisms, including man, and that the mechanisms for insuring survival and continuity of life are extremely numerous and diverse.

To reflect upon the extent to which man, in all his cultural diversity, is united by universally adaptive propensities.[3]

The divergence of opinion concerning the purpose of social studies magnifies the task of the teacher. Before he can complete his basic task of determining the objectives of his program and his method of approach, he must first decide what he considers to be the purpose or purposes of social studies. His decision should be based on

1. the experiential background of the students
2. the intellectual abilities of the students
3. the availability of materials necessary for his approach
4. the goals for the total curriculum of the school
5. the societal factors that affect each and all of us

DEVELOPING OBJECTIVES

Too frequently, objectives for instruction are stated in vague, meaningless terms. Objectives so stated are difficult to implement in the classroom and they do not communicate to others what is to be accomplished by learning experiences. Numerous educators contend, however, that objectives stated in behavioral terms do lend themselves to observation and measurement. Robert Mager defines an objective as

... an intent communicated by a statement describing a proposed change in a learner—a statement of what the learner is to be like when he has successfully completed a learning experience. It is a description of a pattern of behavior (performance) we want the learner to be able to demonstrate.[4]

Mager indicates that when a teacher is writing objectives, either in behavioral or performance terms, it is advisable to include the following information:

First, identify the terminal behavior by name; we can specify the kind of behavior which will be accepted as evidence that the learner has achieved the objective.

Second, try to further define the desired behavior by describing the important conditions under which the behavior will be expected to occur.

Third, specify the criteria of acceptable performance by describing how well the learner must perform to be considered acceptable.[5]

Each objective need not include all of the above information. Initially, objectives are written in broad terms to indicate the type of subject matter to be covered. Secondly, specific objectives are written in behavioral or performance terms to indicate the behavior expected of the individual after he has been exposed to the subject matter. An example of a broad objective is:

The student will acquire knowledge of the history of Mexico to enable him to understand the customs and traditions of that country.

This objective made more specific and stated in behavioral terms might be:

The student will:

Compare and contrast several of the Christmas customs and traditions of Mexico with those of the United States.

7

Identify two of the traditions sacred to Mexican families.

List at least one of the Mexican holidays that is different from those celebrated in the United States.

On the other side of the argument are those educators who believe that behavioral objectives standardize instruction and aim at only measureable results, thus eliminating learning that is self-directed, unstructured, and unpredictable. These educators would recommend objectives that are "specified" rather than "behavioral"; specified by a teacher according to his philosophy and taking into consideration the talents and choices of the children.[6]

The important aspect of stating objectives is whether or not the teacher has communicated what is to be accomplished by the instruction. Not all of the results of social studies instruction (e.g., values, attitudes) can be measured nor is it necessary to attempt this, but the teacher will want to have some means of determining the success of his efforts.

Objectives of the social studies are grouped into four areas: knowledge, understanding, values and attitudes, and skills. Knowledge and understanding are a part of the cognitive (knowing) domain; values and attitudes are a part of the cognitive, as well as the affective (e.g., prizing, feeling) domains; and skills are abilities or proficiencies.

Knowledge

In the social studies, as in any subject, children should not be required to learn facts or knowledge merely to become walking versions of a book. The knowledge they are to acquire should be selected on the basis of its capacity to further their understanding. For example, it would be better to learn that Washington became president of the new nation because the people trusted the leadership he exhibited during the Revolution than merely to memorize the fact that he was our first president. Rather than learn the names of the states and their capitals to reel them off in rote fashion, it would be better for students to learn that state capitals are generally located near the center of the states to better serve the people of that state.

Objectives developed in the area of knowledge are selected to further an understanding. An example of such an objective would be:

The student will acquire knowledge of the minority groups of the United States to better understand how much they contribute to our society.

Understanding

One of the most important aspects of the social studies is the area of understanding. Obviously, facts are of little value unless they increase one's understanding of a subject or problem. Understanding requires the individual to synthesize several pieces of information and relate them to one another to comprehend the connection between the previous knowledge and the newly acquired information. Understanding of a problem is essential before an individual can attempt to solve it. With understanding, various pieces of information can be fitted together for a possible solution.

Measurement of an individual's achievement in the area of understanding becomes difficult unless the individual applies this synthesized knowledge to a new situation. Therefore, objectives under the heading of understanding must include this application.

Examples of objectives for the area of understanding are:

The student will understand that individual abilities differ, and will show this understanding by his ready acceptance of people.

He will understand that the mobility of people is dependent upon a variety of individual goals such as adventure and greater opportunity, and he will identify the different goals of groups he has encountered.

Attitudes and Values

Attitude is a continuing area of concern in the social studies, because it is believed that attitudes determine behavior. An attitude is defined as a relatively enduring organization of beliefs about an object or situation that causes an individual to respond in some manner. A belief

within an attitude organization is conceived to have three components: a *cognitive* component, because it represents a person's knowledge, held with varying degrees of certitude, about what is true or false, good or bad, desirable or undesirable; an *affective* component, because under suitable conditions the belief is capable of arousing affect of varying intensity . . . when its validity is questioned; and a behavioral component, because the belief . . . must lead to some action when it is suitably activated.[7]

Therefore, the cognitive component may affect an attitude as knowledge is acquired about a particular situation, such as viewing films of the modern cities in Africa would change the belief that Africans only live in grass huts. The affective component may be activated by confrontation with behavior that is inconsistent with the individual's belief "on how one should behave in that situation." For example, the teacher displays an interest in and appreciation for the primitive art of Africa and the child has always believed this type of art was "junky." The child will be required to reassess his attitude toward the artwork. The atmosphere of the classroom affects the attitudes developed. If a teacher is attempting to develop an attitude regarding the importance of recognizing the worth of the individual, but does not allow each person to express his opinion nor accept the contributions of each member of the group, it is doubtful that he will convey this attitude successfully to his pupils.

Measurement of attitude is best accomplished by observing the behavior of individuals in a given situation. Undoubtedly, there will be occasions when children will display the actions they feel are expected of them, thereby making measurement difficult. And there also will be times when teachers misunderstand or misjudge the behavior of children and are unable to assess their real feelings or emotions.

Examples of objectives for the area of attitudes are:

The student appreciates that cooperative behavior is necessary to accomplish certain tasks and willingly offers to work with others.

The student values the contributions to our heritage of the many subcultures and expresses an appreciation for them.

" . . . a value, unlike an attitude, is a standard or yardstick to guide actions, attitudes, comparisons, evaluations, and justification of self and others."[8] "A person's value system may thus be said to represent a learned organization of rules for making choices and for resolving conflicts—between two or more modes of behavior or between two or more endstates of existence."[9] Values are much more difficult to change since they are generally learned early in the socialization process, at home and within the peer group.

Previously, values often were taught by the process of indoctrination, where the teacher indicated what was right or wrong based on his own value system. However, studies have indicated that there are stages of development and that the school can best influence the child's values by helping him to grow into the advanced stages of personal development. Children can be helped to clarify their own value positions through the experience of analyzing conflicting value situations and exploring their own feelings and values in different situations. An example of an objective in the valuing area would be:

The student will clarify his value position when confronted with a problem situation by listing alternative solutions, their consequences, and value issues.

Skills

A skill is defined as the ability to become capable or proficient at performing a task or tasks. In stating objectives for this area, the individual's potential should be determined. Because skills are developmental, an acceptable achievement level varies according to the individual,s maturation level. For example, a primary-grade child cannot be expected to perform certain skills with the same proficiency as would an intermediate-grade child.

Skills are developed sequentially—some must be acquired before others. For example, a child must learn to read before he can acquire skill in locating information; or he must understand spatial relationships before he can develop skill in map reading. Skills are divided into three subgroups: social, intellectual, and motor.

Social skills are concerned with the interaction of individuals within a group. Obviously, children who are unable to get along with members of their own class or who constantly display uncooperative behavior will find it difficult to understand and appreciate the necessity for establishing cooperation among other groups or nations. A teacher must first strive to develop the social skills within the classroom. Examples of such objectives would be:

The child will develop leadership ability by assuming the role of committee chairman.

The child will acquire skill in cooperative planning by working in committees.

Intellectual skills include skill in doing research, critical thinking, problem solving, making oral and written reports, outlining, and taking notes. The development of these skills need not be limited to the social studies; they offer an excellent opportunity for integration, especially with the language arts. For example, critical thinking can be introduced in reading and then applied in the social studies. Examples of such objectives would be:

The child will select the important point of a paragraph.

The child will demonstrate his use and understanding of the seven-color key of a map.

Motor skills include proficiency in manipulative activities such as construction, painting, and drawing. Sample objectives would be:

The child will demonstrate skill in the use of a variety of media, including paint, chalk, and charcoal.

The child will construct a relief map using plasticene.

Continued practice is essential to ensure increased proficiency of skills. Some skills which will be practiced relate only to the social studies, while other skills could be used in any of the subject areas.

A crucial part of any social studies program is the development of a set of relevant objectives. Such objectives are related to purposes, understandable to all, and many can be measured by the student's behavior. For instruction to be valuable, the teacher should have a clear idea of how his instruction will affect his students' behavior.

CONTRIBUTIONS OF THE SOCIAL SCIENCES

The content of the social studies is derived from the social sciences, which study the actions of humans engaged in the process of living. Each of the social sciences contributes its method of inquiry and its knowledge of human actions. Each of the social sciences (history, geography, political science, economics, sociology, anthropology, psychology, and philosophy) views humans from a different vantage point and uses a unique method of inquiry to acquire its knowledge. What are the vantage points, methods of inquiry, and contributions of each social science?

History

The historian looks at the past, from which he attempts to obtain a record of human actions. Because he can find only facts that have been preserved, his record is limited. Basically his method of inquiry is to collect as much data as possible, organize and test it. In his reconstruction of the facts, the historian extrapolates, using the bias within his own frame of reference. Thus, to fully understand the historian's record of the past, we must know his particular frame of reference. His primary purpose is to interpret the present through an understanding of the past, and in so doing, to chart a general course for the future.[10]

The contribution of history is its accumulation of knowledge of the past, which provides meaningful insight into what is happening

13

in the present and what to expect in the future. It can be an explanation of the cause and effect relationship of events. Events do not occur in a vacuum—something must precipitate them and something will be effected by them.

The contribution of history to the social studies is illustrated in this example. Suppose you were studying the local community with your class. The children do not understand why their community grew as a railroad town because now the railroad line is no longer used. It would be necessary to pursue the historical development of the community to learn how it was started, why it grew, and the possible basis for discontinuing the railroad.

Geography

The geographer views man in terms of his physical environment and its effect upon his actions. The geographer describes the characteristics of places on the earth, distinguishing one area from another and categorizing them into regions. He is interested in man's activities in these regions to determine whether man is dominated by his environment or has learned to cope with it. In learning to cope with his environment, man—working within his cultural framework—has utilized the available resources and given character to the region.

The geographer's primary method of inquiry is the regional approach, whereby a geographical area is identified "in terms of the specific criteria chosen to delimit it from other regions."[11] The criteria include conditions such as climate, land form, vegetation, manufacturing industries, and internal organization.

Geography's contribution to the social studies is best described by Broek:

The geographer must learn about the biophysical features of the earth; is deeply interested in the interrelations between society and habitat; needs to read the cultural landscape as the earth-engraved expression of man's activity; inspects and compares distributional patterns and formulates concepts and principles.[12]

Applying the geographer's method to the previously stated problem of the former railroad community, you would investigate the land along the railroad line and discover that it follows the flatland along the river, which may have been the best natural location for the railroad. Also, the community was built at the bend in the river where rich soils had been deposited that are good for growing crops.

Political Science

Man's attempt to bring order to his life is the concern of the political scientist. He studies man's methods of organizing society in terms of authority at both the family and national level. The political scientist seeks to discover why man extends legitimacy of authority—whether by custom, morality, or legality. He is primarily concerned with the functions and levels of government that extend to all people in society. Political parties, lobbies, and individual powers who provide decision-making policies are also of interest to the political scientist.

In recent years, this method of inquiry has become intent upon building a science of political phenomena to express political behavior "in generalizations of theories with explanatory and predictive value."[13] One application of the behaviorists' theory is evident in the study of voting behavior. The behaviorists attempt to discover who votes and why and to generalize from these findings.

Contributing to our knowledge of human actions, the political scientist provides basic information concerning processes, behavior, and institutions of political behavior; political relations among nations; and public policies and ideas about government such as democracy, justice, and equality.[14]

As the political scientist views the problem of the railroad community, he would investigate the existing state laws to determine whether any of them, such as excessive taxes or labor restrictions, might have threatened the railroad company. In addition, he would study whether government intervention or aid would have helped the railroad to continue in its operations.

15

Economics

An economist's major concern is man's ability to adjust his unlimited wants to his limited resources. The economist is interested in man's use of these resources, both human and physical, in producing goods and services and distributing them among people. He seeks to answer questions of what, how, when, and for whom to produce.

Different societies produce different economic systems. "A primary task of economics is to explain both the essential similarities and the nature of the differences in the economic life of different people, so that man may be better able to understand the conditions under which he lives and the alternatives that are open to him."[15]

If the goals of society (e. g., full employment) are not reached, economists attempt to explain this failure and to suggest solutions for fulfillment. Much economic information involves facts and figures, which are measurable and objective. However, the search for answers to economic questions also involves factors such as judgments of conflicting interests and goals, which are immeasurable. The economist contributes knowledge of economic activity in terms of the individual as well as how the system works and the problems encountered.

The economist would define the problem of the discontinuation of the railroad in terms of whether or not it was profitable for the company. If not, is there something the community could do, such as stopping their shipments of products by trucks, to increase railroad business. Also, the economist would investigate whether the community should encourage new industry that would need extensive use of the railroad to come to town.

Sociology

The interactions of individuals with one another and in their associations are of concern to the sociologist. He is interested in man's membership in groups such as the family, school, church, and government. He studies groups—their internal organization, their maintenance processes, and the relations between members. He attempts to determine the influence of these groups upon their members—to recognize the behavioral changes then exhibited by the members.

The sociologist contributes his knowledge of social institutions (where man has organized in groups). He studies their members, behavior, objectives, norms, roles, values, authority, realia, and location. He describes the social processes, from the simplest interaction to socialization, cooperation, competition, and conflict. He attempts to explain why members of a group behave as they do.

The sociologist is restricted in his inquiry to the information he can observe among and within groups and to that which people are willing to tell him. Many private aspects of human behavior are unavailable to him unless people reveal them through question-naires, recordings, or interviews.

The sociologist would be concerned with the effect of the railroad on the groups in the community. Particularly, he would investigate how families would be affected by the discontinuation of the railroad service. If the fathers no longer had jobs, how would this affect the family life? Could they find other work to do? Did the railroad provide any social life for the family in the form of trips to the city or vacations? Had particular types of businesses and services developed to meet the needs of the railroad people? Would these be needed any longer?

Another aspect of the sociologist's concern would be how the railroad had effected the ethnic composition of the community. Had the railroad drawn to the town certain groups of people such as the Germans, Irish, the Polish, or the Italian? Were these groups still living together in certain sections of town?

Anthropology

The anthropologist views man biologically as he adapts to his environment. These adaptations compose man's culture—his cus-toms, laws, beliefs, physical characteristics, and language. An-thropology is primarily concerned with non-Western cultures, although there is increased interest in the study of complex modern societies such as the United States and Europe. Anthropological study involves searching for the artifacts of early cultures, attempting to date their existence, and trying to formulate an understanding of their structure and general characteristics, as well as learning about cultures as they exist today.

Methods of inquiry employed by the anthropologist include field study, whether it is archaeological digging for remains of early people or living with the people whose present culture is being studied. The anthropologist analyzes and classifies the information he collects. Thus, extensive knowledge about the culture of man is provided—knowledge of sources of words in language, physical attributes of different races, customs of marriage and religion, and behavior patterns of members of the cultures.

The anthropologist would view the problem in relation to the total community. What impact had the railroad made on the cultural development of the community? Would the community have been different if the railroad had not been there? Many of the children might have gone to college if they had not found jobs with the railroad. Were the social patterns of the community a result of the types of jobs men held with the railroad?

Psychology and Philosophy

Only recently have psychology and philosophy been included in the social studies, and their contributions become more important as we attempt to help children to understand themselves and the values they possess.

Psychology is man's attempt to understand himself and the actions of those around him. The discipline is involved with the search for the cause-effect relationships of human behavior, and thus, the ability to make predictions about future behavior. Generally, the inquiry is directed toward individuals or small groups.

Philosophy is the search for and the accumulation of truths about reality, value, logic, and knowledge. It has been called the mother of the other sciences—as the individual areas of knowledge increased, they separated from the parent. Philosophy is broad and inclusive and has been described as "an attempt to discover the whole truth about everything."[16]

SUMMARY

Throughout the preceding discussion of the contributions of the social sciences, the tremendous overlapping of the subject areas is obvious. As a result of this overlapping, combinations of the sciences appear such as social psychology, cultural geography, political sociology, cultural history, and economic geography.

The tables that follow should further clarify the contributions of the social sciences and their relationship to social studies.

Table 1.1 illustrates the major concepts and methods of inquiry of each of the social sciences. In addition, it identifies how each of the social sciences makes an important contribution to the social studies. Then in Table 1.2, the concepts, information (pertinent definitions), and generalizations from the social sciences are illustrated as each aspect relates directly to the topic "The Community."

ANTHROPOLOGY

Major concepts
similarities and differences of physical and cultural characteristics of man
relationship of aspects of a culture to whole of a culture
Method of inquiry
archaeological excavations
field studies

Importance
describes the variety of human behavior and aids in the understanding of different cultures

SOCIOLOGY

Major concepts
group life-institutions; small, voluntary stratified groups
relationships among groups
individual's role in the group
Method of inquiry
observation
theorizing
testing theories through questionnaires and interviews
Importance
deals with social forces in our lives and the forces in the lives of others applicable to us

ECONOMICS

Major concepts
human wants are greater than available resources
scarcity, specialization, interdependence, market, public policy
Method of inquiry
definition of problems
analysis of causes
prediction of effects

Importance
deals in economic reality—an important part of everyday living

SOCIAL STUDIES

HISTORY

Major concepts
understanding of the events of the past and how they are related to the present and future

Method of inquiry
collection of available information
testing of information

Importance
aids in understanding of the past, helps slow mistakes, and possible ways to avoid them in the future

GEOGRAPHY

Major concepts
likeness and difference of earth's surface
relationship of physical environment to humans
origins and composition of a group of people as a result of its geography
Method of inquiry
regional method—one region is subdivided into climate, vegetation, land forms
mapping and direct observation
Importance
aids in understanding the relationship between man and his surroundings and in understanding physical features of the earth

POLITICAL SCIENCE

Major concepts
public processes of political systems
ideas and doctrines about government

Method of inquiry
case study
historical development
comparative study

Importance
encourages active participation in the political process and clarifies cognitive images of governments

Table 1.1 Major Concepts, Methods of Inquiry, and Importance of Each of the Social Sciences

ANTHROPOLOGY

Concepts
ethnicity
cultural contributions

Information
ethnic—relating to groups of people with the same ancestry
cultural contributions—shared and diverse values, activities, dress, customs, artifacts

Generalization
cultural contributions are not the monopoly of any one ethnic group

SOCIOLOGY

Concepts
groups—family, friendship, peer, community

Information
A family is a group of people who live together—father, mother, children, aunt, uncle, grandparents
Each member of a family has certain responsibilities. Each family decides these for itself.
Friendship or peer-people who enjoy doing things together
Community—people who live in the same neighborhood who may or may not be organized in their activities

Generalization
man organizes many kinds of groups to meet his social needs

ECONOMICS

Concepts
interdependence
public policy
market

Information
Interdependence—community cannot produce everything it needs; it exchanges surpluses with other communities
public policy—goods and services are received as result of local government
market—supply and demand for local goods

Generalization
the development of a community is directly affected by its economic activities

HISTORY

Concepts
origin of community
development
important events

Information
origin—when, who, and why community began
development—relating origin of the community to the present
important events—what and when they occurred and who was involved

Generalization
a full understanding of one's community requires understanding its past

GEOGRAPHY

Concepts
population
land forms
climate

Information
population—number of people living within community
landforms—mountains, plains, rivers in the area
climate—temperature, rainfall, growing season, and winds

Generalization
man if influenced not only by people but by the climate and physical environment of the community

POLITICAL SCIENCE

Concepts
political institutions
community rules
political roles in community

Information
political institutions—decision-making governing bodies that exist to make rules
rules—laws that groups of people abide by to maintain order
political role—part an individual assumes through interaction with other people

Generalization
there are many political groups within a community for varied reasons

COMMUNITY

Table 1.2 The Concepts, Information (Facts) and Generalizations from Each Social Science as Related to the Topic "The Community."

SELECTED REFERENCES

Banks, James A. *Teaching Strategies for the Social Studies.* Reading, Mass.: Addison-Wesley, 1973.

Clements, H. Millard; Fielder, William R.; and Tabachnick, B. Robert. *Social Study: Inquiry in Elementary Classrooms.* Indianapolis, Bobbs-Merrill, 1966.

Douglass, Malcolm P. *Social Studies From Theory to Practice in Elementary Education.* Philadelphia: J. B. Lippincott, 1967

Dunfee, Maxine, and Sagl, Helen *Social Studies Through Problem Solving.* New York: Holt, Rinehart, and Winston, 1966.

Estvan, Frank *Social Studies in a Changing World.* New York: Harcourt Brace Jovanovich, 1968.

Fraser, Dorothy, and McCutchen, Samuel P., eds. *Social Studies in Transition: Guidelines for Change.* Washington, D. C.: National Council for the Social Studies, 1965.

Gibson, John S. *New Frontiers in the Social Studies: Action and Analysis.* New York: Citation Press, 1967.

Jarolimek, John *Social Studies in Elementary Education.* 4th ed. New York: Macmillan, 1971.

Joyce, Bruce R. *New Strategies for Social Education.* Chicago: Science Research Associates, 1972.

Kenworthy, Leonard. *Social Studies for the Seventies.* Waltham, Mass.: Blaisdell, 1967.

Michaelis, John W. *Social Studies for Children in a Democracy: Recent Trends and Developments.* 5th ed. Englewood Cliffs, N. J.: Prentice-Hall, 1972.

Michaelis, John U., and Johnston, A. Montgomery, eds. *The Social Sciences: Foundations of the Social Studies.* Boston: Allyn & Bacon, 1965.

Muessig, Raymond H., and Rogers, Vincent R., eds. *Social Science Seminar Series.* Columbus, Ohio: Charles E. Merrill, 1965.

Ploghoft, Milton E., and Shuster, Albert H. *Social Science Education in the Elementary School.* Columbus, Ohio: Charles E. Merrill, 1971.

Ragan, William B., and McAulay, John D. *Social Studies for Today's Children.* New York: Appleton-Century-Crofts, 1964.

Ryan, Frank. *Exemplars for the New Social Studies.* Englewood Cliffs, N. J. : Prentice-Hall, 1971.

CHAPTER 2

Social Studies
Curriculum Development

What constitutes an effective social studies curriculum for an elementary school classroom? Should the teacher religiously follow a textbook that has been selected by the school system? Is there a local curriculum guide that suggests topics, learning experiences, and references that may be utilized by the teacher? Has the school system initiated the use of national social-studies project materials? Are there state requirements that must be met, such as citizenship education or state history? Or, is the curriculum a mixture of all these elements?

Every teacher is faced with a group of children who have entered the classroom with *different experiential backgrounds:* Sarah has been to 17 foreign countries, but Robbie has never been outside his home state; *different value systems:* Jay's family believes that the state should take care of them because the father can't find work, while Cindy's dad denounces anyone on welfare because he has worked hard for everything they have; *different skills and abilities:* Scott has an I.Q. of over 140 but doesn't know anything about sports, while Bill struggles with an I.Q. of 89 and hits the baseball over the school-yard fence almost every time; *different interests:* Mary saw that television show about the Tassadays of the Philipines and would like to study them, however, José would like to learn about his ancestors—the Indians of Yucatan; but with *many of the same needs and aspirations:* to have a feeling of worth, to meet with success and to deal with failure, and to learn to live and work with others.

How does the teacher accommodate for these differences? Agencies at the local, state, and national level each develop social studies curriculums, but the ultimate decision about the proper curriculum for the individual classroom rests with the teacher. (See Figure 2.1.)

During the last decade, a battle has been raging over the method of teaching and the content involved in social studies programs in the elementary school. For many years, the expanding horizons or environment theory established by Paul R. Hanna dominated the organization and content of the social studies. This theory advocates that the child should first study the environment around him in terms of familiar basic human activities. For example, in kindergarten or in first grade, the child studies the activities of the family and home. In second grade, his environment is expanded to the school and the local community. Successively, throughout the remainder of the elementary grades, the child is introduced to the community, state, nation, western hemisphere, and world. The theory contends that, initially, a child understands best the environment that is most familiar to him. The curriculum content centers around the human activities involved in production, communication, government, transportation, protection, creation, religion, recreation, education, and the expression of aesthetic impulses.

Many conditions in our society have been responsible for suggested alterations in this theory. Frequently, educators view the

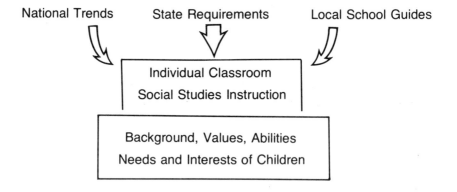

Figure 2.1   Factors Influencing Individual Classroom Instruction

advent of Sputnik as the impetus for radical changes in our educational programs. In the area of social studies, however, it would be unfortunate to fail to point out conditions that initiated change prior to Sputnik.

For example, the position of the United States as a world power following World War II placed greater strain on the social studies to prepare citizens to accept this tremendous responsibility. The United States could no longer isolate itself without concern for what was happening in the rest of the world.

The problems in international relations between the communist and noncommunist countries during the cold-war period necessitated a more thorough study of foreign ideologies. In addition, it was advocated that students needed a broader understanding of our American heritage in order to provide a basis for comparison.

Equally important in the development of new educational programs was the emergence of underdeveloped nations seeking a place in the diplomatic world. Nations such as China, Egypt, and the African countries that in the past were rarely included in the social studies curriculum must now be a part of it.

The availability of transportation, which permits more travel and contact of peoples from around the world, places pressure on the social studies to provide understanding of different cultures. The mobility of people into our communities from other countries adds emphasis to this task.

Educators such as Jerrold R. Zacharias and Jerome Bruner have influenced the social studies curriculum with their research and development programs, which stress the structure of the disciplines and a major change in the theory of instruction. Social studies, however, has been one of the last areas to be affected by these programs.

Project Social Studies, which was initiated by the U. S. Office of Education in 1962 to encourage social scientists and educators to develop new programs, adds its pressure to social studies education. These new programs emphasize the inclusion and extension in elementary social studies of content from all of the social sciences. The impact of these programs is now being realized at most levels.

Federal monies that placed emphasis on educating the culturally disadvantaged resulted in the development of programs and materials for these students. A natural outcome of this emphasis on individual differences was the establishment of programs for students of exceptional ability.

More recently, pressures within our society have influenced the teaching of social studies. The rapid urbanization of our nation has changed the living patterns of people. The close contact of people in an urbanized society requires the development of better human relationships and an understanding of the problems created by crowded cities. Technological advancements also have had their effect. Limited working hours provide more leisure time, which should be channeled toward worthwhile endeavors. Mechanization has virtually eliminated pride in craftsmanship and has created a need for some replacement for this reward. Pressures created by the social and racial problems in our society present a real challenge to the social studies. Content that depicts the white, middle-class American is insufficient in a world that knows of extensive poverty and men of all colors.

The previously discussed conditions have resulted in fervent attempts to initiate changes in social studies education. A discussion of the programs developed by agencies at local, state, and national levels will explain the tremendous divergency of programs currently in existence.

LOCAL

Development of social studies programs at the local level is generally the responsibility of committees of teachers, curriculum specialists, or administrators. Frequently, assistance is solicited from local colleges and universities or the state department.

The type of social studies program established by a local school district results from studies of the conditions inherent in the school environment. The following conditions are examined to help determine the social studies program to be adopted by the district: community environment, socioeconomic level of the students, experiential background of the students, aspiration level of the students, general educational goals of the school, and materials available.

Community Environment, Socioeconomic Level, and Experiential Background

Environmental factors influence the type of social studies program that is introduced into a school system—a meaningful series of learning experiences for children in a rural area would not necessarily prove as fruitful for children in an urban community or in an affluent suburban district. The reason for this variation obviously lies in the everyday experiences of each group of children. Many of the situations confronting the children in the city, the suburbs, and the rural areas would differ greatly.

The socioeconomic level of the children in each area also affects their experiential background. The child from an affluent suburban home may have traveled extensively, been exposed to an enriching vocabulary, and been surrounded by books, magazines, and newspapers. The urban child from a poverty area may have traveled no more than four blocks from home, never have seen books until entering school, and received little direct communication from adults. Because they bring such different experiential backgrounds to the school situation, the children from these two environments certainly should not be confronted with the same social studies experiences. Children with rich, experiential backgrounds benefit from a program that builds upon their experiences and expands their horizons. They are able to handle more abstract material. In comparison, children with a paucity of experiences need a program to provide the experiences lacking in their backgrounds. A major portion of such a program would include field trips, a wealth of visual materials (such as pictures, films, filmstrips, books, and magazines), enriching cultural activities, and concrete experiences for vocabulary development. Obviously, programs for both areas would contain certain basic elements, although they would vary in their approach and content.

Large school districts with varying environmental areas within their boundaries may find it necessary to adopt several social studies programs to meet the needs of their children from divergent backgrounds.

Intelligence and Aspiration Levels of Students

Home, community, and school environments play important roles in the intelligence and aspiration levels children achieve. Studies conclude that socioeconomic factors influence the intelligence level of children—those from lower-socioeconomic groups score significantly lower on intelligence tests than those from middle-socioeconomic groups.[1] School achievement apparently is related as well to socioeconomic status.[2] The aspiration level also is affected by the amount of motivation, interest, and support children receive from their environments, which include the home, the peer group, and the school. Obviously, social studies program planning should be influenced by these factors.

Children with apparent lower intelligence and aspiration levels need enriching experiences to stimulate their interest in learning and increase their motivation to achieve. Teacher expectations for them are important. Goals should not be outlined that would be unreasonable and frustrating to the children, but neither should the teacher possess the attitude "they can't do anything."

The above-average in intelligence should be challenged by more in depth studies of topics and extensive use of their own initiatives in order to complete work; the quality of their work should be expected to be higher; they should be provided with material that will interest and excite them on their intellectual level. An important attitude for the superior student to acquire is one of respect for his own ability plus respect and appreciation for the contributions of those of lesser ability.

Educational Goals of the School

The social studies program planned by the local school district should certainly contribute to the overall goals of the elementary school. If the school's intent is to help each child to develop to the extent of his potential so that he may become an effective member of society, the social studies program should accept the responsibility for helping the student to develop skill in and an understanding of human relationships.

Materials

The extent of the materials necessary to make a program effective should be considered before the program is developed. Some programs require extensive libraries, resource materials, audiovisual aids, and artifacts that may not be available in some districts. However, often overlooked community resources such as the museum, public library, and guest speakers can add considerably to the limited resources of a district.

Other Factors Affecting Local School Programs

Local school programs also are affected by state requirements, which may control both content and materials. Certain states have adopted laws that require the inclusion of topics such as American Heritage or Principles of Communism. Other states designate specific textbooks that must be used by the schools.

National trends advocated by social studies educators development centers, the U. S. Office of Education, and the National Council for the Social Studies frequently influence the programs of local agencies. Often, school districts are requested to field test programs developed by these national agencies.

A sample of a social studies curriculum that was developed by a local school agency is shown in Table 2.1. The school had some specific concerns about its children and wanted to design a program that would attend to those concerns. Many of the children in the school came from lower-socioeconomic homes and lacked social skills that permitted them to get along well with their classmates. As a result, there were frequent discipline problems. Materials that were used in the present program did not relate to the experiences of the children and there was a lack of interest. The value orientations of the children often were different from those of their teachers.

OBJECTIVES
(Attitude/Knowledge/Skill)

LEARNING EXPERIENCES

RESOURCES

OBJECTIVES (Attitude/Knowledge/Skill)	LEARNING EXPERIENCES	RESOURCES
I Knowledge of the democratic process and an understanding of its effect on their lives.	Children make their own rules in class, when possible. Organize a student council for the class or school, if there are decisions such a group can make. As a group such as family or school, etc., is studied, examine how and why rules are made. For example: families have rules; families depend on government that has rules; families teach their children to be good citizens and obey all the rules.	INTERMEDIATE David Guy Powers *How to Run a Meeting, Book 1.* David Lavine *What Does a Congressman Do?* Alvin Schwartz *The People's Choice* (The story of candidates, campaigns, and elections). Ivan Klapper *What Your Congressman Does.* RECORDS Music of the American Indians of the Southwest, *The World of Man,* vol. 2. Religions Israel: Its Music and Its People. Head Start—With the Child, Development Group of Mississippi, John P. Sousa. G. Johnson *Communism, An American View.* I.A. McCarthy *Let's Go Vote.* E. Lundop *The First Book of Elections.*
II Attitude of the worth of each individual as a member of society; developing self-respect and respect for others.	Important considerations—Teacher's treatment of individuals in the classroom. Try to disassociate misbehavior from individual—"it's not you I dislike, but your behavior." Use assembly line to develop something of importance to children. Pull out any individual in the line and discuss what happens without them.	PRIMARY Eva Knox Evans *People are Important.* Peter Buckley and Hortense Jones *Living as Neighbors, Five Friends at School.* Sandra Weiner *It's Wings That Make Birds Fly.* INTERMEDIATE Beryl and Samuel Epstein *Who Says You Can't?* Gudrum Alcock *Run Westy Run.* Robert Burch *Skinny.* Natalie Carlson *The Happy Orpheline, The Letter on the Tree.* Samuel Agabashian *All Except Sammy.* Madeline L'Engle *Meet the Austins.* Eleanor Estes *The Moffats, The Middle Moffat,* Rufus M. Elizabeth Sorenson *Miracle on Maple Hill.* Meindert DeJong *Shadrach.*

Table 2.1 (Roseville) School Social Studies Program

OBJECTIVES (Attitude/Knowledge/Skill)	LEARNING EXPERIENCES	RESOURCES
Similarities in all individuals A. Awareness of traits shared by all people. All "are, feel, do, & have." Recognition of these similarities will be helpful for our students who may feel detached or alienated from other people. *Similarities in groups* B. Awareness of membership in many kinds of groups and similarities between us and other groups of people. Aids in development of positive self-concept.	*Timmy* (gr. K-6) Objective: To stress importance of feelings. To discuss the inability to see feelings. To emphasize people's basic similarities as well as differences. *Sameness and Difference* (gr. 2-4) Objective: To help children see the basic similarities among people as well as their differences. *Sameness and Difference* (gr. 2-6) See A. *Perception of People* (gr. 2-4) Objective: To sharpen children's perception of people. *Is, Feels, Does, Has* (gr. 2-4) Objective: To help children to begin distinguishing between things people do, what they are, how they feel, and what they have. To get children to talk about themselves. *Groups* (gr. 3-6) Objective: To make children aware of the different groups to which they belong; to help children realize how allegiances to groups can overlap. To point out basic similarities of people, and yet show the differences among groups. *Americans* (gr. 3-6) Objective: To develop an awareness of what it means to be an American and how one becomes an American.	The above learning experiences may be found in *The Intergroup Relations Curriculum*, John S. Gibson, Tufts University. *The Magic Circle* activity may be used with all four topics (A, B, C, D). This concept is included in the Human Development Program.

Table 2-1 Continued

31

OBJECTIVES (Attitude/Knowledge/Skill)	LEARNING EXPERIENCES	RESOURCES
Differences in individuals C. An awareness of the uniqueness of each person can and should foster positive self-concept.	*Sameness and Difference* (gr. 2-6) See A. *Perception of People* (gr. 2-4) See B. *Is, Feels, Does, Has* (gr. 2-4) See B. *Individuals* (gr. 1-6) Objective: To start children thinking about people, what they are, do, feel, have. *Describing Individuals* (gr. 1-6) Objective: To develop awareness and to increase descriptive abilities. *The Uniqueness of Individuals* (gr. 2-6) Objective: To develop an awareness of: (1) the difficulty of judging a person by looks alone, (2) the fact that there are some things about a person that you can only know by asking. *Hypothetical Individuals* (gr. 1-6) Objective: To increase children's understanding of the complexity of people; to discover some of their stereotypes and prejudices and to help them become aware of their own mistaken generalities and definitions. *Who Am I?* (gr. 1-4) Objective: To increase awareness of the visible and invisible aspects of a human being.	The above learning experiences may be found in *The Intergroup Relations Curriculum,* John S. Gibson, Tufts University.
Difference in groups D. Awareness of differences between and among groups as well as differences of individuals within any one group helps to eliminate tendency to prejudge and misjudge people because they belong to a certain group.	*Role Playing* (gr. K-6) Objective: To help children to gain an understanding of different roles of members of same group. *Sameness, Difference* (gr. 2-6) See A *Perception of People* (gr. 2-6) See B *Is, Feels, Does, Has* (gr. 2-4) See B	

Table 2-1 Continued

OBJECTIVES
(Attitude/Knowledge/Skill)

LEARNING EXPERIENCES

RESOURCES

The *Magic Circle* activity may be used with all four topics (A, B, C, D). This concept is included in the Human Development Program.

Groups (gr. 3-6) See B
Americans (gr. 3-6) See B
Describing Individuals (gr. 2-6) See C
Skin Color (gr. 2-6)
Objective: To put the socially laden fact of skin-color differences into a context that makes the matter primarily a question of: what is skin? what is color? To provide an opportunity for children to discuss skin-color differences without using the word *race*, while treating the fact of skin-color differences as a matter of shades.

Apply knowledge to concrete situations such as buying groceries, using ads from the paper, buying a home, studying geography and cultures of countries where boys may go for military service, setting comparative clothing costs, learning where foods come from, selecting nutritious foods, understanding the concept of work and how we depend on one another, examining welfare-value whether temporary or permanent. Students also will give examples of knowledge needed for the future—what happens after you have all the money you need—how to appreciate other than material things.

III Attitude toward the value of learning and its potential for future worth of the individual.

PRIMARY
Muriel Stanek *How People Earn and Use Money.*
Frederic Rossomando et al *Earning Money.*
Spending $. K. Guy *Money Isn't Everything.*
J. Mother *Ideas About Choosing.* Shay *What Happens When You Put $ in the Bank.*

-IV Ability to work with a group to the completion of a task.

Use committe work.
Establish guidelines
1. responsibility of chairman
2. responsibility of members.
Be sure a goal has been established for group—evaluate work of committees each day.
Play simulation game "Production Line."

Table 2-1 Continued

33

OBJECTIVES
(Attitude/Knowledge/Skill)

V Ability to control their behavior through understanding their feelings and those of others.

VI Ability to participate in the planning of learning experiences with the teacher.

VII Ability to recognize problems and to find solutions to those problems.

LEARNING EXPERIENCES

Use of children's literature books
Use of pictures displaying emotions
Games such as "Is, Feels, Does, Has and Go Away Prejudice"
School exchange—cultural, art pictures, writing letters, and play day.

Each activity planned with children and teacher.
Children set goals for what they want to accomplish.
Self-evaluate—how well goals were achieved.

Group focus on identification of problem—establish goals
Holding forces—why couldn't it happen?
Helping forces—what would make it different?
Brainstorm alternative solutions
1. smaller group chooses alternative and role-plays solution for larger
2. use situations from unfinished stories
3. "You Are There"—problems presented by roving reporter.

RESOURCES

Fannie R. Shaftel and George Shaftel, John Gibson (previously listed). Ruth Sawyer *Maggie Rose, Her Birthday Christmas*. George Smith *Wanderers of the Field*. Kate Seredy *A Tree for Peter*. Hel Griffiths *The Greyhound*. Lois Lenski *Strawberry Girl, Texas Tomboy, Corn Farm Boy*. James Garfield *Follow My Leader*. Eleanor Estes *The Hundred Dresses*. Jerrold Beim *Trouble After School, The Smallest Boy in the Class*. Emily Neville *Seventeenth Street Gang*. Mary Urmston *The New Boy*. Mary Stolz *The Noonday Friends, A Dog on Barkham Street, The Bully of Barkham Street*.

Table 2-1 Continued

As the teachers worked to delineate the objectives for the program, it was obvious that the major focus had to be developing good self-concepts, clarifying value positions, investigating one's feelings, acquiring the ability to work with individuals and groups, and acquiring the ability to recognize problems and to solve them.

Table 2.1 contains a selected number of the key objectives of the program, the learning experiences to develop them, and the necessary resource materials. The specific school where this program was developed is not identified.

STATE

Responsibility for social studies curriculum development at the state level generally rests with the curriculum specialists of the state departments, often with assistance from public school personnel and university and college professors of social science and education. State departments establish broad guidelines for local districts, interpret state laws, and provide leadership for initiating change within the existing programs.

Previously, state departments issued curriculum bulletins that were followed religiously. Deviations from the established program were not encouraged and few opportunities for creative teaching were possible. In addition, adjustments necessary to provide meaningful programs adapted to local needs were lacking. Now, however, a trend toward more flexibility in the use of these bulletins is apparent; generally, they are used as guides to instructional programs. The establishment of broad guidelines from the state departments gives the needed direction and continuity to the local programs, but permits the variations necessary for adaptation to local situations.

State requirements established by the legislature are interpreted to the local districts by the state departments. Frequently, they are also responsible for establishing programs to implement state requirements. In states where textbooks are adopted on a statewide basis, it is the responsibility of the textbook committee of the state department to make these selections. Thus, the type of text materials to be utilized by the districts is often a state responsibility.

By using its guidelines and considering national trends, the state department can evaluate current programs more objectively than can local departments. The Oregon Council for Curriculum and Instruction, for example, developed a project whereby the state was divided into ten regional districts for preevaluation of current programs before instituting any major revisions.[3]

Leadership for introducing change in the social studies curriculum should be provided at the state level. Certain states have been more active in this respect than others. The state departments of Wisconsin, Minnesota, Indiana, California, New York, and Connecticut are among those that have either organized or encouraged curriculum revisions.[4] A more detailed look at the Wisconsin program will provide opportunity for a comparison of the programs developed at local and state levels.

A Conceptual Framework for the Social Studies in Wisconsin Schools was the result of collaboration between the Wisconsin Social Studies Committee and research scholars from colleges and universities. The bulletin's introduction gives an explanation of its basic philosophy:

> Factual knowledge is one aspect of the curriculum that most teachers recognize, teach, and test. Until recently most teachers, consciously or otherwise, have accepted the idea of the existence of a body of "conventional wisdom." This information answered the question "What should be known?" or "What should be taught?" Such a viewpoint is incomplete. While much of the knowledge that has stood the test of time will continue to merit consideration, much new, vital information has been generated. Not all facts can or should be learned; furthermore, these fragments of information often have little relevance in themselves. To resolve this problem, teachers should help students to collect and organize into concepts the multiplicity of facts that confront them.[5]

The bulletin contains introductory statements concerning the disciplines, history, geography, anthropology-sociology, economics, and political science. It also offers generalizations incorporating major concepts of each discipline and topic variants for each discipline for grades kindergarten through 12. Suggested use of the bulletin by teachers is identified thus:

The pages within this bulletin attempt to demonstrate how the course content at each grade level can be used to develop these concepts and generalizations in a spiralling manner from kindergarten through the 12th grade. By following any strand, the reader will note that the developmental variants emerge in greater depth and sophistication at each succeeding grade level.

This bulletin suggests the interrelated nature of history, geography, and the social sciences. An "orchestration" of these areas is implied in the developmental variants which appear at each grade level. This approach would encourage the teacher and students to draw against the concepts and structure of the several social studies areas in the consideration of any topic or problem.

It is not intended that the statements of the basic concepts nor the variants will be taught as items to be committed to memory but rather as illuminating ideas or analytic generalizations which will emerge from what has been studied. Care should be taken that the concepts *do* emerge and then are applied to new situations. Mere verbalization of rules or masses of information is not effective social studies education. Students should be helped to acquire meaning by use of the common elements presented. As students use the conceptual strands they should be given new challenges and presented with opportunities to see new applications at even higher levels until they gain the habit of arriving at valid analyses and generalizations of their own.[6]

The guide then lists the topics to be introduced at each grade level, selected major concepts from each discipline and the developmental variants for each topic. Because of the constant demand for the publication and the increased concern for the inquiry, problem-solving/teaching-learning procedure and the valuing process, another pamphlet *Knowledge Processes & Values in the New Social Studies* was published. The first section of this guide deals with knowledge and its attainment through concept development and generalization attainment. In the second section, the 11 major social studies processes are identified and related to the problem-solving procedure. (See Figure 2.2.) We can look at the social studies processes and problem solving as being interdependent. The last section discusses the valuing process and how it relates to the school.

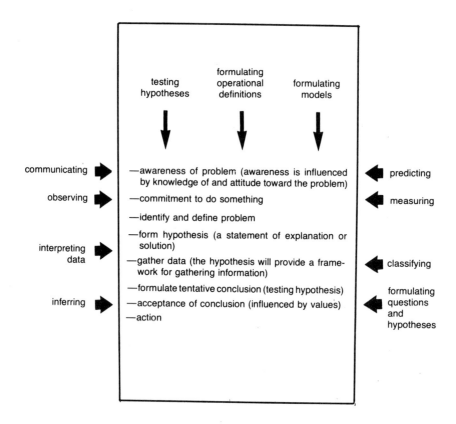

SOURCE: *Knowledge Processes & Values in the New Social Studies (Madison: Wisconsin Department of Public Instruction, 1968–70), p. 35. Reprinted by permission.*

Figure 2.2   Problem Solving

Values and the Schools

In a society in which there is general consensus on values, the public schools' role is quite clear. It is expected to reinforce and build into its curriculum and procedures the prevailing values. But in a situation of change and controversy about basic social norms, the position schools should take is not as easily determined. Each of the competing segments of the society—special interest groups, economic and business interests, political organizations, religious and ethnic groups, professional organizations, and so forth—all such groups believe that what they desire for themselves is also good for everyone, and they want to influence the training of the young in the desired directions. The school board, the administration, the teachers, and textbook publishers find they are being pushed and pulled by these interest groups each of whom wants the schools to foster its values and beliefs.

Traditionally there was little question that the schools should promote such values as the following:

1. Respect property.
2. Be respectful of adults.
3. Say please and thank you at appropriate times.
4. Do not use profane language or bad grammer.
5. Be neat and clean.
6. Do not lie or cheat.

Now, however, in some situations these are quite controversial. Many lawsuits and community controversies have focused on the meaning of "neat and clean," for example. Several recent surveys indicate that cheating in school, rather than being unacceptable, has become the norm, and most students feel no guilt about cheating. Standards of profanity are constantly changing and words that one rarely heard used in public a few years ago are now heard a great deal. While many may not like these developments, it is very necessary for teachers to recognize that they are taking place.

It is important to understand, too, that the school as a social institution, as a place where adults and youngsters live together for a large portion of the day, promotes many values simply in the way it is organized and run. Students may learn that:

1. Boys should be interested in sports. Girls should be interested in reading, clothes and jump rope.
2. Fear and sadness are acceptable emotions for girls but not for boys.

3. As an individual, I don't amount to much. Or, as an individual, I have considerable skill and talent and people like me.
4. Teachers and adults generally have the answers and know what is good for me. Or, everyone affected by a social situation should share in controlling and assessing it.

While it is beyond the scope of this project to deal with the subtle but very powerful set of relationships that exist among students, teachers, and administrators in the school as a social structure, it is hoped that this brief mention will encourage teachers and administrators to look at it carefully. A somewhat polemical but very provocative commentary on the problem is Edgar Friedenberg's *Coming of Age in America.* [7]

Teaching strategies for valuing to use at the various stages of development complete the guide.

NATIONAL

At the national level there are a number of agencies that are involved in curriculum development, many of which influence social studies education. For a number of years, the National Council for the Social Studies, a department of the National Education Association, has devoted itself to the improvement of social studies education. *Social Education,* the official journal of the organization, provides information representing the current thinking in social studies. Its yearbook and other publications pinpoint problem areas in social studies and supply needed guidance and material to aid in their solution.

The National Council for Geographic Education, through the *Journal of Geography,* and the American Historical Association expend considerable effort toward improving the teaching of their respective disciplines in the elementary school. Both provide leadership and materials to stimulate interest in and concern for social studies education.

The Joint Council in Economic Education is an example of a national group committed to the improvement of economic education.

In 1964, the group initiated a project entitled "Developmental Economic Education Program" (DEEP). The three major objectives of this project are "(1) to build economic understandings into school curricula, (2) to improve teacher education in economics and (3) to develop and test new teaching materials at all grade levels."[8] DEEP supplies a variety of materials for students in grades 1 through 12, a teacher training program via television, and clearing house services for economic materials.

By means of its financial assistance to Project Social Studies, a part of the Cooperative Research Program initiated in 1962, the United States Office of Education supplied a major impetus for curriculum change in the social studies. These projects, initiated at major colleges and universities across the nation and involving social scientists and educators, have approached change from a variety of viewpoints. For example, Roy Price, Syracuse University, sought to identify major social science concepts and to utilize them in developing instructional materials. John Michaelis, University of California, prepared teaching guides and materials on the Asian Countries for grades 1–12. New approaches and materials for a sequential curriculum on American society for grades 5–12 became the concern of John Lee, Northwestern University. Charlotte Crabtree, University of California at Los Angeles, was involved with teaching geography in grades 1–3.

Project Social Studies at the University of Minnesota under the direction of Edith West develops concepts from each of the disciplines. The interdisciplinary units for grades K–12 use culture as the core concept of the program. *The Family of Man* multimedia kits for grades 1–4 focus on a family or community such as the Hopi, Japan, Ghana, Israel, and New England.

The *Social Science Laboratory Units* were developed at the University of Michigan with authors Ronald Lippitt, Robert Fox, and Lucille Schaible. These units for grades 4–6 are concerned with the causes and effects of human behavior. First, children study what and how social scientists work. They learn to observe, make inferences, value judgments, and identify cause and effect relationships. Then, they work with hypothetical cases of social behavior, which they analyze with the tools acquired earlier.

41

Intergroup Relations Curriculum for grades K–6 was produced under the direction of John S. Gibson at the Lincoln Filene Center for Citizenship and Public Affairs. The objectives for the program are

1. to advance the positive self-image of the child
2. to reduce prejudicial thinking and discrimination toward all groups
3. to help the child realize the many cultural and ethnic differences among people
4. to give the student a realistic picture of America's past and present, including the contribution of its many groups
5. to encourage the child to participate actively in the learning process
6. to suggest ways individuals can foster a truly democratic society.[9]

With the political science concept of the "governing process"as the core, the materials focus on human behavior and why individuals, groups, and cultures differ.

Development of a Sequential Curriculum in Anthropology for Grades 1–7 was instituted at the University of Georgia by Wilfred Bailey and Marion Rice. The Anthropology Project was a cooperative venture involving members of the Department of Sociology and Anthropology and the College of Education. The rationale of the project is based upon these premises:

1. Any field of knowledge, such as anthropology, consists of a system of symbols, or word labels, which is used to express ideas and describe relationships. An understanding or mastery of any field of knowledge begins with an understanding of the symbol system, the meaning of which expands and develops as the knowledge of the discipline is extended.

2. Symbol systems are usually organized for transmission of a core of congruent ideas, usually referred to as subject matter, discipline, or field. For almost thirty years, the social studies movement has contended that a subject approach to the transmission of social studies is inappropriate for the elementary grades. It is thought that any type of organization of material, irrespective of its method, is designed to transmit knowledge, and there is nothing incompatible, except preference and tradition, with a subject presentation of a social science in the elementary grades.

3. Anthropological material is frequently used in the public school, but, in the absence of emphasis on anthropological concepts and terminology, the contribution that anthropology has to make to an understanding of man and of different cultures is frequently obscured. The material deliberately introduces anthropological terminology which may at first be somewhat difficult for the student. As his familiarity with these terms increases, however, it is expected that they will help him to organize and interpret in a more meaningful manner the world in which he lives.[10]

Organization of the program follows a cyclical pattern, with concepts developed in the primary cycle repeated and enlarged in the intermediate cycle. *The Concept of Culture* is the topic presented for grades 1 and 4. In grade 1, three ethnographies—the American, Kazak, and Aruntas—are presented through oral discussion by the teacher and with a picture text for the children. The comparison cultures of Kazak and Aruntas were chosen because they would be little known by teacher and pupil, and stereotypes of them would not have been established. Grade 4 develops the same topic; however, it emphasizes a more analytical approach with the organizing of cultural constructs.

The Development of Man and His Culture is the topic presented for grades 2 and 5. Units on *New World Prehistory* for grade 2 and *Old World Prehistory* for grade 5 are provided.

A project such as the Anthropology Project stresses the importance of social science content beyond the usual history and geography for children in the elementary school. It also stresses the value in helping the children to act as social scientists, learning their method of inquiry, and attempting to study the problems of society.

Other organizations at the national level have been responsible for the development of materials. One group is the Boston Children's Museum, which developed MATCH units under the direction of Frederick H. Kresse. These unit kits organized around topics of *The City, House of Ancient Greece,* and *The Japanese Family* contain realia, films, filmstrips, pictures, games, maps, records, reference books, and a valuable resource—the teacher's guide. The philosophy guiding the development of these materials is that when children are involved with nonprint material, learning is real.

Man: A Course of Study (MACOS) was produced by Education Development Center with Jerome Bruner as the major director. It is designed as a fifth-grade course with its focus on three questions: What is human about human beings? How did they get that way? How can they be made more so?

Man: A Course of Study defies the subject matter, content, and grade-level classifications normally used in describing curriculum materials and underscores the notion that "all things that are, are in all things." The core discipline of the course is anthropology; but, because man is the subject, the scope of the curriculum ranges freely between the biology of man's origins and the humanities of his own creation.

Some organizing concepts of the course are life cycle, adaptation, and natural selection, which are introduced through the study of the salmon. In the herring gull studies, the same concepts are repeated, with the focus on adaptation, territoriality, parenthood, and aggression. The study of baboons includes all of the earlier concepts, but shows the unique social organization which allows the baboon to survive in his hostile environment. The highest-order concepts are introduced through a study of the Netsilik Eskimo. The examination of this microculture highlights the humanizing forces that have shaped man. The student must relate to this alien culture, and in the process of understanding the Eskimo, will understand the forces which have shaped his own culture and behavior patterns.[11]

Taba Program in Social Science was initiated in Contra Costa, California under the leadership of Hilda Taba, San Francisco State College. A detailed look at this program will aid in comparison of programs developed at each level. The rationale of the program is outlined as follows:

Today's curriculum must cope with many problems. One is the explosion of knowledge. A vast array of ideas has been added and is being added to the curriculum each year. Since the curriculum is already overcrowded, the pressure to cover an increasing range of content creates a severe problem. To encompass expanding knowledge without aggravating the problem of coverage, it is necessary to make a new selection of content. Otherwise, additions of content without deletions will dilute what is being offered.

Obsolescence of descriptive knowledge creates still another difficulty. Much of what is covered in schools, such as political boundaries or production statistics, changes constantly. This means, for example, that much of the descriptive knowledge learned by a fifth grader will be out of date before he reaches the twelfth grade.

There is also a need in curriculum for concepts from a wider range of the social sciences. If students are to acquire the needed knowledge and skills for effective living in the complex society of today, which includes an understanding of the many cultures in the world, it is necessary to introduce concepts not only from history and geography but also from anthropology, economics, sociology, political science, philosophy, and psychology.

The cumulative effect of these problems requires a new look at what kind of knowledge is most durable and valuable. We must reconsider the role of specific descriptive knowledge in curriculum implementation. If descriptive knowledge changes rapidly, we are wasting time with any attempt to cover specifics for permanent retention. A new function must be found for descriptive knowledge.

To complicate this matter further, recent studies of learning and experimentation with curriculum have greatly extended the scope of responsibilities of the schools. For example, the current emphasis on creativity, on autonomy of thinking, and on the method of inquiry represents a renewed concern with thinking and cognitive skills. The development of cognitive powers now is recognized as an important aspect of excellence. This extension of objectives beyond the mastery of knowledge requires us to reexamine learning experiences. We no longer can assume that mastering well-organized knowledge automatically develops either autonomous or creative minds.

Another problem is that the range of ability and sophistication in any classroom has expanded both up and down. In many ways, the students of today are more knowledgeable and capable than we assume. At the same time, because of higher retention of students in schools, there are students in the ninth grade whose intellectual equipment is functioning on the level of an average second grader. This problem of heterogeneity may be severe enough to require measures other than ability grouping or changing the pacing while covering the usual ground. When the heterogeneity in ability is combined with the problems of emotional disturbance, frequently created by increasing urbanization, offering a fixed traditional curriculum becomes futile.

In other words, the curriculum must simultaneously build a more sophisticated understanding of the world, use a greater range of knowledge, be applicable to pupils having a greater range of abilities, and deal with expanding content. All of this has made it necessary to develop a new curriculum pattern.[12]

Objectives include the acquisition of selected knowledge; development of thinking skills; formation of selected attitudes; and development of academic and social skills. As an example, topics for grade 3 include:

The Bedouin of the Negev
    A Bedouin Family
    Winter at Wadi Juraba
    Spring on the Desert
    Summer Months
The Yoruba of Ife
    Twins in Yorubaland
    In the Country
    The Special Times
The Thai of Bangkok
    Bua Comes to the City
    Getting Ahead
The Norwegians of Hemnesberget
    The Time of Dark
    The Time of Light[13]

The topics are organized around the key concepts that follow: it is not expected that any of the Key Concepts will be developed fully in any one unit or even at any one grade level; they must be dealt with on all grade levels. The concepts must be visualized as threads which appear over and over again in a spiral which is always moving to a higher level. As the student's experience broadens and his intellectual capacities develop, he is provided with repeated opportunities in a variety of contexts to develop an increasingly sophisticated understanding of the Key Concepts. The sentences following each concept word provide illustrations of the way the word is used in THE TABA PROGRAM IN SOCIAL SCIENCE.

Causality

Events often can be made meaningful through a study of their antecedents. Hence, to some extent, future events can be predicted.

Events rarely have a single cause, but rather result from a number of antecedents impinging on one another in a given segment of time and space.

Conflict

Interaction among individuals or groups frequently results in hostile encounters or struggles. Conflict is characteristic of the growth and development of individuals and of civilization as a whole.

There are culturally approved and disapproved means for resolving all varieties of conflicts. Irrational conflict is reduced by recognition of the inevitability of differences and of the difficulty of determining their relative value. In most situations, some form of compromise is necessary because of the serious consequences of sustained conflict.

Cultural Change

Cultures never remain static, although the context of change (economic, political, social, and technological), the speed of change, and the importance of change vary greatly.

Cultural change is accelerated by such factors as increased knowledge, mobility, and communication, operating both within and between cultures.

Differences

The physical, social, and biological worlds (including human beings and their institutions) show extreme variation. Survival of any species depends on these differences.

Conflicts and inequities often result from assigning value to particular categories of differences, such as skin color or high intelligence.

Institutions

Societies develop complexes of norms and roles which guide their people toward the satisfaction of needs. These complexes of norms and roles define proper and expected behavior.

Social institutions include organizations such as the family, and perform an important function in socializing the individual and establishing his status. Political institutions include rules and laws and serve to maintain order, to compel obedience to existing authority systems, and to provide the means for change in such systems. Economic institutions are organized around the production, distribution, and consumption of goods and services, and provide for the material needs of society members.

Interdependence

All persons and groups of persons depend on other persons and groups in important ways. These effects on others are often indirect and not apparent.

The solution of important human problems requires human beings to engage in joint effort. The more complex the society, the more cooperation is required.

Cooperation often requires compromise and postponement of immediate satisfactions.

Modification

As man interacts with his physical and social environment, both he and the environment are changed.

Man has often exploited his physical environment to his own detriment.

Power

Individuals and groups vary as to the amount of influence they can exert in making and carrying out decisions which affect peoples lives significantly.

As a strong motivating factor in individual and group action, the desire for power often leads to conflict.

Societal Control

All societies influence and attempt to mold the conduct of behaviors of their members. The techniques used include precept, example, and systems of reward and punishment; the specifics of these techniques vary greatly from one society to another. Written laws are an attempt to clarify the rules by which society operates and to promote impartial treatment of its members.

Marked differences in child-rearing practices often exist among societies.

Everyone belongs to many groups with overlapping membership, different purposes, and often conflicting demands on members in terms of duties, responsibilities, and rights; each, by exerting social controls, shapes the personality structures and behaviors of its members.

Tradition

Societies and the groups and individuals within them tend to retain many traditional values, attitudes, and ways of living and dealing with current problems, whether or not that behavior is appropriate.

Certain institutions in societies, such as family, religion, and education, tend to change less rapidly than do other elements of societies.

Values

Those objects, behaviors, ideas, or institutions which a society or an individual considers important constitutes values.

Whether or not a person holds a value can be inferred by others only on the basis of an extensive sample of his behavior.

Societies and individuals often differ significantly in the values they hold.

Values develop through both nonrational and rational processes.

The survival of a society is dependent upon agreement on some core of values by a majority of its members. The greater the variety of values within a society, the greater the likelihood of disagreement and conflict; in some societies such conflict is accepted as necessary to the realization of core values.[14]

SUMMARY

Agencies at each of the levels—local, state, and national — provide social studies programs that represent interpretations of what should compose social studies education. An analysis of the examples from each level reiterates the presence of the quite divergent programs to be adopted by school districts.

The local school system can provide specific objectives and a more detailed presentation of its program based on the needs and interests of its children. State programs are broad and general, indicating a framework from which the local school districts can build their own curriculum guides. National programs for curriculum development exemplify the current thinking of educators and social scientists. National programs are designed to provide exacting information and guidance for teachers and children. Their goal is to affect the curriculum development of the local and state agencies.

SELECTED REFERENCES

Bailey, Wilfred, and Rice, Marion. *Anthropology Curriculum Project* Athens: University of Georgia, 1966.

Banks, James A. *Teaching Strategies for the Social Studies* Reading, Mass.: Addison-Wesley, 1973.

Chase, W. Linwood, and John, Martha Tyler. *A Guide for the Elementary Social Studies Teacher*. Boston: Allyn & Bacon, 1972.

Fraenkel, Jack R. *Helping Students Think and Value: Strategies for Teaching the Social Studies*. Englewood Cliffs, N. J.: Prentice-Hall. 1973.

Gibson, John S. *New Frontiers in the Social Studies: Goals for Students, Means for Teachers*. New York: Citation Press, 1967.

Goodlad, John. *The Changing School Curriculum*. New York: Fund for the Advancement of Education, 1966.

Hoffman, Alan J., and Ryan, Thomas F. *Social Studies and the Child's Expanding Self*. New York: Intext, 1973.

Knowledge Processes and Values in the New Social Studies. Madison: Wisconsin State Department of Education, 1968–70.

Massialas, Byron G., and Smith, Frederick R., eds. *New Challenges in the Social Studies*. Belmont, Calif.: Wadsworth, 1965.

Muessig, Raymond H., *Social Studies Curriculum Improvement: A Guide for Local Committees*, Bulletin No. 36. Washington, D. C.: National Council for the Social Studies, 1965.

Social Studies Framework for the Public Schools of California. Sacramento: California State Department of Education, 1967.

Taba, Hilda. *Teachers' Handbook for Elementary Social Studies*. Reading, Mass.: Addison-Wesley, 1967.

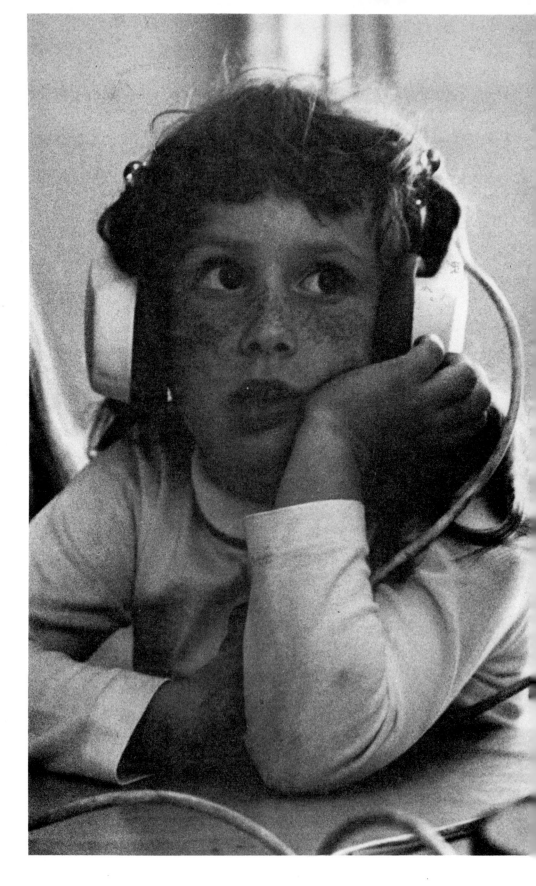

PART II

Methodology

Although textbooks and state and local curriculum guides are provided for teachers, a teacher ultimately must design a social studies program to meet the needs of the children in his classroom. What method will he use? Method here is defined as the procedures followed in achieving the goals of the social studies program. For example, should children learn to solve problems through the method of inquiry? Are learning experiences better organized with a unit approach? Should children learn social science concepts by studying the structure of the discipline? Should children learn to think and behave as social scientists? Do disadvantaged children learn most effectively through concrete experiences? Should a variety of approaches be used throughout the year?

This section will discuss several approaches: (1) problem solving through inquiry, (2) unit development, (3) method derived from the structure of the social science disciplines, and (4) method for the disadvantaged child. Each discussion will include a definition of the method and an explanation of the objectives, philosophy, selection of content, and organization of the program, with an appropriate example. Also included and equally important is the comparison of the advantages and disadvantages of each method.

CHAPTER 3

Problem Solving Through Inquiry

The method of teaching problem solving through inquiry often has been misunderstood and misused because of discrepancies in the definitions given for the terms "problem solving," "inquiry," "reflective thinking," "inductive reasoning," and "discovery." Frequently, these terms are used interchangeably without explanation of their different meanings.

Problem solving is the process whereby an individual identifies a problem situation, formulates tentative explanations or hypotheses, verifies these tentative hypotheses by gathering and evaluating data, and restates the hypotheses or arrives at generalizations. The individual may then apply these generalizations to new situations.

Many authors use reflective thinking and inductive reasoning to identify the problem-solving method. Early in the thirties, Dewey referred to the identification of the problem as the prereflective period, to the search for an answer as the reflective period, and to the dispelling of doubt as the postreflective period.[1]

Inductive reasoning or inductive teaching is described as the process of leading an individual toward solving a problem by providing him with sufficient stimulation and a direction based on hypotheses. In contrast, inquiry is the method of searching for the solution to a problem.

Inquiry is not conducted as an indiscriminant search for facts; it is instead, an organized, directed search.[2]

Hypotheses direct its activities. . . . Hypotheses determine what facts will be selected as relevant to the problem. They influence what interpretations are formulated and accepted in the end.[3]

Discovery may occur as the individual is conducting his search— he reassembles or reorganizes information based on previous and newly acquired learning and gains insight into the problem.

Bruner states that discovery

. . . is in its essence a matter of rearranging or transforming evidence in such a way that one is enabled to go beyond the evidence so reassembled to new insights. It may well be that an additional fact or shred of evidence makes this larger transformation possible. But it is often not even dependent on new information.[4]

Therefore, inquiry and discovery can be defined as steps in the problem-solving process.

The problem-solving approach in teaching rests solidly on the ability of children to think effectively. Taba relates, "The task of instruction is to provide systematic training in thinking and to help students acquire cognitive skills which are necessary for thinking autonomously and productively."[5] There is a sequential order, as Piaget shows, in the development of forms of thought from childhood to adult hood; each step is a prerequisite to the next. A student should manipulate concrete objects in order to develop an intuitive grasp of the abstract concepts before he engages in abstract reasoning. Teaching strategies require the following of a proper developmental sequence.[6]

The teaching strategies which helped students advance to higher levels of thinking involved what questions were asked; what the teacher gave or sought and at which point in the proceedings; or bypassed elaboration and extension of ideas; and whether or not there were summaries of ideas and information before inferences of higher order were sought.[7]

As Taba so aptly points out, teaching children thinking skills depends more on what we get out of the children than on what we put into them.[8] The basic philosophy of the problem-solving approach is one of developing thinking skills in children that enable them to formulate generalizations about a given situation. These generalizations should be ones that can be applied in new situations, specifically in the problems in the everyday lives of the children.

QUESTIONING

If teachers are to help children develop thinking skills, they must know how to ask the right questions at approximately the right time—when the child appears ready for the question. Research has indicated that teachers tend to ask questions that are at the lowest level of the hierarchy of questioning, concrete questions that require the individual to recall information. Several models of questioning have been advanced to increase the teacher's ability to ask questions at higher levels of thought. One example is Taba's model based on three cognitive levels: concept formation, interpretation of data, and application of principles. At the first level, *concept formation*, the child is asked to list, group, and categorize through such questions as what did you see, hear, note? What belongs together? On what criterion? What would you call these groups? What belongs under what?

Next, the child is requested to *interpret the data* collected, draw inferences, and generalize through questions such as what did you notice? see? find? Why did so and so happen? What does this mean? What picture does it create in your mind? What would you conclude?

The last level, *application of principles*, requires that the child hypothesize about what he thinks will happen in the new situation and to support his prediction. These questions are like What would happen if? Why do you think this would happen? What would it take for so and so to be generally true or probably true?

Applying this model to the following picture, several concepts can be developed through a different focus of the questioning.

Note that the beginning questions are those that any child should be able to answer, and act as a motivator to encourage him to continue. Try to identify the level of each question.

CONCEPT ONE—Humanistic—Develop good self-concept
Many People Feel the same way when they face problems.

Questions

Tell me what you see in the picture?

How do you think the boy is feeling?

Why do you think he feels that way?

What makes you think he feels that way?

Have you ever felt that way? When?

Why do you think he set up the lemonade stand? What are some possible reasons?

Have you ever wanted to have a business of your own? Why?

CONCEPT TWO—Economic
There must be a demand for your product in order for it to sell. Costs cannot exceed money taken in if you are to make a profit.

Questions

What is the boy in the picture doing?

Is there something wrong?

What expenses does he have?

Why do you suppose he wants to make a profit?

Why do you suppose business is bad?

What could the boy do to improve his business?

CONCEPT THREE—Citizenship Education
Responsibility must be accepted as a part of individual freedom.

Questions

Do you think the people in the neighborhood would mind having the lemonade stand?

What are some problems that might occur?

How could the boy avoid these problems?

Why must we think of others when we plan to do things?

If children are to receive maximum benefit from the questioning strategies and continue to engage in the problem-solving approach, then the role of the teacher and the classroom conditions are crucial factors.

CLASSROOM CONDITIONS

The atmosphere of the classroom must foster a feeling of trust and security within the children. Students need to know that they will receive help and understanding from the teacher and that they can ask questions and offer acceptable answers without fear of being wrong. The classroom environment should provide excitement and stimulation for learning. Materials should be available to supply the needs of searching minds. The teacher should create an atmosphere of mental freedom that enables each individual to think without concern for boundaries.

How can this be accomplished? The responses given by a teacher, verbally and nonverbally, will relay much to the children. Encouraging responses such as "that sounds interesting," "what a thought-provoking solution," "good thinking," and "what a good idea," should be utilized. However, facial expressions and tone of voice should convey the same messages. To state flatly "you're wrong" or "what a ridiculous answer" to a child in front of his peers will cause him to be much more cautious with his next response, if he responds again.

ROLE OF THE TEACHER

In an inquiry-oriented classroom, the concept of the teacher's role undergoes a change in emphasis. Previously, the teacher assumed the major roles of information giver and disciplinarian with only minor roles of motivator, referrer, counselor, and advisor. (See Figure 3.1.) However, in an inquiry-centered classroom, the teacher assumes the primary role of motivator, while remaining an information giver, disciplinarian, counselor, referrer, and advisor. (See Figure 3.2.)

As motivator, the teacher stimulates and challenges his students to think. He initiates problem situations for the children to identify. His questioning provides the focus and direction for the children's search. He assumes the role of information giver only

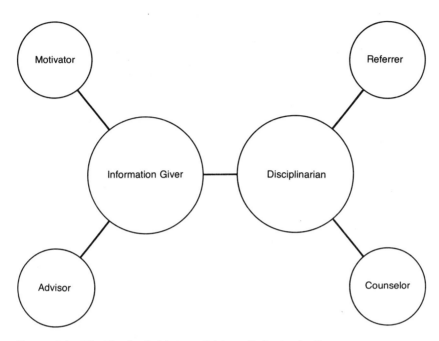

Figure 3.1 The Teacher's Major and Minor Roles in the Past

when his students request it or when it becomes necessary to redirect activities that may have wandered from the original goal. As referrer, he guides children to materials and sources of information. As advisor and counselor, he supplies children with encouragement when it is needed and he diagnoses difficulties and gives assistance. Discipline is necessary to avoid chaos; however, it is vital that children be guided toward self-discipline, which is important in the problem-solving approach.

To summarize the teacher's role, it is one that:

1. helps children seek an answer rather than being a fountain of knowledge
2. provides motivation and direction for the inquiry
3. establishes an effective classroom climate where children can question and can seek answers without fear of being penalized for wrong answers
4. provides materials expressing different points of view
5. helps children to learn to accept the opinions of others

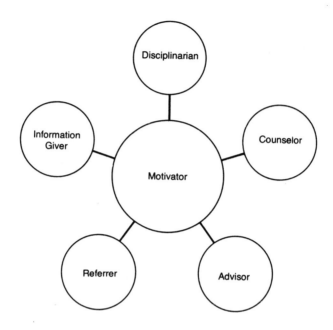

Figure 3.2   The Teacher's Major and Minor Roles in an Inquiry-centered Classroom

6. helps children develop an organized method of thinking about and dealing with information so that they will become independent thinkers
7. becomes an effective questioner—leading children from the concrete to the abstract level of thought.

Teachers should be aware that the use of the inquiry process in the classroom does require more planning time on their part. They must know how they will initiate the activity, what questions they will ask, and how to refocus the thinking of children. To accomplish these tasks it is necessary to have sufficient background knowledge of the problem from a variety of sources.

OBJECTIVES

The objectives of the method of problem solving through inquiry are based on the processes or steps in which children are involved (identifying a problem, stating and testing hypotheses, and generalizing).

These broad objectives are outlined as follows:

Develop the student's ability:

To identify and define a problem situation in relation to the social sciences and to apply this knowledge to everyday life.

To formulate hypotheses for tentative problem solutions utilizing the information presented and previously acquired knowledge.

To compare and evaluate various theories, data, and generalizations in testing tentative hypotheses.

To select relevant facts necessary for testing hypotheses.

To state generalizations from results and apply them to new situations.

Acquire skill:

In the use of a variety of materials to secure information relative to the problem.

In discovering the relationships between previously and newly acquired information to acquire new insight into the solution of a problem.

In rational thought processes by constructing hypotheses and testing, revising, and refining these hypotheses.

In expressing opinions on issues after an analysis of available information.

Acquire knowledge:

Of problem-solving techniques.

Of methods of inquiry used by social scientists.

Of recall information necessary for problem solution

Develop an attitude:

Of open-mindedness toward all sides of an issue before arriving at a decision.

Of accepting opinions of others and understanding why opinions vary.

Of concern and interest in the problems of society by active participation in problem-solving activities.[9]

These objectives are general and based on the major values of the problem-solving methods as purported by its many advocates. More specific behavioral objectives should be developed within the content boundaries and needs of the individual classroom.

PROBLEM SELECTION

Quickly acknowledged is the fact that the success of the problem-solving method lies in the selection of problems for inquiry. Dunfee and Sagl suggest the following criteria for problem identification:

1. Does the problem challenge the children intellectually, stimulate critical thinking, allow them to seek cause-and-effect relationships, and offer opportunity for formulating and testing generalizations?
2. Does the problem relate directly to the lives of the children, based on their past experiences, and have an impact upon them presently?
3. Is the problem concerned with a basic human activity and does it thus illumine man's efforts to meet his needs?
4. Are there sufficient community and classroom instructional resources available for developing the problem?
5. Does the problem offer opportunities for expansion of interests?[10]

Does following the guidelines of a structured plan restrict the problem-solving method? Should teachers be permitted to provide alternatives to the suggested outline of study? Freedom of choice in what Clements, Fielder, and Tabachnick call "Big Questions" for inquiry study is "justified by the demands of a particular teaching-learning situation and its potential for increasing the efficiency with which children learn."[11] The choice of alternates for study should be based on:

1. Children's interests, questions, and attempts to interpret events.
2. Teacher's experiences and participation in community events and concerns.
3. Consideration of the work of various social scientists such as historian, geographer, or anthropologist.[12]

The "Big Questions" or problems should be interesting and should initiate inquiry. It should be possible to translate them into small questions that can be answered by simple observation and lead to increased understanding. By selecting concepts and ideas that help answer the small questions, answers to the "Big Questions" can be formulated.[13]

Fox, Lippit, and Lohman, of the University of Michigan, assume "that the way for children to inquire in a social science area is to begin with incidents that are microcosms of the larger scene — incidents that are representative of their own life experiences."[14] An adaptation of their model of inquiry is presented:[15]

1. *Identify problem.*

   Set goals.

   Make design for study.

   Why do people behave in this way?

2. *Observation data collection.*
   Children look for clues to determine why things turn out the way they do.

3. *Advance theories for causes of behavior.*

4. *What behavior might lead to better consequences?*

   Make hypothesis.

   Test hypothesis.

5. *Draw conclusions.*

6. *Research theories of others.*

7. *Generalize.*

   How can I apply this to my own life?

An example of the method of problem solving through inquiry will be developed with adaptations from the above model.

Initiation

The initiation (designated in the model as Step 1) sets the stage for the problem-solving situation. It should stimulate inquiry and develop a continuing interest in the problem. Unless sufficient background is provided, problem identification will be difficult; however, too much information may stymie the quest. The initiation establishes the focus or direction of the search and serves as a springboard for action. The most effective initiations are those that actively involve the children, either mentally or physically. Possibilities for this stimulation are contained in these illustrations of initiations.

Incident

This example from a sixth-grade classroom is designed to initiate inquiry. Step 1. The teacher, without giving any reason for his action, uses chairs and desks to build a separating wall between two sections of children in the classroom. He deliberately separates good friends and any brothers or sisters. The children soon ask questions. "Why are you doing this? What have we done to deserve this? My best friend is on the other side, when will we get to sit together again? How long are you going to leave this here?" As a result of this experience, the children begin to analyze the motives for and results of such actions. The remaining steps of the model are easily identified. Step 2. Observe the behavior of the children as the incident takes place. Help the children look for clues to understand their own behavior. Step 3. Advance theories about causes—what negative or positive feelings were produced? Step 4. What behavior might lead to better consequences? Was there some way to avoid the building of the wall? Make and test an hypothesis by classroom action. Step 5. Draw conclusions and summarize learnings. Step 6. Discuss places in the world where cities or countries have been divided in such a manner—Berlin, Korea, Vietnam. By introducing questions and materials, the teacher can provide direction or focus toward one of these areas if he desires. The inquiry can now take on as much emphasis as necessary through research, reading, and discussion. Step 7. Generalizations can be drawn from the study. Final applications are made to the children's own life—a possible question might be "What behavior leads to hostile feelings toward me?"

PROBLEM-SOLVING ACTIVITIES

Presentation of Facts

Another activity designed to initiate inquiry is this graduated presentation of a series of facts about a country to a fifth-grade class.[16]

FIRST TRANSPARENCY

Information about a country

Area: 760,000 sq. mi.	Birthrate: 42.5/1000
Texas: 267,339 sq. mi.	Birthrate of U. S.: 18.2/1000
Population: 48,313,438	Suicides: 1.6/100,000
Texas: 11,196,730	Suicides in U. S.:11.1/100,000
	Life expectancy: 1940—39
	1968—67

Questions

As you compare the area and population of this country with those of Texas, what conclusions can you draw?

What does the comparison of birthrates indicate?
What does the comparison of suicide rates suggest about the country?
From your limited knowledge of this country, identify any problems you think it might have.

Some problems the children might suggest would be overpopulation and lack of food.

SECOND TRANSPARENCY

Major Crops

coffee	rice	garbanzos	bananas
corn	tobacco	cocoa	sisal (50% of world's production)

Questions

What indication of the physical features of the country do these products give you?
What type of climate do these crops suggest?
What discrepancies in the climate might these crops suggest?
Do the crops indicate the country's location?

THIRD TRANSPARENCY

Minerals

silver (world's leading producer)	copper	tin
gold (7.5 million U. S. 63.1 million)	zinc	coal
lead	antimony	iron ore

Questions

Do the minerals indicate anthing different about the physical features?
What can you hypothesize about the technology and industries of the country?

FOURTH TRANSPARENCY

Industrial Products

cotton	iron and steel	rubber
cloth	chemicals	paper
beer	electrical goods	handicrafts
sugar		

Questions

What can you conclude about the country from its industrial products?
Would you change any of your previous hypotheses as a result of this added information?

FIFTH TRANSPARENCY

Imports: $2,442,000
Exports: $1,374,000

cotton	cattle
coffee ($1,000,000 annually)	fruit
cane sugar	fresh & frozen meat
tomatoes	

Questions

What does the imbalance between exports and imports suggest about the economy of this country?

69

Do the products indicate any of the industries in the country?
Hypothesize concerning the problems you see this country facing.

SIXTH TRANSPARENCY

Tourism

$320 million long-stay/yr.	Texas
$540 million short-term	$500 million/yr.

Questions

Does the information about added income from tourism change any of
*   your hypotheses?*
Try to identify the country.

The country is Mexico. The class can now begin to seek information to test their hypotheses about the country. The information on the transparencies was selected to focus primarily on economics, but other facts can be selected to change the focus.

Wastebasket Technique

The teacher collects assorted articles from the wastebasket in one of the rooms of the house or one from another classroom in the school. For example, from the kitchen: a cereal box with the vitamins listed; soft drink can, be sure to include the pull ring; frozen orange juice can; other vegetable or fruit cans; pair of scissors; find a box or can that has a person's picture on it; a knife and fork; ice cube tray; a penny; plastic milk carton, can opener; and glass bottles. Other materials may be added as the teacher plans to focus the search for information. Pose the problem thus: If you were an archeologist in the year 2500 and during a dig had unearthed these articles from a lost culture, what could you hypothesize about that culture? Could you draw any generalizations about the culture without further information?

This type of activity should increase the child's skills of observing, classifying, and interpreting data and formulating hypotheses. Another approach to this same type of activity would be to substitute artifacts from other cultures such as a tribal spear, war mask, and figurines from an African country.

Discrepant Data

The utilization of the discrepant data technique[17] is intended to create cognitive dissonance within the individual, which should help him to break down his own stereotypes.

For example, to introduce the study of another culture, choose slides or pictures that would reinforce the stereotypes about that culture—such as wooden shoes, windmills, tulips, and chocolate from Holland. Present the slides or pictures to the children and ask them to formulate a generalization about the culture. An example of the generalization they might arrive at would be: most people in Holland wear wooden shoes and grow tulips.

Then introduce the discrepant data in the form of slides or pictures featuring large cities and factories to show the modern aspects of Holland. Ask the children to restructure their generalization to accommodate the new information. The restructured generalization might be formulated thus: some people in Holland still wear wooden shoes and grow tulips, but many live in modern cities and work in factories.

Role playing

Role playing is an activity that can be used for initiation in any grade. Following is an example of its use at the primary level. The teacher presents and discusses a particular situation with several selected children who, in turn, role play for the class. Their dialogue follows:

KEVIN: Did you hear what happened to Billy on the playground yesterday?
SARAH: No, I was absent.
KEVIN: He was sliding backwards down the slide and cracked his head.
JESS: He's in the hospital with a concussion.
SARAH: I'm sorry, but he knows we shouldn't slide backwards.
KEVIN: He always did like to show off.
JEFF: Other kids do it all the time and don't get hurt, so why shouldn't he?

Question

Why do you suppose Billy behaved this way?

The class discusses the situation and recognizes the problems and consequences of breaking safety rules. They try to understand why things turn out as they do. Why did Billy get hurt when others do the same thing without being hurt? What type of behavior would lead to better consequences? The class makes and tests hypotheses and draws conclusions. The teacher may then direct the search for information in any direction he prefers—for example, bike safety, home safety, or highway safety.

A variation of this initiation can be accomplished by role playing using an unfinished story for which the children seek solutions. An example might be:

Terry had borrowed a really neat snake book from Kim to finish his report for science. While he was working at the kitchen table (where his mother had told him not to do his homework), eating cookies and drinking a glass of milk, his baby brother knocked over the milk, drenching Kim's book. What should he do? His mother wouldn't allow him to go on the trip to the zoo Saturday if she knew he had disobeyed, but he couldn't return Kim's book the way it looked now.

Children can take turns playing the roles of mother, Terry, and Kim as they work out the solutions to the problem. Other similar role-playing situations can be found in *Role-Playing for Social Values* by Fannie R. Shaftel and George Shaftel.

Tape Presentations

Another interesting technique to utilize is a taped presentation which provides the opportunity to include several voices and sound effects. Taping segments of historical diaries or fiction stories that introduce problem situations can be quite effective. An example of one follows:

Rob Nelson added a flashlight to the collection of clothes and other articles he had placed in his gym bag. He thought he'd better go to the kitchen and get some cookies and a sandwich or two since he didn't know when he might find food again. Rob was running away from home. He was tired of all the rules, rules, rules. Go to bed by 9:00 o'clock, you can't watch T.V. on school nights, and on and on.

Rob left the house and started for the main highway where he hoped to get a ride. Rob walked for a long time, but no one seemed interested in giving him a ride. When he spied a police car coming down the road, he quickly dashed off into the woods. All of a sudden from the direction of his city came a blinding flash and loud booms. Rob dove for a covered ditch and that was all he remembered.

Hours later Rob came to; he ached all over. Gradually he crawled toward the opening, which was almost closed with debris. He looked out and was stunned at what he saw. The landscape was scarred and nothing could be seen. No sound, human or mechanical, could be heard. No birds sang.

For a while he just stood there. Then he . . . .

The generalization to be reached by the children from a discussion of this episode is:

Written laws are an attempt to clarify the rules by which society operates and to promote the impartial treatment of its members.

Dialogue between teacher and children might go like this:[18]

T: What would be one of the first things you might do?

S: I'd run.

S: I'd look around and maybe just go back and see what happened.

S: I'd just run as fast as I could the opposite way.

T: Well, suppose you did look around; what might you look for?

S: Some way to survive.

S: For people.

T: Why would you look for people?

S: To see if any were alive.

S: You heard the big sound (on tape) and then you couldn't hear anything after that.

T: Is there any reason that you would look for people? Do you think that perhaps others escaped?

S: Yes.

S: Yes, you need to start working together and build to survive. Everything is barren.

S: It's natural to look for somebody else.

T: Why do you say that?

S: I don't think one person could live in a destroyed city by himself.

S: Yeh, he's right there—you need someone to help you. You can't do everything yourself. You need help.

T: Good!

S: If the city was destroyed, I'd try to get out of there and go someplace else.

T: Suppose you do find a few more survivors; perhaps some had hidden in a cave, and soon you found 5 or 6 people. What would be one of the first things that you people might do?

S: Look for food and shelter.

S: Yes, you would be hungry after a day and you can't go without it.

S: You need shelter.

T: Remember, everything was destroyed. What would you use for food and shelter?

S: You would look for plants and stuff in the ditch.

S: I think you would look for food or anything left over you might be able to find.

T: What might be the safest thing for you to eat?

S: Something that was in your ditch because everything else could have been poisoned by the explosion.

T: What kind of food would you look for?

S: Mostly plant life—that would be about the only thing left.

T: Could you eat the top of the plant?

S: You could eat the root.

T: Why would the roots be the only thing left really?

S: Because the top of the plants would be destroyed and the roots would be left underground.

T: You're right; you remembered in the story that everything was scarred. Do you know anything about plants that might tell you about a water supply? What do you know about plants?

S: They need water, sunlight . . . .

S: The roots, they collect something like that so I guess you might get something out of the roots to eat.

T: Good! Now we've discovered people. We've discovered our next basic need is our food, water, shelter . . . .

S: Well, water, that might be our first. It depends. It may be way back in a cave and there would be blind fish, lobster, crab . . . .

T: Ok, after we get our food, water, and our little group of people, what are we going to have to do now? For example, when you go on a camping trip, what do you do to make things easier?

S: You work together.

S: Yeh, you work together in groups.

T: How do you work together?

S: Have somebody go get firewood, and some get water. . . .

S: Some get water, and you know—that was everything destroyed?

T: Yes, that's good. I'm glad you came up with the idea of organizing; this is what you have to do. Now suppose you have this group of people, how are we going to make sure everyone plays fair? For example, if we have a big, strong man over here and also someone who was hurt in the blast and is not too strong, who do you think should get the most food?

S: He would.

T: Who would?

S: The injured guy.

T: Why?

S: Because he'd need the nourishment.

S: I don't agree with that because there may be so little food that they will have to fight over it and the stronger one is going to take it.

T·   Do you think that the strong should take it?

S: No, I think that it should be divided, but that's not the way it is. If I was in that position, I'd probably take the most if I could, or as much as I could.

T: But, what do you think we could do to make this a little more fair? We may have some strong people and some weak people. . . .

S: I think we should give the weak person more food and he might get better and then we would have another person helping. I don't know.

T: What can we do to make sure this doesn't happen, that one person gets all of it?

S: Split it up evenly or something like that.

S: Depends on how many people you had in on this. It might be easier, you know, if we had five or six people, or it might be harder to find that much food. But if there were three or four people it might be easier, I think.

S: Make rules.

S: Make the rules and everybody gets the same amount of everything.

S: Like in Monopoly you would get the same amount of money, even though you aren't equal at the end of the game.

T: That was the important thing; you said you need a set of rules, good!

S: And Jim was trying to get away from rules. (referring to tape)

S: Ah-hh.

T: Yes, he was, wasn't he?

S: Uh-huh.

T: What do you think might happen if we didn't have any rules at all?

S: You couldn't do a thing. If you wanted to play a game, you couldn't play it.

T: Why not?

S: Because one guy could say, well, there's no rules and I can have as much money as I want.

T: And who do you think is going to?

S: The stronger person.

S: It's right there. If you don't have rules, the stronger person always gets it. You know it's that way!

T: Suppose someone breaks the rules?

S: Give him a penalty.

T: What kind of penalty?

S: Depends on what you're doing.

T: Suppose we catch one of the people in our group stealing food.

S: Make his next ration less than he usually gets.

S: See how much he took. If he took an awful lot and if he had any extra, put it back and he can't eat for the rest of the day or something.

T: What else could you do? What do you think some people might want to do to him?

S: Physically hurt him.

S: That's a good idea—ha, ha!

T: How could we decide on a proper punishment to give a person? If we find someone taking more than his share—in other words, breaking a rule—how can we punish him?

S: Make him have a little less than his share.

T: Ok, thinking over the little story you have just heard and the discussion we've had. What would you consider an important idea you developed? Everyone think carefully! What is one important idea you came up with from today's story and our talk?

S: Well, rules are very important because if somebody breaks them, the stronger person always gets his way, then it's just no fair to the weaker person.

T: Anyone else have an important idea?

S: Well, if a person is going to participate in something, everyone has to work together. . . .

S: And play fair and not break the rules.

S: Because there are too many people in the world to live without rules.

S: Laws you mean.

Continuing Activities

After the problem has been initiated with the class, testing the hypotheses may take many forms, depending on the needs of the class. For example, the class could be divided into committees (to be discussed in chapter nine), with each committee selecting an hypothesis to test and then reporting back to the class on their findings. At that time, the class can decide on the basis of the information given whether to accept or reject the hypothesis or determine whether additional information is needed. Another approach would be for each child to test his own hypothesis.

Gathering data may take many forms—such as viewing films or filmstrips, listening to tapes or records, interviewing people in the school or community, and utilizing resource books or textbooks. After the hypotheses have been tested utilizing the data collected, the children should draw generalizations based on their new knowledge. When possible, these generalizations should be applied to the child's own life.

Responsibility of the Child
in an Inquiry-centered Classroom

The child becomes an active inquirer into his own education. He makes decisions about his learning experiences and interacts more with his teacher and peers. He is an active thinker—seeking information, probing and processing data, and asking questions rather than always being questioned. The child poses the problem to be solved, suggests the hypotheses to be tested, searches for the necessary information, determines the discrepancies in the information, accepts or rejects the hypotheses, and draws his own generalizations. He participates in the self-discovery of certain basic concepts and principles as he moves from observation, classification, interpretation, and application to generalization. The child acquires insight into his own behavior that will enable him to apply the generalizations to his own life. He also learns to express himself so that all may understand his views; while learning to be openminded and willing to accept the thoughts and opinions of others.

ADVANTAGES AND DISADVANTAGES OF PROBLEM SOLVING THROUGH INQUIRY

Advocates of the method of problem solving through inquiry stress the value of developing rational thought and of the act of discovery encountered during the search for solutions to a problem. Bruner hypothesizes that discovery in learning "helps the child to learn the varieties of problem solving, of transforming knowledge for better use, helps him to learn how to go about the very task of learning."[19] Retrieval of the information learned through discovery is more easily accomplished. [20] Research indicates that as the child progresses through elementary grades his inquiry ability increases.[21]

Motivation for learning becomes internal for the learner in the problem-solving situation because he is actively seeking knowledge to solve a given problem. The excitement of discovery encourages him to continue his search; he learns by doing. The problems presented to the learner are concrete and are related directly to his own experiences. The child can suggest a variety of solutions, but the situations remain open ended, which can lead to further study.

Those who question the emphasis on the act of discovery of the inquiry method suggest that it places too little attention on the crucial role played by facts and skills in a student's mastery of a body of knowledge. Ausubel relates that "abundant experimental research has confirmed the proposition that prior learnings are not transferable to new learnings unless they are first overlearned."[22]

Friedlander questions the value of a child's curiosity in operating as a motivator and incentive for academic learning. He claims that children's curiosity may be unsystematic, noncumulative, immediate, and easily satisfied. He suggests that a child's curiosity may be satisfied with incorrect or partial information and that it may be strongest with issues not necessarily the proper concern of the school.[23]

Concern is voiced by many for the inquiry method's practice of accepting "any answer." This group stresses the fact that the child might not have the opportunity to test all of his answers and it questions how the child will know if his answers are right or wrong. Continued research is necessary to answer the claims of both the advocates and the opponents of this method.

SELECTED REFERENCES

Beyer, Barry K. *Inquiry in the Social Studies Classroom.* Columbus, Ohio: Charles E. Merrill, 1971.

Brubaker, Dale L. "Indoctrination, Inquiry, and The Social Studies," *The Social Studies* 41 (March 1970): 120-24.

Bruner, Jerome. *Toward A Theory of Instruction.* Cambridge: Harvard University Press, 1966.

Clements, H. Millard; Fielder, William R.; and Tabachnick, B. Robert. *Social Study: Inquiry in Elementary Classrooms.* Indianapolis: Bobbs-Merrill, 1966.

Dunfee, Maxine, and Sagl, Helen. *Social Studies Through Problem Solving.* New York: Holt, Rinehart, and Winston, 1966.

Fair, Jean, and Shaftel, Fannie R. *Effective Thinking in the Social Studies.* Washington, D. C.: National Council for the Social Studies, 1967.

Fenton, Edwin. *Teaching the New Social Studies in Secondary Schools: An Inductive Approach.* New York: Holt, Rinehart, and Winston, 1966.

Goldmark, Bernice. *Social Studies, A Method of Inquiry.* Belmont, Calif.: Wadsworth, 1968.

Massialas, Byron G., and Cox, Benjamin C. *Inquiry in Social Studies.* New York: McGraw-Hill, 1966.

Schwab, Joseph J. *The Teaching of Science as Inquiry.* Cambridge: Harvard University Press, 1962.

Servey, Richard. *Social Studies Instruction in the Elementary School.* San Francisco: Chandler, 1967.

Skeel, Dorothy J., and Decaroli, Joseph G. "The Role of the Teacher in An Inquiry-Centered Clasroom," *Social Education* 33 (May 1969): 547-50.

Suchman, J. Richard. *Developing Inquiry.* Chicago: Science Research Associates, 1966.

CHAPTER 4

Unit Development

Current interpretations of unit teaching are equal in variety and number to those of problem solving. The *Dictionary of Education* defines the unit as "an organization of learning activities, experiences, and types of learning around a central theme, problem, or purpose developed cooperatively by a group of pupils under teacher leadership."[1]

Michaelis identifies a unit as "a plan to achieve specific objectives through the use of content and learning activities related to a designated topic."[2] Another definition suggests "The unit represents a way of organizing materials and activities for instructional purposes."[3] Each definition recognizes the importance of organizing learning activities. This organization is the key to unit planning—one learning experience must be related to another in order to avoid fragmentation. A unit contains learning experiences that are related to other curriculum areas—for example, language arts, math, science, physical education, art, and music. Problem solving may be incorporated in the unit, but a unit can be developed without its use.

Basically, there are two types of units—the resource unit and the teaching unit. Resource units, as the label indicates, contain extensive suggestions of learning experiences, content, and materials for developing a selected topic with children. In contrast, a teaching unit is created to meet the needs and interests of a specific group of children. The teacher may draw upon the contents of a resource unit for the development of a teaching unit. A teaching unit may become a resource unit when used by another teacher with a different group of children.

The organization of a unit consists of:

1. purpose—the reason for teaching the unit
2. objectives—the goals that will be reached in the process of teaching the unit
3. content—primarily the background information for the teacher or an organization of the knowledge necessary to achieve an understanding of the topic
4. activities—including initiation, individual and group experiences, integration with other subject areas, and culmination
5. bibliography—references for the teacher and children and materials such as records, films, filmstrips, and games
6. evaluation—a measure of the success achieved in accomplishing established objectives.

Variations occur in this suggested organization, but most units contain the same components.

OBJECTIVES

Objectives established for the unit method of teaching overlap with those of problem solving, because both methods are concerned with similar goals although they attempt to achieve their goals by different means. Broad objectives for unit teaching include:

Acquire skill:

In working cooperatively with members of a group through committee participation.

In the use of a variety of materials including books, primary sources, magazines, and pamphlets.

In communicating with members of a group through reports, plays, panel discussions, and interviews.

Develop an understanding:

Of the importance of establishing effective human relationships to achieve established goals.

Of the interrelationship of content areas.

Of the importance of social studies in relation to everyday life.

Of the democratic process and the responsibility of each individual to make the process effective.

Acquire knowledge:

Of facts and information sufficient to develop an understanding of the topic under study.

Of methods to secure accurate information about the topic.

Obviously, these objectives are quite general and are based on the elements of unit teaching that are emphasized. More specific behavioral objectives could be formulated with a definite topic in mind.

Unit teaching is based on the theory that the child is motivated to learn material that he helps to select and to plan in cooperation with his teacher. The theory also suggests that a child can understand a topic more readily if he studies it in the context of various subject areas, for he is then able to realize the interconnectedness of the content areas. For example, following this method, a child who is attempting to understand Russian culture learns about the country's music and art and participates in games played by Russian children in addition to learning about Russia's government, education, history, geography, and economics.

The unit is a blueprint for broad or depth coverage of a topic. Topics can be covered in breadth, including as many aspects as possible, or in depth, emphasizing only selected aspects. A unit generally requires a longer period of time than does a problem-solving situation. However, a problem-solving situation may be included as part of a unit. The unit method places more emphasis on content acquired than does the method of problem solving, but content is not its primary goal. The processes the child uses (communicating, cooperating, researching, and analyzing) as he acquires his information are still the primary goal. The fact that a unit-teaching situation provides opportunities to meet individual differences is one of its vital facets.

Role of the Teacher

The teacher's major role in unit teaching is one of motivator; however, more of the initial motivation should come from the child's involvement in the planning. Since the teacher has developed the unit plan, he supplies more guidance for the organization of the study. There is cooperative teacher/pupil planning of the learning experiences to permit children to participate in the decision-making processes. The teacher plans activities particularly designed to meet individual needs. If Janice is shy and needs the experience of working with others, the teacher places her in a group where she won't be dominated, but where she can accept responsibility and develop her leadership skills. Or, the child like Terry who has exceptional art skills can be utilized in the development of an authentic African war mask.

The referrer role is expanded since more information is provided directly by the teacher in the initiation and by supplying materials for research and suggesting activities for reporting. Advisor and counselor roles may be expanded particularly if the groups have difficulty working together. It may be necessary for the teacher to counsel groups on ways in which they can work out their problems. For example, Jimmy isn't doing his share of the research and the committee wants to drop him from the group. The teacher talks with Jimmy about his responsibility and also with the rest of the committee to find out how the issue can be resolved. Much of the discipline is handled through group participation and decision making.

Role of the Children

Children's responsibilities during the development of a unit are extensive. They should actively participate in the planning stage of the unit, fulfill their committee obligations, enter into discussions, and report research findings to others. The children are involved in some discovery in pursuit of information, but it is not as greatly emphasized in unit teaching. In addition, they should exhibit interest in the other children's reports, ask questions, and evaluate the performance of themselves and others.

Guidelines for procedures are formulated by the children, and it is each individual's responsibility to abide by the established rules. Group cooperation is essential to accomplish the selected goals.

Conditions of the Classroom

The atmosphere of the classroom is created by the group's decisions concerning the regulation of their activities. Through cooperative planning, the children and teacher develop suggested behavior standards for working in committees, doing research, and presenting information to the class. The teacher's primary responsibility is to guide the children's thinking toward reasonable decisions. Extensive materials are necessary for research, and physical conditions should lend themselves to small group activities.

UNIT SELECTION

Numerous criteria are suggested for selecting units of study around children's interests. Some of these criteria are:

1. the unit's general utility
2. its social significance
3. its ability to increase and extend the children's background knowledge
4. consideration of the needs and demands of society.[4]

If the processes in which children are involved (communicating, cooperating, researching, and analyzing) constitute the primary goal of unit development, should the content of the unit be based on the interests of children? Will children become more involved in a unit based on their interests? What are the interests of children at the various grade levels? Research indicates that children are interested in:

First grade—Trips or journeys to extraordinary and different places such as dry, wet, hot, or cold lands. Also, cowboys and Indians of early American history.

Second grade—Areas of the earth different from their own immediate environment such as Africa, Japan, the North Pole. Historical background of national symbols as Fourth of July, Statue of Liberty, the President.

Third grade—Big oceans and big continents, historical background of people such as Indians, soldiers of the Revolution, the person who discovered New York.

Fourth grade—Genuine interests in particular areas of the earth—Japan, England, the Congo and general social features of these such as the Queen of England, the religion of Japan.

Fifth grade—Those geographic areas which dominate the current news—Middle East, Russia, China and the historical reason for some of the large social problems that appear on the national and international scene.

Sixth grade—Similar interests as the fifth grade, but more penetrating. Also, interest in the poverty of the masses in Latin America, social differences in East and West, beginnings of Communism, and development of the Cold War.[5]

Do the children's interests change as the times change? Are their interests universal, or do they differ from school to school and from classroom to classroom? How can the teacher determine the interests of the children in his classroom?

The teacher can develop an interest inventory to aid in determining the focus of his students' interests. The children answer the teacher's questions by checking the appropriate column, for example, "like," "dislike," or "not sure." Sample questions might be:

1. Do you like to learn about the following?

    a. People from countries such as
       Japan?
       Vietnam?
       Africa?
    b. The way a country runs its government?
    c. Why many people in the world cannot find work and do not have enough to eat?
    d. Famous people such as
       John F. Kennedy?
       Queen Elizabeth?
       Charles De Gaulle?
    e. How people transport goods from place to place by
       Trains?
       Airplanes?
       Ships?

Teachers formulate questions based on current topics in the news, suggested topics from curriculum guides, and knowledge of the children's interests gleaned from class and informal discussions. Other types of interest inventories might involve short answer questions, children's autobiographies, or individual pupil/ teacher conferences.

DIRECTING CHILDREN'S INTERESTS

Children's interests can be directed toward topics that the teacher deems important for study. The techniques that the teacher employs to introduce the topic as well as the interest displayed by him are important factors. What topics should be included in elementary school social studies? The basic human activities involved in the expanding communities of men (in the family, school, neighborhood, local county and metropolitan area, state, region of states, U. S. national, U. S. and inter-American, U. S. and Atlantic, U. S. and Pacific, and in the World), as identified by Hanna, are frequently used as a basis for determining content. These activities are:

1. producing, exchanging, distributing, and consuming food, clothing, shelter, and other consumer goods and services
2. communicating ideas and feelings
3. organizing and governing
4. transporting people and goods
5. protecting and conserving human and natural resources
6. creating tools, technics, and social arrangements
7. providing recreation
8. expressing religious impulses
9. expressing and satisfying aesthetic impulses
10. providing education.[6]

Equally important to consider for inclusion in a social studies unit are topics that aid in developing the selected generalizations from each of the social sciences: history, geography, sociology, economics, political science, anthropology, philosophy, and psychology.[7] An awareness of our current social, economic, environmental and political problems should certainly direct the teacher's selection of topics.

DEVELOPMENT OF A UNIT

Initiation

The teacher is responsible for providing the setting for the study. Sufficient information is necessary to stimulate continuing interest in a topic. However, too much information will not leave enough questions to be answered and may stifle interest. The ability and experential level of the children will serve as possible guidelines for determining the amount of information to include in the initiation. A problem-solving situation, as suggested in chapter three,

Kindergarten	First Grade
Who Am I?	Our Community
Where We Live	Pollution in Our Town
Where Other People Live	How Do We Communicate?
Our Animals	Homes in Other Lands
Animals from Other Lands	Japan
Working Together	Mexico
	Africa
Second Grade	**Grade Three**
Our Shopping Center	How Communities Grow
Interdependence of People	Big Cities
How Do We Transport	New York
Our Goods?	Boston
People Who Are Poor	Los Angeles
Our National Parks	Houston
	Other Communities
	Bombay, India
	Melbourne, Australia
	Manila, The Philippines
Grade Four	**Grade Five**
Pollution of the World	Our Nation Today
How Do We Govern	How Did It Grow?
Ourselves?	What Problems Did It Face?
How Do Other People	Our Nation and Its Neighbors
Govern Themselves?	Our European Neighbors
People of Latin America	
Our State and Its Problems	
Grade Six	
World Neighbors	
What Are the Problems?	
People of China	
What's Happening in the	
Middle East?	
People of East Africa	

Table 4.1 Sample Unit Topics for Each Elementary Grade.

can be used for the introduction in order to combine the methods of problem solving and unit organization. Other initiation activities might include an arranged environment, exploratory questioning, films, stories, poetry, and folktales.

Arranged Environment

Use of a number of prepared exhibits and bulletin boards creates a classroom atmosphere that lends itself to the topic for study. Bulletin boards supply two types of stimulation: (1) information about the topic—presented by charts, pictures, and newspaper clippings, or (2) the presentation of a series of searching questions to be answered during the study.

Displays would include books and magazines that present discussions of the topic at varying levels of reading difficulty. The books should contain stories as well as facts. Other displays might show selected artifacts relative to the topic. Criticism of the arranged environment points out that it lacks pupil/teacher planning and creates an artificial beginning for the pursuit of the study. Gradual development of the bulletin boards and exhibits by the children throughout the study is suggested.

Exploratory Questioning

Teachers need to know the extent of their students' understanding or misunderstanding about a topic before beginning the study. Introducing a topic through a stimulating question period provides the teacher with information to help him plan the direction and depth of the study. It also creates excitement about the topic. Such questioning can be incorporated with any initiation or used exclusively for the initiation. For example, when the topic is concerned with the study of Africa, the teacher might have the children react to questions such as: What do you think of when someone mentions Africa? How would your life change if you moved to Africa?

What are some of the contributions that Africans have made to our heritage?

Generally, more information about individual understanding can be obtained when children are requested to write their answers; however, oral questioning stimulates more interest in the topic. Assessment of the answers in terms of general misconceptions as well as the amount of present knowledge about the topic should direct the focus of the study.

Film or Filmstrip Presentation

A film or filmstrip used to introduce the study can present information and/or questions. Those that provide provocative information may foster immediate interest that may not be sustained.

Reading Stories, Poetry, or Folktales

Stories relative to the topic that present situations similar to those in the children's lives provide stimulation. Poetry and folktales also catch the interest of children. *Children's Books to Enrich the Social Studies*[8] is a good source for information concerning this type of material.

TEACHER/PUPIL PLANNING FOR THE UNIT

After the initiation, the course of action for the study should be planned cooperatively by the pupils and the teacher. The initiation in this example presents on a transparency a map of Africa indicating the natural resources of the continent.[9] The dialogue that follows might introduce the transparency and continue the pupil/teacher planning.

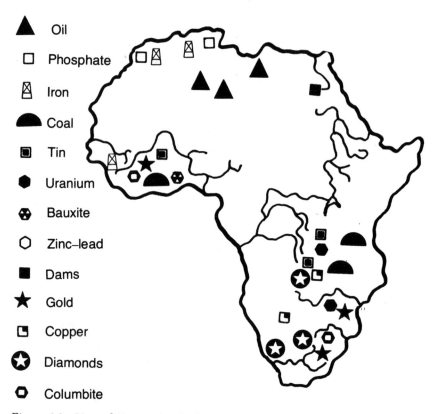

▲ Oil

☐ Phosphate

⌖ Iron

◖ Coal

▣ Tin

⬣ Uranium

✦ Bauxite

○ Zinc–lead

■ Dams

★ Gold

⌸ Copper

✪ Diamonds

⬡ Columbite

Figure 4.1 Natural Resources of Africa

TEACHER:	What can you learn about Africa from the map?
SANDRA:	It has many natural resources.
TOM:	Not so many when you think how large Africa is.
TEACHER:	Can you tell anything about the physical features from the resources?
JEAN:	Many of those minerals are found in mountainous regions.
BUZ:	Not all. Oil is found in flat areas, also phosphate.
JIM:	Yes, and I've seen copper mines on plateaus.
TEACHER:	So far we think there are mountains, plateaus, and plains. What do the rivers tell you about the land?

MYRTLE:	Usually, the sources of rivers come from mountains.
TODD:	Look at that large area where there aren't any rivers. That must be all desert.
TEACHER:	Can you hypothesize about where people might live?
SHERMAN:	It seems more would be concentrated near the resources and rivers—the eastern and southern sections.
REED:	They have so many different resources, there must be lots of industries.
MARIA:	No, I don't think Africa has that much technology. Those are different countries with the resources and maybe they don't trade with one another.
SCOTT:	Don't some European countries control the resources in Africa?
TEACHER:	You've raised a number of questions about Africa. What type of information do we need to answer them?
SCOTT:	Physical and political geography.
MARIA:	The history of the countries and how they developed.
RON:	I want to know what industries are in the country. Most of the time you think of jungles and huts.
RUTH:	What is the climate like and how do the people dress?
GRACE:	Let's find out about the music and art of Africa.
TEACHER:	Africa is such a large area, do you think we should try to learn about the whole continent?
SCOTT:	Let's find out general information about all of Africa, then we can decide if there's an area where we may want to concentrate.
TEACHER:	All right. We've listed several topics for research —physical and political geography, climate,

	how the countries developed, industries, music, art. Look carefully and decide which one you want to choose for research.
SCOTT:	Can we work in committees, so several people can look for information on each topic?
TEACHER:	Good idea. We should find more information when we work together on a problem.

Children become more actively involved in their learning experiences when they have an opportunity to share in the planning. The teacher can easily guide the discussion toward the goals he plans to accomplish.

INDIVIDUAL AND GROUP ACTIVITIES

Unit organization has the advantage of providing the opportunities to meet individual needs. Children who have special interests or skills can be guided toward tasks that fulfill these needs. Research can be conducted in areas of a study that are of particular interest to individual children. Those of exceptional ability can engage in research in greater depth and thus can acquire skills beyond the normal level. Children who have talent in music, art, writing, or drama have an opportunity to use these skills.

In the above dialogue it's obvious that Scott is outgoing and probably possesses leadership ability. He easily can assume the responsibility for organizing a committee where he can help other children. Maria, on the other hand, would prefer to pursue the topic of technology on her own. Tom and Reed are both talented in music and art. Continuing in this manner, other group or individual activities may be organized around the interests and abilities of the other children.

Group activities contribute to the individual's development. For example, the child who has difficulty in getting along with other children who is assigned to a group activity of real interest to him, hopefully, will acquire skills of cooperative behavior. Equally important is the opportunity for the child with leadership ability to channel this energy into worthwhile activities. Shy children who would hesitate to enter into activities and discussions in front of the whole group will often do so within small groups. Activities that encourage discussions of important aspects in the study aid the development of oral language skills.

INTEGRATING ACTIVITIES

The development of an understanding of the relationship of one subject area to another is made possible through integrating activities, which helps children realize that knowledge in one subject is related to other subject areas. These activities also provide meaningful practice of skills acquired in other areas.

Language Arts

Skills introduced in the language arts acquire more meaning when they are applied in the content areas. Children realize a purpose for acquiring skills when they can put them to use. Unit teaching provides numerous opportunities for the use of language skills.

Methods for encouraging the development of oral language skills might include reports of individual or committee research, panel discussions or debates on facets of the study, role-playing incidents to clarify understandings, and class discussions about the topics. Interviewing individuals to secure information also develops oral language skills. Listening skills, too, are sharpened during these experiences.

Outlining, note taking, and preparing written reports are skills needed for research activities. Locational skills involving the use of the table of contents, index, cross references, and appendix are necessary when seeking information during the study.

Art, Music, and Physical Education

Construction activities such as building a model Indian village or a salt and flour relief map add considerable understanding to a study and correlate learning experiences. Painting or drawing murals provides opportunity for interpreting events. Making artifacts from various cultures (for example, making cornbread when studying Indians) makes a study more realistic.

Frequently, topics provide opportunity for integration with music (for example, constructing maracas or drums when studying Mexico or listening to the music of the country). Learning the dances native to a country helps develop an understanding of its people. Children enjoy learning the games that are played in the countries under study.

CULMINATING ACTIVITIES

Culminating activities draw together the learning experiences of the unit. These activities should emphasize the main points, identify the interrelated ideas, and provide a compositive view of the topic. As a result of these activities, children should be able to formulate generalizations that can be applied to new situations. Examples of culminating experiences follow.

Committee Reports

The completed research of the committees can be presented in a variety of ways—T.V. or radio productions; talks illustrated with prepared charts, bulletin boards, and realia; or a movie roll that includes information from every committee.

Tours

The study of a country provides the opportunity for planning a guided tour to emphasize the important historic, recreational, and geographic points of interest. Illustrative materials such as maps, murals, and pictures supply background.

Dramatizations

The production of dramatic presentations requires interpretation of the information secured and insures better understanding of the topic. Children portraying the landing of the Pilgrims or the Boston Tea Party will understand better and retain longer the information acquired.

Films and Filmstrips

Audiovisual aids such as films and filmstrips can be used effectively for culminating activities when they review information previously investigated.

BIBLIOGRAPHY

An extensive bibliography listing the materials available for the teacher and the children should be included in the unit. Resource books, films, tapes, records, pictures, community resources, and suggested field trips should be included for reference.

EVALUATION

The methods of evaluation to be utilized during and at the completion of the unit must be planned. These evaluations are attempts to determine whether or not the objectives of the unit were successfully achieved. Evaluations must be made in terms of the success with which individual and group performance meets the objectives. Continuous evaluation throughout the unit guides its direction. The teacher should be evaluating his teaching procedures and his effectiveness in guiding the activities of the children. An assessment of the kinds and uses of materials is also important. Evaluation methods will be discussed in greater detail in chapter thirteen.

A SAMPLE RESOURCE UNIT

Africa will be the topic used to illustrate the development of the aspects of a resource unit: purpose, generalizations, objectives, activities, and bibliography (See Table 4.2). The content or background information for the teacher is too extensive for inclusion here, however, a skeletal outline is provided.

AFRICA—A LAND OF CONTRASTS

Purpose: Africa is a continent that is experiencing rapid changes. Countries that for many years were ruled by European nations have gained their freedom and are struggling with the problems that face all new governments attempting to be recognized by the modern world. For too long, the ideas and impressions that children have had about Africa are those from a TV world of animals and jungles. This unit presents a view of Africa with its cities, industries, and problems similar to other countries of the world. An overview of the continent will be developed and will be followed by an in-depth study of one country—Kenya.

Initiation: The unit can be introduced with survey type questions as indicated on p. 92, or with the use of the natural resources map on p. 94. Another possibility would be the use of discrepant data, where you first present a set of pictures or slides that reinforce the usual stereotypes of Africa (jungles, animals, grass huts, tribal costumes) and ask the children to draw a generalization about Africa from these pictures. Then you would introduce the discrepant data with pictures or slides of the modern cities, industries, western dress and entertainment and ask children to restructure their generalization about Africa. What has

GENERALIZATIONS	OBJECTIVES	CONTENT	LEARNING EXPERIENCES	RESOURCES

Geography influences the culture developed within a country and thus modifies the environment.	To acquire knowledge of the physical features of Africa and to understand its effect on cultural development.	1. Geography
		A. Area
		B. Population
		C. Location
		D. Land forms
		  1. Desert
		  2. Plateau
		  3. Mountains
		  4. Great Rift Valley
		E. Rivers
		F. Vegetation
		  1. Rain forests
		  2. Savanna
		  3. Veldt
		  4. Oasis
			Utilize maps in discussion of location of Africa in relation to the United States and other areas of the world.	Relief maps and globes of the world.

	To develop locational skills using maps and globes.		Organize committees to prepare maps indicating the major geographic regions of Africa.	Jarolimek and Davis. *The Ways of Man.* New York: Macmillan, 1971. Shorter; Starr; Kenworthy. *Eleven Nations.* Chicago: Ginn, 1972.
	To develop skill in understanding and using the seven-color key on a map or globe.		Take an imaginary tour through the geographic regions and point out the important features of each area.	O'Hern. *Man and His World.* Morristown, N.J.: Silver Burdett, 1972. *Hi Neighbor.* U.S. Committee for UNICEF.

Table 4.2 Africa—A Land of Contrast

GENERALIZATIONS	OBJECTIVES	CONTENT	LEARNING EXPERIENCES	RESOURCES

Culture is the pattern of interaction within a given group of people; it is determined by the people's shared values, beliefs, and opinions on what constitutes acceptable behavior and customs.	To acquire knowledge of the different cultural patterns of Africa.
	
	To develop skill in locating information through a variety of sources.
	
	To develop the ability to work cooperatively through committee work.
	
	To develop oral language skills by reporting in front of the class.
		G. Natural Resources
		H. Leading Products
		I. People
		  1. Hamite
		  2. Nilote
		  3. Bantu
		  4. West African Negroes
		J. Cities
		  1. Nairobi
		  2. Addis Ababa
		  3. Dar-es-Salaam
		  4. Salisbury
		  5. Capetown
		  6. Lagos
		  7. Brazzaville
		  8. Algiers
		  9. Tunis
		  10. Cairo
		K. Music
		L. Art
		M. Religion
		N. Recreation
			Organize committees to research the different groups of people.
			
			Organize committees to search out information on cities, music, art, and religion.
			
			Have committees present reports to class in the form of dramatizations, panel discussions, murals, graphs, and charts.
			
			Plan trip to Africa including arranging necessary travel plans and passport requirements.
				Children of African People. Afmeric Publications 231 E. 32nd St., New York, N.Y. 10002
				Efua Sutherland, *Playtime in Africa.* Atheneum Press.
				Leonard Doob. *A Crocodile Has Me by the Leg.* Walker and Co., 720 5th Ave., New York, N.Y.
				Fun and Festival in Africa. Friendship Press, 120th St. and Riverside Dr., New York, N.Y. 10027
				African Song Book. Recreation Services, Delaware, Ohio.
				African Musical Instruments. D.C.A. Education Products, 4863 Stenton Ave., Philadelphia, Pa.

Table 4.2 (Continued)

GENERALIZATIONS	OBJECTIVES	CONTENT	LEARNING EXPERIENCES	RESOURCES
The historical background of a country affects its development.	To acquire in-depth knowledge of a major country of Africa—Kenya.	1. Historical Background A. European Influence	Prepare a time line of historical events of Kenya.	*Kenya.* Scott, Foresman: Glenview, Ill.: Spectra Program, People of the World.
Government is an attempt to provide a society with order and stability.		B. Independence C. Struggle for Nationhood D. Government	View films and compare with our way of living.	Film: "Two Life Styles in East Africa." Bailey Films.
Africa is a country rich in tradition, but struggling with social changes.		E. Problems of the People F. Traditional versus Modern	Role play a problem situation of Kenya boy or girl breaking away from tradition or difficulty in finding jobs.	Film: "Malawi: Two Young Men." Churchill Films.
			Develop debates on	*East African Packet,* post cards, charts. African-American Institute, 866 UN Plaza, New York, N.Y. 10017

Table 4.2 (Continued)

103

changed their ideas? Do they have sufficient information about the country? If not, what questions do they need to research? Organization of these research activities can follow a similar pattern as the one indicates for the resource map.

Culminating Activity: Prepare an African Festival with artifacts, murals, music, and foods from Kenya or the continent. Try to find visitors from Africa who will attend in their native dress as well as those who present the modern image of the people.

ADVANTAGES AND DISADVANTAGES OF UNIT TEACHING

Most proponents of unit teaching claim that its major advantage is broad or in-depth coverage of a topic, which provides opportunities for integration with other curriculum areas.

A unit also aids in the efficient organization of learning experiences. The boundaries of content for a topic are established to determine the skills, knowledge, attitudes, and understanding a child will acquire in a specified period of time.[10] The variety of possible activities in a unit provides opportunities for meeting individual needs. Also, this variation promotes the development of a wider range of skills.

The disadvantages of unit teaching are centered primarily on its less effective means of developing thinking skills. Problem solving through inquiry, which can be part of a unit, accomplishes this goal to a greater extent. The boundary lines drawn for the unit's content often do not permit children to pursue interests that may arise spontaneously.

Possibly the most effective way of overcoming the disadvantages of both unit teaching and problem solving is to combine both methods. Hanna relates "that when the problem approach is used as the basis for unit organization the overall problem is analyzed into subproblems and questions, the answers to which are necessary before the overall problem can be solved. Sometimes the larger problem grows out of a perplexity about a smaller, related problem."[11]

Obviously some topics that should be presented by unit organization don't lend themselves to problem solving or present such weak problem situations that they are ineffective. There are also some problem situations that can't be effectively organized as units because of their short-term duration. The teacher must select the most effective method by considering a topic in relation to the interest, ability, and motivation of his children.

SELECTED REFERENCES

Chase, W. Linwood, and John, Martha T. *A Guide for the Elementary Social Studies Teacher*. 2d ed. Boston: Allyn and Bacon, 1972.

Darrow, Helen Fisher. *Social Studies for Understanding*. New York: Teachers College, Columbia University, 1964.

Hanna, Lavone A.; Potter, Gladys; and Hageman, Neva. *Unit Teaching in the Elementary School*. New York: Holt, Rinehart, and Winston, 1963.

Hill, Wilhelmina. *Unit Planning and Teaching in Elementary Social Studies*. Washington, D. C.: U. S. Office of Education, 1963.

Hopkins, Lee, and Avenstein, Misha. *Partners in Learning: A Child Centered Approach to Teaching Social Studies*. New York: Citation Press, 1971.

Jarolimek, John. *Social Studies in Elementary Education*. 4th ed. New York: Macmillan, 1971.

Joyce, Bruce R. *New Strategies for Social Education*. Chicago: Science Research Associates, 1972.

Michaelis, John U. *Social Studies for Children in a Democracy*. Englewood Cliffs, N. J.: Prentice-Hall, 1972.

Michaelis, John U., ed. *Teaching Units in the Social Sciences: Early Grades, Middle Grades, Intermediate Grades*. Chicago: Rand McNally & Co., 1966.

Ragan, William, and McAulay, John D. *Social Studies for Today's Children*. New York: Appleton-Century-Crofts, 1964.

Skeel, Dorothy J. *The Challenge of Teaching Social Studies in the Elementary School: Readings*. Pacific Palisades, Calif.: Goodyear, 1972.

CHAPTER 5

Structure
(Conceptual Framework)
as a Method of Teaching

DEFINITION
OF CONCEPT AND STRUCTURE

What is a concept? As in the case of problem solving, inquiry, and discovery, the term "concept" is interpreted in different ways by different authors. Should time be spent in an attempt to clarify the issue? If there are so many interpretations of concept, it is important for the reader to be aware of this and to attempt to formulate his own ideas about concepts and their utility. Possibly one of the difficulties in explaining concept is inherent in this definition—"a concept is something conceived in the mind—a thought, an idea, or a notion."[1] Another definition adds "a concept is a mental image of something." The "something" may be anything—a concrete object, a type of behavior, an abstract idea. The image has two basic dimensions: the individual components of the concept as well as the relationships of these components to each other and to the whole."[2] While the above definitions discuss what a concept is, the following one suggests what the individual does " . . . concepts are categorizations of things, events, and ideas—a convention, a carrier of meaning."[3] In the first two, the individual conjures up in his mind a way of thinking about "that something," while the third indicates that the individual must be involved in thinking processes—enumerating attributes of the concept, determining if he possesses a previous category for the concept or whether a new one will be necessary. This process is known as conceptualization. It is an on-going process that operates as the individual encounters new experiences with the concept. Thus the "mental image of any given concept will vary according to the background or experience of whoever is conceptualizing."[4] Concepts are stated in a number of forms—concrete or abstract; broad or narrow; single words, or phrases. Some concepts are concrete, e.g., "man"; while others are abstract, e.g., "government." Some are so broad that they are difficult to conceptualize and must be broken down in order to be understood, e.g., "culture"; while others are so narrow they are of limited use, e.g., "homes." Single words such as "work" are concepts as well as phrases like "division of labor."

Why are concepts so important? Concepts permit the individual to organize the information or data he encounters. He places the information in categories or groups and by so doing recognizes the relationships within the data. He asks questions about the data and gains meaningful insight. In the formation of the individual's conceptual framework, openings remain available for new information to be placed as it is encountered.

How are concepts acquired? The individual must formulate his own mental image of a concept. Therefore, experiences must be provided where he will have opportunities to encounter the concept in different situations.

How do concepts and structure or conceptual framework relate to the social sciences? Much discussion centers around the structure or conceptual framework of the social science disciplines. The discussion involves an identification of the concepts of the disciplines and the role of these concepts in teaching. It also involves a determination of what learning experiences allow children to acquire knowledge of a discipline's conceptual framework. Before we define structure or conceptual framework, it would be beneficial to discuss the meaning of "discipline."

A discipline is a body of knowledge about a subject, the individuals who investigate it, the methods of inquiry used by them, and the desired outcomes of the inquiry. It is difficult to determine the membership and organization of the social science disciplines—to identify the disciplines that are significantly different—for they are all concerned with the study of human behavior. In the social sciences, the disciplines have been identified as history, geography, economics, political science, anthropology, sociology, psychology, and philosophy. Some would even dispute whether history should be included in the social sciences. After a discipline has been identified, the nature of its structure is investigated.

Bruner relates "To learn structure, in short, is to learn how things are related."[5] He claims, "in order for a person to be able to recognize the applicability or inapplicability of an idea to a new situation and to broaden his learning thereby, he must have clearly in mind the general nature of the phenomenon with which he is dealing."[6] In other words, the individual must know the structure of the subject. However, to know how things are related without developing "an attitude toward learning and inquiry, toward guessing and hunches, toward the possibility of solving problems on one's own"[7] is learning that is neither usable nor meaningful. Joyce explains structure as organizing concepts which formulate the way we think things are related.[8] These organizing concepts "provide the child with a systematic method of attack on areas where he seeks new knowledge."[9] The difficult task of the social scientist is to "translate the scholarly concepts and methods into forms that can be readily taught to children."[10] When these scholarly concepts have been selected and translated, experiences that permit children to discover their structure or organizing concepts should be selected.

Schwab states that the structure of a discipline is based on two components—concepts and syntax.

The conceptual structure of a discipline determines what we shall seek the truth about and in what terms the truth shall be couched. The syntactical structure of a discipline is concerned with the operations that distinguish the true, the verified, and the warranted in that discipline from the unverified and the unwarranted. Both of these—the conceptual and syntactical—are different in different disciplines.[11]

Should concepts be presented in a sequence to provide an understanding of the discipline? Should all concepts be introduced at the beginning level and further developed at each succeeding grade level, or should a set of concepts be presented at each level? Figures 5.1 and 5.2 will help clarify this.

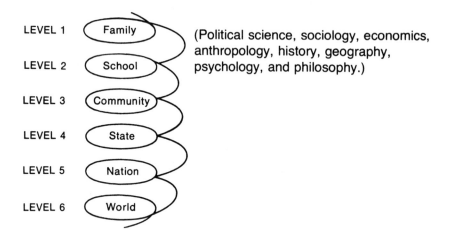

LEVEL 1 — Family
LEVEL 2 — School
LEVEL 3 — Community
LEVEL 4 — State
LEVEL 5 — Nation
LEVEL 6 — World

(Political science, sociology, economics, anthropology, history, geography, psychology, and philosophy.)

Figure 5.1   Concept of Man Organizing Systems to Reach Certain Goals

LEVEL 1

Concept of interdependence of man
(family, school, community, other people).

Concept of man's interaction with his environment
(clothing, food, shelter).

LEVEL 2

Concept of man satisfying his needs with available resources
(money, work, division of labor).

Concept of producing goods and services.

Figure 5.2   Selected Set of Concepts To Be Presented at Each Level

Figure 5.1 illustrates the method of introducing a concept at the beginning level and allowing it to increase in depth at each succeeding level. In both examples, concepts are presented within a structure that is dependent (1) on the depth of the concept and (2) on one's previous set of concepts.

Social studies compounds the difficulty of introducing its structural framework, because it draws its content from a number of disciplines. Should the approach be interdisciplinary or multidisciplinary? Advocates of the interdisciplinary approach view "the social sciences as specializations of a common subject matter. According to this view, one thinks of social science as a substantial subject that proliferates like the branches of a tree."[12] (See Figure 5.3.)

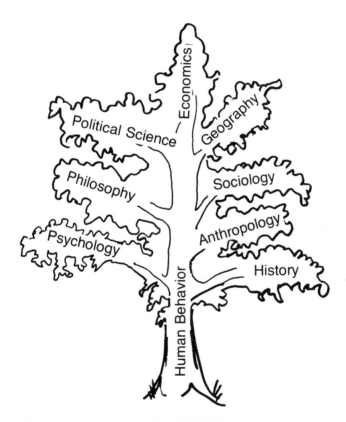

Figure 5.3 Representation of the Interdisciplinary Approach

Each of the disciplines is related to the others through the common core of human behavior.

Advocates of the multidisciplinary position see the social sciences as independent sciences concerned with aspects of human behavior that are related by the fact that the behavior is performed by the same organism. Here the social sciences are not part of a single tree, but are a number of independently rooted trees that happen to grow in the same earth, the study of human behavior."[13] (See Figure 5.4.)

Those favoring the interdisciplinary approach stress the need to understand the interrelationships of the concepts of each of the social sciences. Presno and Presno explain that social science disciplines have some "common elements whatever their unique qualities and differences."[14] Each discipline "addresses itself to the description, explanation, and classification of some aspect of the goal-directed behavior of human beings as they act, either individually or in groups, and as they are influenced by natural and cultural forces."[15]

Opponents of this theory argue that each discipline should retain its unique method of inquiry and conceptual structure. Scriven questions the interdisciplinary approach. He states that "the minute that you merge them, you get a smudge from which very little emerges."[16] Joyce, however, assumes "that the social sciences have much content in common and that a curriculum can be

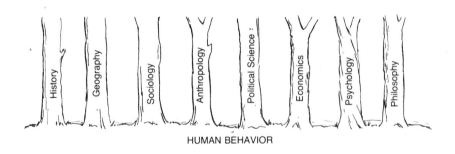

HUMAN BEHAVIOR

Figure 5.4   Representation of the Multidisciplinary Approach

organized which emphasizes the unique concepts of each of them but does not establish separate courses for them."[17]

The multidisciplinary approach might be further identified as a separate-subject approach; however, acquiring knowledge of the discipline without the method of inquiry is not its intent. Programs using both models have been developed. Examples of each will be discussed.

PHILOSOPHY OF THE APPROACH

Differences of opinion arise concerning whether the structure or conceptual framework of a discipline actually provides a method for teaching the discipline. Certainly, the concepts of a discipline can be presented by the unit or problem-solving method; however, if they are not introduced in sequential order, it is doubtful that the structure of the discipline will be discovered. Teachers often have difficulty arranging an effective sequence of activities for programs based on concepts. A study was recently conducted using beginning teachers to determine their ability in organizing a sequence of learning activities for a concept-based social studies program. Findings revealed "that the chief difficulty encountered had to do with selecting and providing relevant learning experiences for pupils. Relating specific learning activities to the attainment of specific concepts and generalizations proved to be particularly bothersome."[18] The prevailing trend in prepared programs based on the disciplines is to provide a sequential development of the concepts constituting a method.

The philosophy underlying the use of structure or conceptual framework as a method of teaching social studies is that the structure dictates what concepts will be presented and when. The prepared programs also suggest activities to be used for teaching the concepts, although variations in these activities are possible.

Programs based on structural framework have tight content boundary lines to avoid confusing the children with other concepts presented at the same time. A logical sequential program is planned, with each activity leading to the development of the intended concept. Each activity in the series builds upon the foundation provided by the previous activity. These programs suggest the procedures to be used to achieve the best results. As previously indicated, the structural framework is used to develop an understanding of the disciplines: the content, method of inquiry, and goals.

MULTIDISCIPLINARY PROGRAM

The following program, selected as an example of a multidisciplinary approach, is *Investigating Man's World*. The philosophy of the series is as follows.

Investigating Man's World is a multidisciplinary program that is meaningful now and will be meaningful for many years. No one social studies discipline—anthropology, economics, geography, history, political science, or sociology—offers all of the tools or experiences children need to learn about and understand man's past, present, and future societies. But children can learn about the world by making use of many social studies disciplines.

The multidisciplinary structure of the material for each grade level leads children to simulate the working methods of anthropologists, economists, geographers, historians, political scientists, and sociologists. Children use the various social studies disciplines to inquire into the physical and man-made features, ideas, values, and problems of the world.[19]

Investigating Man's World accepts the principle that the key to knowledge and understanding lies in the structure and concepts of the social studies disciplines. *Investigating Man's World* is a conceptually structured program. It is organized according to the key concepts and generalizations—the primary ideas—of anthropology, economics, geography, history, political science, and sociology. *Investigating Man's World* asks children to think in terms of these key concepts and to begin to learn to work as specialists in these several disciplines.

Within the framework and sequence of the program for *Investigating Man's World,* the social studies concepts are given extended and expanded treatment to coincide with the intellectual and social growth of children. For example, the basic nature of economic wants, scarcity, and choice are taught simply in a family context in the first primary-level materials. But as the framework of the series expands, the higher grade levels are reached, these concepts of economics are discussed in more complex patterns in regional, national, and international settings.[20]

Regional Studies, the fourth book of Scott, Foresman's program for *Investigating Man's World,* involves pupils in an examination of different kinds of regions beyond local communities. The first region investigated in *Regional Studies* is the state community: Because of its larger resources, the state community is able to provide through public and private institutions many services to the local communities that they themselves cannot provide effectively. Following the examination of the state, the investigation focuses on different regions of state communities.

Regional Studies is primarily a methods books designed to develop in pupils the skills of social scientists. Throughout the text many different states and regions of states are used as prototypes or as case studies to show the pupils how to investigate man's world. Once the methods of investigation have been presented, pupils are given the opportunity to apply them in an investigation of their own state, regions of states, and foreign regions.[21]

The books introduce the topics as they relate to each of the disciplines. The following chart shows how the fourth book, *Regional Studies,* is organized enumerating the disciplines and the concepts introduced from each discipline.

The table on p. 117 is a sample page from the teacher's guide that is concerned with the concept of spatial location from the discipline of physical geography.

INTERDISCIPLINARY PROGRAM

The Greater Cleveland Social Science Program is an example of an interdisciplinary approach to the social sciences. The program

Physical Geography	*Anthropology*	*Sociology*
Spatial Location	Ways of Life	Population
Territory	Early Man	Groups of People
Natural Setting	Races of Man	Change
Natural Resources	Culture	
	Cultural Change	

Economics	*Political Science*	*Human Geography*
Money	Constitutional	Population Density
Market System	Government	Commercial
Public Expenditure	Authority	Agriculture
Public Income	Citizenship	Manufacturing and
Budget	Laws	Transportation
	Politics	

History	*Study of a Foreign*	*Part-One Activities*
Events	*State:* Bihar, India	Study of Your State
Natural Factors	Concepts from	Concepts from
Political Factors	Physical Geography,	Physical Geography,
Economic Factors	Anthropology,	Anthropology,
Social Factors	Sociology, Economics,	Sociology, Economics,
	Political Science,	Political Science,
	Human Geography,	Human Geography,
	and History.	and History.

Table 5.1   Units *(Italics) and Concepts*

SOURCE: *Regional Studies:* (INVESTIGATING MAN'S WORLD) by Paul Hanna, Clyde Kohn and Clarence Ver Steeg. Copyright © by Scott, Foresman and Company, p. 12. Reprinted by permission.

for grades 1-6 contains a number of units to be developed at each grade level. Concepts from each of the social science disciplines contribute to the total program, but selected concepts form the basis for each unit. *The Teacher's Guide for the Primary Grades K-2* explains, "In a sequential program, such as GCSSP, the deepening and broadening of conceptual understandings are the links in the

Each state has a relative location

States with coastal locations Ala., Alas., Conn., Del., Fla., Ga., Hawaii, La., Maine, Md,, Mass., Miss., N. H., N. J., N. Y., N. C., Ore., R. I., S. C., Tex., Va., and Wash.

A state has a location relative to natural features

Georgia has a coastal location. Kansas is far from any ocean. States with coastal locations on Atlantic (includes Gulf of Mexico) and Pacific Oceans are listed above. All others have interior locations.

A state has a location relative to other states

Utah is west from Kansas

Missouri is east from Kansas

Utah is farther from Kansas

Missouri is closer to Kansas

Is your state near an ocean? What states are close to your state? What direction is your state from another state? When you answer such questions, you are describing the location of your state in relation to natural features and in relation to other states. You are describing your state's relative location.

Some states are close to and some are far from natural features such as oceans. States that have an ocean along one or more sides have coastal locations. States that are not near an ocean have interior locations. Look at the map on page 19 to discover how the location of Kansas compares with the location of Georgia in relation to oceans. Does Georgia have a coastal or an interior location? What kind of location does Kansas have in relation to oceans?

Name other states that have interior locations. What states have coastal locations in relation to oceans?

Each state has a relative location that can be described by its direction from other states. Use the map on page 19. In what direction is Utah from Kansas? In what direction is Missouri from Kansas?

Each state has a relative location that can be described by its distance from other states. Compare the distance from Kansas to Utah with the distance from Kansas to Missouri. Which is farther from Kansas? Which is closer?

The 48 states shown on the map on page 19 have a special relationship to one another. They are conterminous states. Each state shares a boundary with at least one other state. On the global map on page 18, you can see that Alaska and Hawaii are not conterminous states. They do not share a boundary with another state.

Answers to review questions.
1. Equator 2. Prime Meridian 3. Global grid 4. States with coastal locations border Atlantic or Pacific Ocean. States with interior locations do not border on an ocean. 5. No. Alaska and Hawaii are not conterminous. Conterminous states share a boundary with at least one other state.

Review of the Concept: Spatial Location
1. Name the 0 east-west line.
2. What is the 0 north-south direction line?
3. What do you use to help you find exact location?
4. What is the difference between a coastal location and an interior location?
5. Are all states conterminous? What is a conterminous state?

SOURCE: Regional Studies: (Investigating Man's World) by Paul Hanna, Clyde Kohn, Clarence Ver Steeg. Copyright ©1970 Scott, Foresman and Company, p. 20.

chain which binds the content at one grade level to the content of the whole program."[22]

The concepts from each of the disciplines are listed in the guide with the caution that they are not to be treated as a rigid, immutable framework, because some concepts are interdisciplinary.[23] The guide explains, "while we must use the disciplines in exploring concepts, we should not regard the concepts in all cases as elements locked in a strait jacket of one particular discipline.[24]

The units presented for grade 1 are: Review of Concepts Developed in Kindergarten, Map and Globe Skills, Transportation in the United States, A Trip to the Capital of Our Country, Allegiance to My Country, Stories About Great Americans Including George Washington, Abraham Lincoln, Clara Barton, and Amos Fortune.

Unit III in grade 1, Transportation in the United States, lists the major disciplinary concepts to be developed.

MAJOR DISCIPLINARY CONCEPTS FOR UNIT III

Economics

Transportation is essential to trade and to the most efficient division of labor.

Division of labor is the key to efficiency. For best results, work must be divided so that each person can become increasingly expert at his job.

The interdependence of our society is very complicated; it is important to realize that millions of people work to serve, feed, clothe, and house one another.

Production is divided between goods and services. Services tend to bulk larger and larger in advanced economies.

It is important to consider which goods or services are best provided by private and which by public means.

Sociology-Anthropology

A society consists of individuals and groups in constant interaction.

Geography

Geography is concerned with circulation, which includes the movement of people and goods, and with spatial relationships.

The ability to locate places on maps and globes is a skill essential to the study of geography.

One of the many duties of government is to make laws regulating transportation.

Government encourages transportation by subsidies and payments raised by taxation.[25]

A sample page from *The Teachers' Guide for the Primary Grades K-2* on Land Transportation—Trains lists the objectives and the experiences designed to meet these objectives.

OBJECTIVES

TO LEARN THAT PEOPLE AND FREIGHT ARE CARRIED BY TRAINS

Vocabulary
passenger train
engine and/or locomotive
freight train
conductor
engineer
railroad track

See Resources for a list of books about trains. The list is by no means comprehensive, but the books included have clear illustrations of the most common types of freight cars and may be helpful in answering questions which may be posed by pupils.

EXPERIENCES

FILMSTRIP

Railway Transportation (see Resources): This filmstrip may be used to introduce the study of train transportation. Nan lives on a farm near railroad tracks. She likes to watch trains pass by, carrying freight and passengers. One day Nan has a train ride. She learns about passenger train cars and the work of the conductor, engineer, fireman, road repair crews, mail clerks, and others.

Suggested Questions

What is the difference between a freight train and a passenger train?

TO LEARN THAT SOME TRAINS ARE SPECIALLY EQUIPPED TO CARRY PASSENGERS

If the filmstrip was used as suggested, instead of explaining the pictures in the *Pupil Textbook*, the teacher may wish to have pupils tell what they know about the trains and workers illustrated.

Explanations given here for each textbook page should be discussed in addition to questions.

What were some things the freight train carried?

What special kinds of cars are there in a passenger train?

Who were some of the workers mentioned in the filmstrip? What did they do?

OBSERVATION—DISCUSSION

Examine and discuss pictures and models of passenger and freight trains. Include pictures showing several different types of freight cars and the interiors of special passenger cars: coach, pullman, diner, railway post office, observation-lounge. Ask pupils to tell about experiences riding trains, or merely seeing them pass by. Mention safety precautions in connection with railroad crossings.

PICTURE STUDY: PASSENGER TRAINS

Pupil Textbook, pages 13-17.

Page 13. "Passenger Train." Explain that this is a picture of a passenger train that can carry people on long trips to many places in our country; it also carries passengers' baggage and mail. It has special cars for

sitting, eating, sleeping. It has a
railway post office car where
workers sort mail as the train
travels from city to city. Trains
travel fast, but not so fast as
airplanes. Compare the
passenger train with the rapid
transit train: How are they the
same? Different?[25]

There is a text for pupils with photographs and explanatory captions and sentences to supplement the study. The guide also contains extensive resources.

ADVANTAGES AND DISADVANTAGES

A program structured in a logical sequential pattern offers the
advantage of providing a continuity of experiences. Too often,
especially in the primary grades, the social studies program may be
a haphazard collection of unrelated experiences. Children thus exposed to a wide variety of experiences may not develop an understanding of the social sciences as disciplines or of their methods of
inquiry.

In a sequential program, the children's maturity level is considered to determine the placement of concepts at levels where most
children will be able to comprehend them. This consideration pre-
vents the presentation of concepts too difficult for the majority of
children at any given level.

Disadvantages of the structured program are its failure to include incidents and problems that arise within the children's environment; the break in continuity caused by interrupting the sequential pattern to pursue an unrelated topic; and the program's
failure to meet individual differences within the classroom. Obviously, some children may not have the necessary background of
experiences to understand the concepts presented. This would be a
prevalent situation in disadvantaged areas.

Another crucial question is whether the children need to understand the social sciences as disciplines, or understand the concepts of the disciplines as they contribute to the understanding of man and his world.

SELECTED REFERENCES

Beyer, Barry K. *Inquiry in the Social Studies Classroom: A Strategy for Teaching.* Columbus, Ohio: Charles E. Merrill, 1971.

Bruner, Jerome S. *The Process of Education.* New York: Random House, 1960.

Conceptual Framework: Social Studies. Madison: Wisconsin State Department of Education, 1967.

Ford, G. W., and Lawrence Pugno, eds. *The Structure of Knowledge and the Curriculum.* Chicago: Rand McNally, 1964.

Fraenkel, Jack R. *Helping Students Think and Value: Strategies for Teaching the Social Studies.* Englewood Cliffs, N. J.: Prentice-Hall, 1973.

Joyce, Bruce R. *Strategies for Elementary Social Science Education.* Chicago: Science Research Associates, 1965.

Moore, Virginia D. "Guidelines for the New Social Studies." *Instructor* 79 (February 1970): 112-13.

Morrissett, Irving, ed. *Concepts and Structure in the New Social Science Curricula.* West Lafayette, Ind.: Social Science Education Consortium, 1966.

Price, Ray A.; Hickman, Warren; and Smith, Gerald. *Major Concepts for Social Studies.* Syracuse: Social Studies Curriculum Center, Syracuse University, 1966.

Schwab, Joseph J., "The Concept of the Structure of a Discipline." *Educational Record* 43 (July 1962): 197-205.

Thomas, John I. "Concept Formation in Elementary School Social Studies." *Social Studies* 63 (March 1972): 110-16.

Womack, James G. *Discovering the Structure of Social Studies.* New York: Benziger Press, 1966.

CHAPTER

Teaching
the Disadvantaged

To provide a chapter in a methods text that can effectively discuss the needs of a large number of the nation's children—the disadvantaged—is not an easy task. One does not wish to label children (lest the label remain with them), but without identifying particular attributes they possess, it is impossible to design educational programs that can adequately develop their potential. These children have worn many labels from "culturally deprived," "culturally disadvantaged," and "underprivileged" to "low-socioeconomic backgrounds." Research indicates that socioeconomic class does affect the level of mental abilities of children and that there are certain patterns of mental abilities found in ethnic groups. Children from lower-class families were found to score lower on mental ability tests than children from middle-class families.[1] "Ethnicity does affect the pattern of mental abilities *and, once* the pattern specific to the ethnic group emerges; social-class variations within the ethnic group do not alter this basic organization."[2] How then do we identify the disadvantaged? How is the term to be defined? To identify them as children who come from lower-socioeconomic levels or minority groups is unfair. Granted, concentrations of the disadvantaged may be found in minority groups and in areas of low-socioeconomic levels, but it is incorrect to label all children from these groups as such. It is also incorrect to assume that disadvantaged children are not to be found in affluent majority groups.

A definition of the term disadvantaged is difficult since different factors contribute to the condition. Larson and Olson identify disadvantaged children as follows:

1. Language development—underdeveloped expressive and receptive skills as well as speech patterns which conflict with dominant language norms.
2. Self-concept—inadequate self-image which will lead to self-doubt and insecurity resulting in low school achievement and a lessened feeling of of personal worth.
3. Social skills—possess a minimal amount of skill in conventional manners and social amenities; unskilled in relating socially to peers and authority figures; and unable to function effectively in school group.
4. Cultural differences—most come from lower income and minority groups and will possess beliefs and behaviors which may differ from dominant groups in school.[3]

The reader must be aware that these children have developed language abilities to function within their own groups, but their language frequently conflicts with the expectations of the school. Most teachers react negatively to these children who come to school with experiences, values, language, and behaviors different from those expected of them. Teachers find three basic problems in their adjustment to teaching these children: (1) presenting learning experience, (2) discipline, and (3) moral acceptability. These students do not meet the specifications of the "perfect student," and the usual teaching techniques are inadequate. However, disadvantaged children indicate a natural responsiveness toward a person who reacts favorably to them; they demonstrate a keen desire to be noticed and respected as persons, and they have a general liking for school.[4] Teachers must be selected who have a basic understanding of the disadvantaged and a conviction that these children must not be rejected because of their "cultural peculiarities."[5] How can teachers with these qualities be found?

Research conducted with a group of student teachers found that using a "Cultural Attitude Inventory" was significant. To select student teachers who were successful with the disadvantaged, the inventory required reactions to statements such as:

Children from disadvantaged homes need socialization experiences, but time in school should not be wasted on these experiences.

Disadvantaged children should not be given help, but be taught as other children.

Teachers should respect disadvantaged children rather than pity or love them.[6]

Disadvantaged children have been present since schools were established, but their increasing numbers and our lack of effective programs have created tremendous educational and social problems. The impetus for alleviating this situation has been provided by federal monies directed toward improving educational programs for the disadvantaged. This effort, however, may be too little too late. Unless individual teachers accept the responsibility for adapting their educational programs to the needs of the disadvantaged, a portion of the potential talent of our nation will be lost.

Another imposing problem of working with the disadvantaged is the lack of materials specifically designed to meet their needs. A book that describes the pleasantries of a middle-class white family where Daddy goes to work every day and Mom stays home with the children has little appeal for the child living in a ghetto. Or, the social studies book that discusses community helpers such as the butcher, the librarian, and the policeman provides little interest for the child whose world is filled with welfare workers, attendance officers, and probation people.

The teacher of the disadvantaged, whether all the members of his class or only one or two fit into the category, faces a number of challenges:

1. possessing and exhibiting the proper attitude toward these children
2. compensating for their learning problems
3. selecting appropriate materials or preparing them if acceptable ones are not available
4. adjusting teaching techniques to coincide with learning styles

These challenges are present no matter what the subject area. Possibly, the challenges are even more demanding in the social studies because the concepts developed are so dependent on the extent of previous experiences.

OBJECTIVES

Social studies objectives for the disadvantaged are formulated with consideration for their learning problems and environmental factors. Broad general objectives include:

Acquire knowledge:

Of the history of minority groups and their contributions to the cultural heritage of the nation.

Of the child's immediate environment in order to enable him to understand its relationship to the larger world.

Of the democratic process and the importance of the individual assuming his responsibility.

Acquire an understanding:

Of the contribution that each individual makes to the group in which he is a member.

Of the reasons prejudice occurs and its effect on society and the relationships of people.

Of the problems of poverty and prejudice that occur in other cultures of the world.

Of the relationship of what is learned in school to the child's everyday activities.

To develop an attitude:

Of the worth of each individual as a member of society.

Of the value of learning and its potential to provide a better future for each child.

Develop skill:

In communicating with others through oral and written methods.

In getting along with others in the immediate group and in society.

In acquiring information through critical reading, listening, and observing.

These objectives vary according to the specific needs and background of the group. The emphasis here is placed on the necessity for experiences in social studies to compensate for the disadvantages the child brings to school with him. Obviously, most of the problems the disadvantaged child faces as he enters school are the result of cultural experiences in his early formative years. Nursery and "Headstart" programs are aimed at attempting to add to these experiences. However, the child still enters school disadvantaged in the previously outlined areas. His future appears quite different to him from that of the average child. He sees little offered by the traditional school that applies to his life. Therefore, teachers must adapt their programs to meet the needs and interests of these children; but what adaptations are necessary?

Before planning educational programs, the teacher would be wise to investigate common conditions in the experiences of disadvantaged groups that have contributed to their early learning. These factors, however, are not to be used as excuses for lack of success with disadvantaged children; rather, they should increase the teacher's understanding of the experiences and expectations they bring with them.

Most of these children come from large families, which precipitate crowded living conditions, limited parental attention, and excessive inappropriate stimuli such as shouting, crying, and loud radio or TV playing. The children's parents often lack formal education and social know-how, are unemployed or in low-paying, unskilled jobs, move frequently, and these same conditions are perpetuated in their children. Discipline in the home is often of a physical nature—authoritative, inconsistent, and immediate—to alleviate a present situation as soon as possible. Patriarchal authority reigns in the home with the exception of the black family, which is most often dominated by the mother.

Children are given responsibilities early—for example; the care of younger children; or particular household chores. This tendency results in less concern for the self and more group orientation. Early independence gives way to peer domination, which replaces the family as a socializing agent and source of values.[7] Frequent illness and lack of proper food; health; and dental care decrease the learning efficiency of the children.

Equally and possibly more important, as Riessman points out, are some of the positives of the culture of the disadvantaged. Riessman feels that these include an interest in vocational education; parents' and children's respect for education in spite of their dislike for school, where they sense a resentment toward them; the children's slow cognitive style of learning; hidden verbal talent; freedom from self-blame and parental overprotection; lack of sibling rivalry; informality, humor, and enjoyment of music, games, and sports.[8] These positives may provide a basis on which teachers can build a more adequate educational program.

Initially, experiences offered these children should be vital and motivational. They should build upon the children's present backgrounds. First, the children should be reintroduced to their immediate environment and helped to understand it. Then, their horizons should be expanded to a wider environment. Have the children ever been on a bus, gone to the supermarket, visited a museum, baked cookies, had someone really listen while they talked, or experienced approval upon completion of a task?

"Bereiter and Engelmann claim that enriching experiences are not enough. They claim that the disadvantaged do not have enough time to participate in the same experiences as privileged children. Therefore, selection and exclusion of experiences is necessary to provide those activities which will produce a faster than normal rate of progress."[9] Their discussion primarily is aimed at a preschool program; however; it certainly should be considered when planning programs at any level.

Cultural deprivation is synonymous with language deprivation. It is apparent that the disadvantaged child has mastered a language "that is adequate for maintaining social relationships and for meeting his social and material needs, but he does not learn how to use language for obtaining and transmitting information, for monitoring his own behavior, and for carrying on verbal reasoning."[10] The disadvantaged child cannot use language "to explain, to describe, to instruct, to inquire, to hypothesize, to analyze, to compare, to deduce, and to test."[11] If such language deprivation has not been corrected by the time the child enters the formal school, it certainly should affect the approach used for teaching social studies.

Research indicates that the following factors should be considered in planning educational programs for the disadvantaged:

1. children's interest and concern for the here and now
2. extensive concrete examples are necessary for their cognitive style of perception and learning
3. the children experience difficulty in classifying, relating, and integrating knowledge
4. learning is most successful when the process is self-involving and of an active nature
5. the teacher should show an expectation of success
6. repetition of information is necessary through a variety of approaches
7. there should be continuous feedback to the student on his progress.[12]

Conditions of the Classroom

More than any other single factor, the importance of providing an interesting and stimulating classroom cannot be overemphasized. Children need to feel that the classroom is a place where they will learn and be respected as individuals, not rejected because they have had different experiences. Examples of some items that should be included in the environment are small animals such as rabbits, snakes, or birds, or a plant. Such items present the children with an opportunity to learn to care and be responsible for living things, which are often not a part of their world. Equally important is the experience of sharing the responsibility for the upkeep of the classroom. Pictures of people and places within the community should be used to help children to identify school with the outside world. Books, books, books are needed at varying levels of difficulty and containing stories of experiences related to and expanding upon the child's experiences. Vast amounts of concrete materials and visual aids are necessary.

Role of the Teacher

The presence of a teacher who can be trusted is crucial to the success of disadvantaged children in school. The teacher must understand and be sincerely interested in the children. He must be cognizant of the most effective teaching techniques for these children. Also, he must be willing to accept the children as they are and help them to learn as much as possible.

Teachers with middle-class backgrounds will need to learn about the cultures of the disadvantaged and about how to work cooperatively with the parents to achieve the best results. The teacher is an important link between the home and the school. He should never discredit the values, beliefs, and customs of the disadvantaged; yet, he should offer the children an awareness of another way of life. Parents are interested in the practical value of schooling for their children, and they should be made to feel welcome and involved in school activities.

A tremendous responsibility is placed on the teacher, since motivation for learning is often lacking in the disadvantaged. Generally, such motivation can be created by a responsive teacher using carefully selected materials, methods, and topics.

SELECTION OF CONTENT

As previously pointed out, there are certain factors inherent in the social studies that are not as problematic in other subject areas. Webster relates the following: "the content in social studies is of highly verbal nature—more reading is required than in almost any other subject; topics are frequently removed from realities of life chronologically and spatially; and many of the values, attitudes, and behaviors advocated are contrary to those of the disadvantaged."[13] Also, the materials available portray experiences that are often remote from the lives of the disadvantaged. An awareness of these factors will permit teachers to compensate for them. Considering the learning experiences of the disadvantaged as well as the problems inherent in the social studies, what should be included in the content of the social studies program?

The goal of such a program is for the disadvantaged to learn the same basic concepts of social studies as any elementary school child; however, adaptation will be necessary to relate the content to their everyday lives. The following model serves as a basis for planning programs for the disadvantaged, whether they be urban or rural.

IMMEDIATE ENVIRONMENT   REMOVED ENVIRONMENT

Kindergarten—Grade 1

His home, family and school—Discussion centers on the type of family relationships that occur in the environment of the child—an example might be the presence of additional adults in the home, such as aunts, uncles, grandmothers, or the absence of a father. No attempt should be made to place emphasis on the typical mother-father-child relationship of the middle-class home. To develop the self-concept, stress should be placed on the individual and his role.

Values of individual. Comparison of values in classroom.

Local community—Stress available libraries, museums, parks, recreation areas, and community services.

Important people—Discuss leaders in the community and nation but, most important, select leaders from the children's culture, such as Martin Luther King for black children.

Select a culture that has a similar family relationship—for example, have Mexican-Americans study Mexican customs.

Grade 2

Democratic processes—Discuss the problems of minority groups, using those apparent within the classroom—for example, the failure to choose a favorite game or the presence of more girls than boys.	Group minority problems in national relationship.
National heritage—Stress contributions from their particular culture such as music, art, etc.	Symbols such as flag, holidays, freedom.
Economic concepts—Work in the family, neighborhood, school. Study problems of lack of money, resources, unemployment.	Other areas of the nation with similar problems.
Environmental problems—neighborhood playground, garbage, streams, air.	Worldwide pollution problems.

Grade 3

Historical—Choose a local memorial, monument, or early settlement of the area.	Early pioneers, Indians, people who came from lands specific to the group's ancestry.
Relationship of urban and rural areas—Children in rural areas learn about their contributions to cities in terms of food, labor, purchases; children in the city learn of their contributions to the country.	Cities or rural areas beyond local environment.
Communication—Within the classroom, use methods beyond spoken language, e.g., facial expressions, actions.	Systems including different languages relating to their cultural background.
Transportation—Stress modes used in their community and the problems presented.	Link to previous study of cities and their available modes of transportation.
Develop a community project.	

Grade 4

Geographic concepts of locale—Study climate, rainfall, and terrain.

Similar geographic conditions in other areas of the world. Contrasting geographic conditions existing in close proximity to the local environment and in other parts of the world.

Social, economic, and political problems of the community. How values affect decisions that are made.

National and world problems of a similar nature.

Grade 5

Governmental processes—Begin with class organization, school, and community.

State and national government and relation to early development and birth of the nation. Contrasting governments.

Local racial or nationality problems.

Discuss the Civil War, Spanish-Cuban-American War, etc., to help the children understand the possible origins of the problems.

Grade 6

Family background of children in classroom. Neighboring community's ancestral background. Community projects—Neighborhood improvement, visiting home for elderly, vocational opportunities.

Nations of children's ancestors.

United Nations.

This model does not provide an exhaustive list of the content to be included in the social studies, nor are the grade lines intended to be restrictive. The model attempts to show a pattern of relationships between the concerns of the immediate environment and the removed environment. This model stresses the necessity of beginning with the here and now and expanding to that which is distant and past.

SPECIAL INSTRUCTIONAL CONSIDERATIONS

Adaptation of the content is important, but it is not sufficient to allow the disadvantaged learner to receive maximum benefit from the instruction. Other necessary considerations involve organizational patterns, teaching methods, activities, and materials.

Organizational Patterns

The organization of the class affects subject areas other than the social studies, and it is an important consideration. Team teaching has been used successfully with disadvantaged children.[14] A faculty team comprised of a team leader, four teachers (each with a class), a college intern, and a team mother provides more individualized instruction, increased motivation for learning, different teaching styles, and flexibility in scheduling. Disadvantaged children need the opportunity provided by the team to identify with many adults. Discipline is maintained more readily and neophyte teachers are more effectively introduced to working with disadvantaged children in a team-teaching situation.

Organization based on nongraded continuous progress is beneficial because it removes the failure complex and emphasizes individualization of instruction. Children are grouped by ages; they begin working at their respective levels, and they move ahead as rapidly as possible. Interest grouping across class or grade lines, specifically in social studies, provides increased motivation because children are encouraged to select their own group based on their interest in a topic. Within-class grouping, organized according to specific skills or friendship groups, adds to both the interest and the flexibility of the program. Children can learn to work more effectively with others and move freely from group to group.

Teaching Methods

This chapter previously stated that disadvantaged children have difficulty with abstract reasoning and need more concrete experiences to facilitate learning. Teachers must adapt teaching methods to avoid pursuing abstractions without providing concrete examples. However, it is important for teachers to move from the concrete to the abstract.

The teacher should use open-ended questioning to motivate thinking and to remove the block of the one-right-answer syndrome. Repetitive use of this method is necessary because first experiences may be discouraging. An example of the type of open-ended inquiry that should be used with the children to help them understand their problems is portrayed by the following dialogue.[15] There has been an argument between two children in the group. The teacher pursues the causes of the argument with the children:

T: What was the fight about?
P: About Tanya and him shooting each other.
T: Why do you suppose he pulled the chair out from under Tanya?
P: Because Tanya was hitting him.
T: Why was she hitting him?
P: Because he was bothering her. She was bothering me.
T: Why was she bothering you?
P: Because I didn't let her use my Footsie [a toy attached to the foot for jumping].
T: So what seems to be the trouble between the two of them: What was the problem?
P: That Michael . . . .
T: What was really the problem?
P: He could of told on her.

135

T: Now stop and think about it. What was really the trouble? What do you think the real problem was?

P: That I didn't let her use my Footsie.

T: In other words, she wanted something that you had. So what really was the problem then? What do you think it was? Yes, he wouldn't share with her. Can you think of what might have been a different way to behave?

P: Everything would have been all right—if he hadn't pulled the chair from under her.

T: You think that if they had shared, everything would have been all right. Tanya and Michael, will you show us how it would have been if you had shared? Show us what would have happened if you would have shared.

[The children role play the sharing process]

T: All right, what makes the difference here?

P: He shared with her so no fight would start.

T: Why do you suppose people behave the way they do? Who do you suppose. . . .

P: Because they don't want to get in trouble.

T: Stop and think a moment, Tanya, why is it that people don't want to share? Or why is it that they behave the way they do?

P: Because they don't like the other people. Sometimes they are spoiled.

T: What do you mean by spoiled?

P: They always want their way.

T: Anyone else?

P: They aren't bothering other people. But Tanya asked Michael for a Footsie and then they ask someone else and they say no. Like if they ask someone else and they say yes, they are a nice guy.

P: Like if Tanya had Footsie and Michael asked for it and Tanya wouldn't let him, so if Michael had a Footsie. . . .

P: If Lanie and Robert had a Footsie and Lanie asked Robert could he use his Footsie and Robert went home and Lanie came back with his Footsie, Robert asked him and Lanie said no.

[The teacher switches to another incident that had occurred in the hall.]

T: Now something happened out in the hall while these children were out there—you tell us what happened.

P: There was a boy out in the hall and his name was Brian and he was looking at us while we were playing our play and then Jeffrey went over there and pushed him.

T: All right, why did Jeffrey push him?

P: Because he was nosey. Because he was waiting for somebody and Jeffrey didn't know it.

T: Why did he push him, Tanya?

P: Because he was going to tell everybody else.

P: He could have been meddling, picking at him and stuff.

T: You boys aren't thinking carefully enough. Why do you suppose—here we are out in the hall and Brian is not really a part of our group you see out there. He was just standing there; now what did Jeff really do when he went over and pushed him?

P: Meddling. . . .

T: No, I think you are using a word you don't really know. What do you mean by meddling?

P: Picking on him.

T: He wasn't picking on him.

P: They don't know. They weren't even out there.

T: That doesn't make any difference. Don't you think they can tell just by thinking about it? Why do you suppose—now picture us out there in the hall. Here we are, the four of us, talking and standing over there in the corner and the boys here think, "he is listening to our conversation and what we are doing," and so Jeff goes over and pushes him. Why do you suppose he went over and pushed him? What was he saying to Brian by pushing him?

P: To get out of here.

T: Why do you suppose he wanted him to get out of here?

P: So he couldn't listen.

P: Now can I tell the rest? He was waiting for somebody. . . .

T: Wait a moment, before you tell us that. . . .

P: Jeffrey didn't know he was waiting there for somebody and then Jeffrey pushed him.

T: We still haven't really answered why he pushed him.

P: I know, I know. Because Jeffrey didn't know Brian was waiting for the lady and the girl.

T: This is very true. But don't you think there is some real reason behind it?

P: Brian might tell somebody or something.

T: Do you think that he was worried about Brian telling someone? What do you think was his real reason for pushing him?

P: He didn't want nobody to know about it.

T: All right. Here we were, a small group, and he didn't want him to get into the group, did he? Can you think of other times when people do this?

P: When they don't want nobody to listen in their conversation.

T: Is it only listening in their conversation? What are some other times when you don't want someone to get into some activity or something that you are doing?

P: Because they are disturbing you?

T: Do you think it was because they are disturbing you? What is another reason?

P: They are supposed to be in a classroom and they might be tardy. They might be tardy and we don't want them to get in trouble.

P: They would get a bad report on their report card.

T: All right, can you tell me what would have been a different way that he could have acted toward Brian? What could he have done?

P: He could have said, "Why are you waiting out in the hall when you should be in the room?"

T: All right, he could have said to him, "Why are you waiting out in the hall?" All right, what else could he have done?

P: I could have said, "What are you doing out there, Brian?" He could have said, "I am waiting for somebody." I could have said, "Ain't you going into the room," and then he would say no, he was waiting for somebody there.

T: Think of another thing.

P: That is a good way to start a fight.

T: So what might have happened?

P: They might have had a fight in the hall and get a paddle from Mr. Gregory.

P: Jeffrey could have said, "You are going to be tardy."

T: All right, that is another thing he could have done.

P: I know another one. He was getting kind of cold as he was soaking wet.

T: That is true. Brian was wet. Now what would you say would have been the best way for him to behave?

P: Just go over there and ask him why he was waiting in the hall. And Brian could have told him and Jeffrey would have walked back and sat down and started listening what you are saying.

T: That is right. So why do you suppose people behave the way they do?

P: Because they don't want other people to listen to their conversation and they don't want to start a fight.

P: And they don't want other people—they want other people to mind their own business.

The main difficulty for the children in this discussion was the ability to concentrate for any length of time and to stick to the line of questioning. However, they have sophisticated insight (possibly more than the middle-class child) into their own and others' behavior. The repeated use of this same approach will lead to improved concentration on the part of the children, and they will be better able to follow the questioning. In this activity, the children were participating in inquiry; they identified a problem (group behavior problem), suggested hypotheses (other ways to behave to avoid the problem), tested out their ideas and arrived at some generalizations (they think most want people to mind their own business). By beginning the inquiry process with a problem that is a part of their daily experiences, the teacher is able to motivate more active participation on the part of the children in the class. Everyone has had the experience of an argument and can contribute to the discussion. This activity then leads to the presentation of a problem that is abstract—out of the immediate environment—

a community problem: Why can't people agree on a location for the new school? or Why is there pollution in our city or local community?

It should be remembered that in addition to enabling children to acquire inquiry skills, this activity is contributing to the alleviation of aforementioned factors that define the disadvantaged. The children are improving verbal skills and their own self-images through successful participation, and are learning the social skills of give and take in a discussion.

It is important to relate the activities of school to the children's outside world. Therefore, current affairs and controversial issues must be a part of the instruction. Children soon realize that what they are learning aids them in solving their daily problems and provides an understanding of the problems of others. They soon realize that history is happening right now and that there is a relationship between the past and current events.

A variety of approaches to the same topic should be used. Only unlearned content should be repeated. Ausubel suggests that material should be thoroughly learned before new material is presented.[16] Disadvantaged children need more guidance from the teacher; however, eventually this guidance should lead to independent action. Both problem solving and unit teaching methods should be used.

Activities

Role playing is regarded as a most effective technique to use with the disadvantaged.[17] It permits children to physically work out a situation, or to be active participants in an incident.

An increasing number of experiences should be provided for the use of oral language. Verbalization in discussions, role playing, reporting, and dramatizations are all vital methods to be used. Talking first in small groups will increase the child's confidence in meeting a larger group situation. By reading information and stories to the children, the teacher facilitates learning for the disadvantaged reader and increases listening skills. However, care should be exercised in making certain children understand the vocabulary and the concepts of what is being read. Concrete materials should be used to illustrate the reading.

It is important to get the children out into the community to become acquainted with the conditions and problems that exist. For example, the students could do a local traffic survey; inspect housing conditions; make a photo scrapbook of the community; interview local public officials and community members about community problems; tackle some local clean-up problem or help some elderly members of the community. These types of activities have been successfully initiated in many school districts.[18]

Simulations, or simulations games—as they are frequently called—present a possible way for more active involvement in learning. A simulation, through its materials—whether films, tapes, graphic prints, or printed material—is intended to re-create a situation as close as possible to real life. The players take the roles of the individuals in the simulation. A problem with several alternatives (with no one *correct* alternative) is presented for the players to solve through the simulation. The more sophisticated games produced commercially, such as Ghetto and Sunshine (originally for high school, but can be adapted for the elementary school), are aimed at improving race relations; the City Game[19] gives children the chance to engage in planning to improve conditions in the city during the next 20 years.

A less sophisticated form of simulation is the role-playing situations developed by Shaftel and Shaftel,[20] which are problem stories for children to portray.[21] Teachers can produce their own simulation games inexpensively and thus build them around the problem areas that are most relevant to their particular classrooms.

Games and simulations are purported to be motivating and competitive and should help in the development of decision-making skills. However, further research is needed to prove this assertion. Research questions needing answers include: Are there lasting effects upon children's values? Does competitiveness developed in the game carry over into other daily activities? Can children handle the power they acquire in the game situation?

Situations for children to express their feelings and emotions must be provided. Honest appraisal of feelings such as hate, love, trust, distrust, and honesty should be included. These experiences help children understand themselves and others. Experiences in which each child meets with repeated success are vital to the disadvantaged. Praise and encouragement should be built-in factors of every experience.

Materials

Excessive use of conventional textbooks is unfortunate, for they are often unrelated to the children's experiences and difficult in terms of conceptual development and vocabulary usage. "Textbook programs in social studies do not work because: a) they do not match individual needs; b) they are artificial and superficial; c) readability is erratic, varying from 2-9 in most books and d) they are biased on such topics as race, economics, nationalism, creeds, politics, governments, etc." The teacher should select materials specifically related to the culture of the child.[22] Extensive use of concrete materials and visual aids is a necessity in teaching the disadvantaged. Teachers should develop a storehouse of their own materials related to their children's needs.

ROLE OF THE DISADVANTAGED CHILD IN THE CLASSROOM

Teachers need to explain the role expected of the child in the learning situation. This explanation frequently has not been reinforced by the home environment. The child first must be motivated to learn. By showing he expects the child to be successful, the teacher assists him in building a good self-concept. As the child gains confidence, he becomes less dependent on the teacher. As he becomes involved in learning activities, his interest increases. Hopefully, he will then understand his role as learner.

In the beginning, the environment should be more structured in order that the child may learn the advantages of organized behavior. Freedom of decisions and choices can be permitted as he learns self-discipline.

Benefits from Teaching the Disadvantaged

A rather obvious benefit in teaching the disadvantaged is the increased interest and motivation on the part of the children. Higher achievement levels can be expected, as well as a decrease in the dreadful waste of the disadvantaged child's potential. Difficulties involved in teaching the disadvantaged include the need for increased commitment and dedication on the part of the teacher. Any child will progress when nurtured in an environment of respect and understanding, but the disadvantaged child needs even more. He needs the expenditures of enough time, energy, and money to enable him to develop to his full potential. It might be argued that the methods and materials discussed in this chapter would be advantageous to any child. This is probably true; but for the disadvantaged child, the use of these methods is crucial.

SELECTED REFERENCES

Banks, James, and Joyce, William, eds. *Teaching Social Studies to Culturally Different Children.* Reading, Mass.: Addison-Wesley, 1971.

Bereiter, Carl, and Englemann, Siegfried. *Teaching Disadvantaged Children in the Preschool.* Englewood Cliffs, N. J.: Prentice-Hall, 1966.

Grambs, Jean D. *Methods and Materials in Intergroup Education: Annotated and Selected Bibliography.* College Park: University of Maryland, 1967.

Harvard Educational Review. "Challenging the Myths: The Schools, The Blacks, The Poor." no. 5, 1971.

Hickerson, Nathaniel. *Education for Alienation.* Englewood Cliffs, N. J.: Prentice-Hall, 1966.

Kozol, Jonathan. *Death At An Early Age.* Boston: Houghton Mifflin, 1967.

Moore, G. Alexander. *Realities of the Urban Classroom: Observations in the Elementary Schools.* New York: Frederick A. Praeger, 1967.

Passow, A. Harry; Goldberg, Miriam; and Tannebaum, Abraham J., eds. *Education of the Disadvantaged.* New York: Holt, Rinehart, and Winston, 1967.

Ponder, Edward G. "Some Psycho-Social Phenomena of the Disadvantaged and Social Studies Learning." *Social Education* 33 (January 1969): 61-65.

Riessman, Frank. *The Culturally Deprived Child.* New York: Harper & Row, 1962.

Skeel, Dorothy J. *Children of the Street: Teaching in the Inner-City.* Pacific Palisades, Calif.: Goodyear, 1971.

Taba, Hilda, and Elkins, Deborah. *Teaching Strategies of the Culturally Disadvantaged.* Chicago: Rand McNally, 1966.

Warner, Sylvia Ashton. *The Teacher.* New York: Simon and Schuster, 1963.

Webster, Staten W., ed. *The Disadvantaged Learner: Knowing, Understanding, Educating.* San Francisco: Chandler, 1966.

PART  III

Selected Content For Emphasis

The national and international problems facing our country today require that particular emphasis be placed upon teaching current affairs and international understanding in our elementary schools. If children are to be active participants—assuming the responsibility that citizenship affords them—they should begin early to be knowledgeable about the events that happen around them. Controversial issues should be presented with an open-minded attitude. All sides of an issue must be viewed, and children should be encouraged to take a position on the issues in question. Only through intelligent, critically thinking citizens will we find solutions to our domestic and foreign problems.

Our world has grown too small, as a result of our fast transportation systems, to allow us to be unfamiliar with the customs and cultures of people around the world. The close contacts today between all peoples require that children build an understanding of cultures different from their own and an appreciation of the similarities among all peoples. In their home or community environment, children are often exposed to unfavorable attitudes toward other cultures. Consequently, the school must assume the responsibility for fostering better relationships among men.

This section discusses the rationale for teaching current affairs and international understanding and presents activities that can be initiated for the development of these topics.

CHAPTER

Teaching Current Affairs— Social, Economic, Political, and Environmental

Numerous purposes can be listed for teaching an elementary school child about the daily events that happen around him; however, none is so pressing as the need for helping each child to become a knowledgeable citizen—one who is an interested and active participant in the affairs of his world. Perpetuation of our democratic way of living requires the attainment of this goal.

Another vital purpose involves the development of the child's awareness concerning the social and political problems that exist in our country. The discrimination against racial and minority groups that causes serious difficulties within many cities and towns, the extreme poverty that deprives people of a decent living, the differences of opinion in our political parties concerning important issues, and the environmental concerns are only examples of the many problems that we face. The early attitudes that children develop about these problems and their ability to attempt to solve them are important outcomes of instruction in this area.

Our rapidly changing world affects each child's life. Failure to understand the reasons for and the effects of change is frustrating. Through the study of current affairs, the child becomes aware of and is more willing to accept the changes in his world. Because our nation is so often affected by events in other parts of the world, children must be aware of the complicated relationships that create these situations. Out of this understanding, will come an awareness of the power wielded by their own and other nations.

Research and discussion of the events that happen in their daily lives permit children to relate school to the outside world. They realize that what they learn in school aids them in solving their own daily problems and provides them with an understanding of the problems of others. Children soon begin to see that history is also what is happening right now and that there is a relationship between past history and current events.

Through the study of current affairs, children will acquire the habit of reading newspapers, listening to news reports, and discussing these events with others. This habit should be retained throughout adult life. The children will find it difficult to understand completely many of the items they hear or read about, and it is important to discuss and clarify these items. The children can also increase their skills in critical reading, looking at all sides of an issue, evaluating the source of information, oral language (through reporting and discussion), vocabulary, recognizing propaganda techniques, recognizing important news events, and summarizing news reports.

Objectives for teaching current affairs are:

To develop knowledgeable active citizens of the community, nation, and world.

To develop an awareness of the tremendous social, economic, political, and environmental problems of our nation.

To facilitate the understanding of the nature of change.

To appreciate the position of the United States as a power in the world community.

To enhance the relationship between school learning and events in the children's daily lives.

To increase proficiency in the language art skills of critical reading, thinking, evaluating, oral language, vocabulary, and summarizing.

WHEN TO START

As soon as children come to school, they should be introduced to the current events within their understanding. As an introduction, teachers can start with reports of events in the children's lives. The first concept to be learned is that events make news. The next step is to learn what news is important. Many teachers start the day with the development of a class newspaper containing items about the children's lives. After the children understand what a newspaper should contain, items are included from other rooms in the school, the community, the nation, and the world. An example of what such a newspaper might contain follows:

Today is October 24, 19__. The weather is warm and sunny.

Sharon Gray's house burned last night. It is located at 24 Locust Street.

Shadyside School will hold an Ice Cream Social. It will be Wednesday at 8:00 in the evening.

The Riverside Community Park will build a swimming pool. Boys and girls can learn to swim.

Learner Creek is polluted. Plans are being made to help clean it.

National elections will be held next month. Our parents will elect a President of the United States.

Some variations of this activity are: small groups of children might prepare their own newspaper or draw pictures of current events and discuss them with the class. Teachers can clip pictures from newspapers and magazines and discuss them with the children, who can then develop captions that demonstrate their understanding of the events in the pictures. These pictures also provide display material for the bulletin board.

To provide children with a thorough understanding of important events occurring locally, nationally, or world-wide, the teacher should plan problem-solving situations or units of study. Examples of such events might be: a natural catastrophe such as a flood, tornado, or hurricane; political campaigns; space events; wars and confrontations; and events that relate to past or current topics of study.

Continuation throughout the elementary school grades of these and other activities concerning current events will foster favorable attitudes toward and natural concern about world affairs. The enthusiasm and interest displayed by the teacher are vital factors in the success of these activities.

SUGGESTED ACTIVITIES

Bulletin Boards

A bulletin board should be reserved for displaying news items or pictures relating to current affairs. An important point to remember is the necessity for the frequent change of its contents. Captions on the board such as "What's New?" "What in the World is Going On?" "News of Our World" stimulate interest.

Division of the board into areas for local, state, national, and international items helps children differentiate the news events. The use of a world map on the board enables children to locate the area of the news event and helps them develop map skills. A thread of yarn attached to the location of the event and leading to the written report helps the children associate the place with the event. Responsibility for the bulletin board can be assigned to committees of children or be a dual obligation of the teacher and children.

News Reporting

A variety of organizational patterns can be used to assign children the responsibility of reporting the news. For example, a child might be assigned the responsibility for the news of one day or one week, or committees of children can be assigned the responsibility for a certain period of time. Tape recording of these reports provides some variety.

The establishment of a mock radio or TV station within the classroom supplies greater reality for the news-reporting situation. Special broadcasts or programs can be planned when outstanding events take place. Some classrooms may wish to conduct a daily morning news broadcast with reporters assigned specific areas of the news. Intermediate-grade children may provide the news program for the entire school over the public address system. Included in these programs may be school news of interest to all.

Items for children to remember when reporting the news:

1. Do I understand what is happening in the news event?
2. Can I discuss it with the other children?
3. Do I know enough about it to answer most of the questions the children might ask?
4. Are there any words that I'll need help in pronouncing?
5. Is the event of interest to most of the children, or will it add knowledge to a topic we are studying?

Class Newspaper

The organization of the class into a newspaper staff to publish and distribute a school newspaper provides realistic experience for news reporting. Reporters can be assigned to secure news of the different classes, the school office, and special events. Additional reporters can use outside sources to obtain significant local and national news. Many language skills, as well as social skills, are developed by interviewing people and writing news reports. A sample front page from a school newspaper is shown on p. 155.

The entire school can be organized to prepare the newspaper if an individual class doesn't want to take on the total responsibility. Generally, one of the intermediate grades handles the organization of the paper, and reporters are selected from the other classes.

A field trip to a local newspaper provides background information and increased interest in newspaper publication. If a field trip is not possible, a resource person from the newspaper could visit the classroom.

Role Playing, Discussion, and Debates

Role playing can be used to advantage with news events. It requires that children have a thorough understanding of the event before they attempt to act out the situation for others. Dramatizing a summit meeting or the speech of a famous person helps children realize what the event was like.

Discussions can be organized in many ways. The total class might research a specific topic and attempt to present different points of view, or a news program might be watched on TV—either at school or at home—and discussed. When differences of opinion occur within the group, a debate provides a valuable experience. Both sides can present their views and the children in the class can decide which side presents the best argument. Before the debate takes place, ground rules must be established for time limits on speaking, the use of notes, and the manner of answering the opposition.

Reading Newspapers

The presence of a daily newspaper in the classroom or library is excellent stimulation for developing the habit of reading newspapers. It is also advisable to secure several popular news magazines to complete the resources. Even primary-grade children can benefit from the pictures presented.

Mere reading of news material without learning to recognize biased presentations and propaganda techniques is useless. Providing children with news materials that relate differing points of view helps them to understand how the same news events can be reported quite differently, depending on the viewpoint of the reporter. Propaganda techniques such as use of emotionalized words, vague, general statements, name calling, or the bandwagon, testimonial, or plain-folks treatments are examples that elementary school children can recognize.

Emotionalized words are those that stir very strong feelings within us whenever we hear them. "Loved ones," "mother," "home," "our rights," and "our duties" are examples of words used to blind us with emotion, and thus, distract us from the main point of the discussion. An example of their use might be "Vote for Joe Doakes, he'll protect your home and loved ones." We are so

THE TOWER

STOP! LOOK! AND THINK!
by the Sixth Grade

STOP!

Did you know that ice is very dangerous? Well it is! Accidents on ice can cause serious injuries, especially when you are fooling around. If you don't watch out you might break an arm or leg. There have been too many accidents this year because someone wasn't thinking.

LOOK!

Look where you walk. Be careful where you play. Don't play on ice or very slippery snow. Watch when crossing the street. Don't run.

Let's say that you are walking along and all of a sudden your feet fly up in the air and you are flat on your back. You know it was ice that made you fall, but you didn't see it. Ice is very dangerous in dark and shady places where the light cannot shine on it.

THINK!

You just can't stop and look, you have to think! You have a better chance of not getting hurt if you think, so Stop! Look! and Think!

WORLD NEWS

Many nations of the world are concerned about the problems of our environment. At a conference of representatives from these nations, they adopted a document entitled, "Declaration on the Human Environment." This will protect the ecology of the world.

FROM THE OFFICE

Dr. Brown is pleased with our assembly programs. He hopes that we will have more assemblies in the next part of the year.

On February 11th and 12th a visitor from Spain will be at our school. Her name is Senorita Maria Asuncion Sole. She is from Barcelona, Spain.

concerned about our home and loved ones that we are willing to vote for Joe Doakes without first determining if he has the proper qualifications. Newspapers and magazines use emotionalized words to excite people about reading certain articles. We frequently see headlines such as "Mother Loses Home," "Rights Are Blocked," or "Children Beaten."

Children often use the bandwagon technique to secure permission for something they wish to do—it is the "everyone's-doing-it, why-can't-I," trick. It is the idea of following the crowd or jumping on the bandwagon to attain a goal.

The testimonial is frequently used in advertising. If a famous personality uses a product, then the product must be good for everyone. In politics, too, a candidate supported by a person who is well known gains additional support from the public.

The plain-folks technique is used by politicians. They appear to dress, act, and think like the people from whom they are seeking votes. An example of this is the politician who visits the farm, milks the cows, pitches hay, or drives the tractor to convince the people that he is really one of them. Actually, he may never have done these things before.

Name calling is used by various individuals and groups to label someone favorably or unfavorably. Many people automatically stop listening to or reading about someone who has been labeled by a name that is unsavory to them. Names such as "communist," "liar," and "traitor" influence people against the individual so labeled. "Good guy," "patriot," and "democrat" are names that may influence a person favorably.

Vague general statements about a topic confuse individuals. Failure to include any proof of a claim makes it difficult to determine its accuracy. "Many politicians are crooked" is an example of a vague, general statement.

Children should be able to identify and give examples of the different propaganda techniques, and they should relate this understanding to the material they encounter in newspapers and magazines and on television. Here are some sample statements:

1. *Plain folks.* Sam Arthur, a man of the people, one who came from humble beginnings, is the man for you.

2. *Name Calling.* Joe Doakes is a communist and should not be permitted to run for office.
3. *Testimonial.* Mr. President endorses candidate John Smith for governor. You'll want to vote for him.
4. *Emotionalized words.* He is a protector of our rights.
5. *Bandwagon.* Millions of people use Granny's Glue and so should you.
6. *Vague, general statement.* Everyone agrees that new sidewalks are needed in Jonesville.

Examples of activities that provide children with the opportunity to recognize these propaganda techniques follow:

1. Bring a radio to class and listen to some popular newscaster as he makes statements such as the above.
2. Suggest children listen to TV at home and bring to class examples of these statements.
3. As the children become more sophisticated, they can identify how people use voice inflections and facial expressions to convey the same messages.

CONTROVERSIAL ISSUES: SOCIAL, ECONOMIC, POLITICAL, AND ENVIRONMENTAL

For a variety of reasons, many a teacher steps lightly when controversial issues arise in the news or in the classroom. Fear of losing his job, his own prejudices, lack of knowledge of the issue, school policy, community feelings, or a lack of concern are all possible causes for a teacher's timidity in this area. Controversial issues—from racial problems to the populations explosion—are found in almost every newspaper or newscast. How can they be avoided? Should they be avoided?

Certain controversial issues should be discussed in the elementary school, for children need the opportunity to study all sides of an issue and to make their own decisions. Teachers should use discretion when selecting issues for study. Several criteria should be applied:

157

1. Are the children mature enough to thoroughly understand the issue?
2. Do the children have sufficient background experiences to critically appraise the issue?
3. Will the study of the issue help attain the goals of the school and the community?
4. Is the issue of social, political, economic, or environmental significance?
5. Does the policy of the school permit the study of such an issue?
6. Will the children become better-informed, thoughtful citizens as a result of the study?

The manner in which a teacher approaches the study of controversial issues is of vital importance. The teacher who has a chip on his shoulder about an issue or one who is prejudiced, opinionated, or possesses an extreme point of view and teaches only one side of an issue would be wise to ask someone to assist him with the study. A teacher who feels he cannot discuss an issue without showing his prejudice does his children a disservice in attempting the study. One of the main purposes in having children research issues is to develop in them the habit of approaching any issue with an open mind, securing the facts on all sides, and then making a decision when necessary. A prejudiced teacher who permits that prejudice to show defeats this purpose.

Most controversial issues can be so charged with emotion that it is difficult for the teacher to ask children to assess all sides of an issue unemotionally. A teacher may not always be successful in this task, but he should encourage his students to attempt to control their emotions and view issues objectively. Simple issues such as resolving the fair treatment of others in the classroom may be the starting point for understanding differences of opinion.

SOCIAL

The teacher must decide whether the social issue will require an extensive study or can be handled in several class discussions with individual and group research. This decision will depend upon the children's expressed interest in the issue and the issue's relation to the previously stated criteria for selection. The approach to a social issue requires objectivity on the part of the teacher and the supplying of materials that present all sides of the issue.

Suppose a riot or some other type of confrontation among groups in the community took place in your town last night. Today, depending upon the person reporting the event, it is being given labels such as "racial," "vandalism," "a demonstration against injustice," or "an attempt to overthrow the law." The children arrive in school very excited about the event and eager to discuss it. What do you do? How do you approach it? Obviously, you can't ignore the issue because it is a part of the children's world. Rather than permit the children to tell what they have heard about the riot, the teacher might suggest that they list a series of questions for which they will be required to secure answers.

1. How did the riot (or the confrontation) start?
2. Where did it start? or why did it start?
3. Is it known who was responsible for starting it?
4. How much damage was done? or what were the outcomes?
5. Why did the riot begin?
6. Will it happen again?
7. What can be done to prevent it from happening again?

Answers to these questions should be found by listening to news reports (in school when possible) presented by several stations, reading papers, and talking to several people who were in the area, if this can be arranged. All children should record the answers they secure, give the source, and then compare them the next day in school. If it is determined that the riot was caused by some deep-seated community problem, a thorough study of the issue should be undertaken by children in the intermediate grades, if school policy permits. Young children should pursue the topic to the depth of their understanding and ability to secure information. Children should interview citizens of the community, assess their feelings about the problem, find out what laws govern the problem, and determine whether the laws are being enforced. The teacher should provide the opportunity for children to discuss possible solutions to the problem. Children should learn that the true facts involved in this type of situation are often difficult to find. They should assess the validity of the information they secure. Other examples of social issues that could be researched and discussed are abortion, population control, capital punishment, drug abuse, and school busing.

ECONOMIC

Most communities are faced with economic problems similar to those faced by the nation—welfare programs, high prices, unemployment, strikes, etc. To study a local issue first may prove beneficial before attempting to understand a national problem because some of the children's families may be affected by the local problem. If this is true, care should be exercised to avoid embarrassment for these children.

Within any community, there is an area where people in lower-socioeconomic levels are living. Depending on the community, conditions will vary from run-down tenements along garbage-lined streets to neat, small dwellings. People here have few modern conveniences, many live on welfare or have low-paying jobs where they do not earn sufficient money to care for their families. Frequently, this means that children do not receive adequate medical and dental care, do not have clothes for school, and do not have recreation opportunities such as playgrounds, pools, or any type of camping or vacation experiences. Some communities provide these services for lower-income families while others do not. How should teachers approach this issue, or should they? It is extremely difficult for children to understand why these conditions should continue to exist, especially if they live within them, and equally as difficult to comprehend, if they live in affluent areas. Why do some people live in large, beautiful homes and are able to take care of all their own needs while others live in crowded, run-down areas and need welfare programs to care for their families?

Older children should tackle such an issue. Questions similar to the following should be pursued:

1. Are there sufficient jobs available in the community?
2. If not, why not?
3. Do the unemployed have the training or skills for the available jobs?
4. If not, why not?
5. Does the community provide the same services for the poor areas as for the affluent—garbage collection, playgrounds, pools, recreation programs, schools, vocational training?
6. Can volunteers provide medical and dental care?
7. Are there any solutions available?

Much of this information will have to be secured from public officials through interviews or letters as well as through public documents in the library and court house. Any follow-up action that can be taken should be done—such as writing letters to public officials discussing the findings or any solutions the children might have concluded. If it is a solution the children can accomplish, such as cleaning up a park or helping to paint houses, then these should be attempted.

POLITICAL

During any preelection period there are political issues that should be pursued. For example: there are two candidates running for office and it appears from the newspapers and T.V. ads that one candidate is using smear tactics to try to win the election. The children should attempt to investigate the charges by either attending speeches made by the candidates and asking questions, or by inviting the candidates to the classroom. It may not be possible to determine whether the charges are true or false by these activities, but the children will better understand the candidates and their positions. If additional investigation is warranted, the children may interview residents in the community to learn their feelings about the candidates, or utilize any records—such as previous issues of the newspapers—which might contain information about the candidates' charges.

ENVIRONMENTAL

Historically in our nation, the people have not been concerned about preserving the environment or our natural resources. When the country was founded, it was believed that there were unlimited resources for man to use in any way he wished. Trees and sod were destroyed to clear land for farming without any concern for their replacement or what ecological imbalance this might create. Disposal of wastes was not a problem as long as one did not contaminate another man's water supply. As the population increased and the industrial revolution advanced, pollution became a critical problem; but unfortunately, the cultural habits of the people had been established. Those who have worked hard for an improved standard of living do not want to give up the goods and services they have earned; even though the increased production of these goods and services increases pollution. Also, historically we have believed that the people should make decisions about pollution control and protection of natural resources. Often, law makers do not pass strict control laws if these would cause financial burdens to certain interest groups; or local voters won't support a bond issue for improved sanitation if it will increase their taxes. Another difficulty in fighting pollution is the importance that is placed upon technology. Many believe that technology can accomplish anything— including saving our environment, or producing synthetic resources when the natural resources are depleted. How can these cultural habits be changed? Obviously, it is crucial that young children develop an awareness of the gravity of the issue.

The issue is not only a national one; for man has advanced technologically to the extent that his activities affect the rest of the world. There are no local problems any more that can be left to local economic or political convenience. "We have now reached a point in human affairs at which the ecological requirements for sustaining the world community take precedence over . . . the more transient value systems and vested interests of any local society."[1] But how does man solve these tremendous problems? What solutions does he seek? "The next fifty years may be the most crucial in all man's history. . . . The knowledge with which we might make the correct decisions is barely adequate—yet our gross ecological errors may reverberate for many generations."[2]

Environmental issues may appear to be more difficult to approach since they are global, but are they different from others in terms of the number of different views that are held, solutions advanced, and positions represented? Possibly they are different in that the individual does not really know how grave the situation has become. Will we be without air to breathe, water to drink, and food to eat? Are our energy sources in danger of depletion? Many danger signs point in this direction and thus it is of utmost importance that children learn about the environmental issues if they are to survive.

How does the teacher present these issues? There are a number of approaches that might be used, but it is crucial that children be confronted with an actual situation, since reading about it or watching films will not bring about the same level of awareness.

One first-grade class filled their aquarium with water and then threw litter into it. They observed what happened to the water and the debris in a very short time. You may want to place a fish in the water to demonstrate how difficult it is for him to get sufficient air when the water is polluted. With the cooperation of the custodian, you could permit each child in the class to throw one piece of paper on the floor each day and leave it there until the end of the week, so the children will realize how rapidly they can pollute their room with litter.

Another type of activity that is a confrontation situation is to either shut off the drinking fountains for a day and not permit the children to have any water. This type of activity should be done only after a letter has been sent home informing the parents of the purpose of the activity. You may want to extend this to the elimination of lunch for a day to emphasize what it would be like to go without food. After the environmental issues have been brought to the awareness level of the children, it is important that they apply the problem-solving and decision-making skills to these issues.

The teacher may want to approach the issue from the viewpoint of one of the social science disciplines. Suppose the children start with the economist, since everyone claims that pollution control would either cost too much money or too many jobs if it were strictly enforced. There are numerous newspaper and magazine articles which express the views of the economist on pollution. Children can discover that the economist expresses the view that pollution can be reduced by producing fewer goods or a different variety of goods, by recycling more of what has been produced, or by changing the form of wastes or their manner of disposal. Here the decision-making skills of the children can be increased. How do you decide which goods you would be willing to go without or have in limited amounts? Do you cut down production of goods and be faced with unemployment? Is this the best solution?

Changing the form of wastes or their disposal seems to be a more possible solution. The economist looks at the amount of money to be spent to control wastes and the amount of value that would be received as a result of it. For example, the disposal of solid wastes—garbage—is one that plagues every large city. Each person in the United States throws away eight pounds of garbage a day. What can be done with it? There are areas, such as outside of Chicago, where garbage is used in land fill projects to provide recreational areas. This land-fill area has been constructed with alternating layers of clay and garbage; eventually it will become a ski and toboggan slope. The economist determines whether the cost of hauling the garbage to the location will be less than the profits gained from the recreation area. The cost of this eventually will be paid by the people who use the recreation facilities. Also, property values around the area will increase once the land fill has been completed. The main problem is moving the garbage from areas of concentrated population, where there is limited use of land-fill techniques, to areas where the garbage can be used. The economist will question—does it pay? In most cases, his answer would be yes.

Another approach would be that of the geographer. He does not look at the problem in terms of specific pollution, but rather in terms of the overall effects of pollution on the earth. "How is man changing the environment by the enormous waste products he deposits in the air, water, and earth?" One of the long-range problems that concerns the geographer is the effect of pollution on climatic changes. Can continued pollution of the earth cause irreversible changes in the climate? Not all geographers agree. The manner in which a geographer measures climatic change is by the temperature of the atmosphere taken at the earth's surface over the whole earth. The temperatures are averaged over a year's time. Between 1880 and 1940, the average temperature increased by 0.4° C. During the last 25 years, it has decreased by 0.2° C.[3] How does this affect man? When the temperatures were increasing, the ice boundaries moved northward and the south-central regions of Eurasia and North America became drier. With the decrease in temperatures there has been a southward movement of ice boundaries and increased rain in these previously dry regions. The North Atlantic has an increased ice cover, which prevented Icelandic fishermen from completing their usual fishing season, but increased the rains in India, which improved the wheat harvest. What the geographer still cannot answer is whether these climatic changes were a result of man's technological advancement and pollution of the environment or of natural phenomena.

However the teacher chooses to approach environmental issues, it is important that an awareness of the problems be accomplished with young children. Any vital social studies program must include the study of current affairs. If this study is omitted, the children are growing up outside the mainstream of society.

SELECTED REFERENCES

Chase, W. Linwood, and John, Martha Tuler. *A Guide for the Elementary Social Studies Teacher*. 2d ed. Boston: Allyn & Bacon, 1972.

"Controversial Issues: Can You Keep Them Down?" *Grade Teacher*, February 1969.

Crowder, William W. "Helping Elementary Children Understand Mass Persuasion Techniques." *Social Education* 31 (February 1967): 119-21.

Gratz, Pauline. "The Environment and the Teacher." *Social Education* 35 (January 1971): 58-62.

Howitt, Lillian C. *Enriching the Curriculum With Current Events.* New York: Teachers Practical Press, distributed by Atherton Press, 1964.

Jarolimek, John. *Social Studies in Elementary Education.* New York: Macmillan, 1971.

Long, Harold M., and King, Robert N. *Improving the Teaching of World Affairs: The Glens Falls Story.* Washington, D. C.: National Council for the Social Studies, 1964.

Meadows, Douella H., et al. *The Limits To Growth.* New York: Universe Books, 1972.

Michaelis, John U. *Social Studies for Children in a Democracy.* 5th ed. Englewood Cliffs, N. J.: Prentice-Hall, 1972.

Sheridan, Jack. "Thursday Is Current Events Day." *Social Education* 32 (May 1968): 461.

Ward, Barbara, and Dubos, Rene. *Only One Earth.* New York: W. W. Norton, 1972.

CHAPTER 8

International Understanding

RATIONALE FOR SPACESHIP EARTH

You are one of the nearly four billion passengers now on spaceship earth as it slowly makes its appointed rounds in space. Soon there will be more of us aboard this tiny craft. In a short time there will be four billion of us. Then five billion. Then six billion. And then—more?

(Kenworthy)

167

We are going to have to learn to live together or perish together. Our choices are limited; our alternatives, few. It is international community or international chaos. It is international society—or international suicide. Or possibly one more alternative—the precarious position of competitive coexistence.[1]

Can you think of radical changes occurring thruout the world that might suggest a message such as Kenworthy's? Do you feel that his statements are too extreme or that the alternatives offered are too limited? Do the concepts "spaceship earth" and "international community" offer new directions for social studies instruction? Why? How does Kenworthy's message focus attention on the need for including international understanding at the elementary school level?

Concepts such as spaceship earth, global society, and world community—to mention only a few of the popular themes of contemporary international understanding—highlight the "wholeness," the "systemness," and the "interdependence" that has come to characterize the modern world and the resulting need to seek to develop some understanding of the earth perceived as a totality.[2]

Lee Anderson of Northwestern University pursues the concept of "systemness" as he outlines the broad objectives of international education for a global society.

1. The development of students' understanding of global society implies developing students' understanding of the planet earth viewed as one planet among many entities in the larger cosmic system.
2. The development of students' understanding of global society implies developing students' understanding of mankind viewed as one species of life among many forms of life.
3. The development of students' understanding of global society implies developing students' understanding of the international social system viewed as one system among many social systems in which they participate and through which human values such as wealth, health, power, safety, respect, and enlightenment are created and allocated.[3]

The fact that educators are prompting students to perceive the world in its totality and not as a collection of strange lands and far away places implies that our earth is shrinking. This "shrinking-globe" concept can be explained in a variety of ways. For example, world population is growing rapidly and steadily reducing the per capita global supply of living space.[4] The world's transportation systems are rapidly improving from a time when man attempted to go "around the world in 80 days" to the present when man can orbit the earth in less than 80 minutes![5] Also, the world's communication systems have advanced to the point of transmitting events instantaneously from anywhere on the globe—as witnessed by the TV coverage of Nixon's visit to China and the 1972 Olympic Games in Munich. These changes in population, transportation, and communication are making inescapable the fact of interaction on a global scale and are definitely affecting the earth as a planet and mankind as a species.

Spaceship Earth in the Classroom

Since it is apparent that the future is going to be dependent on interactions with people from all over, how can students best be prepared to meet and deal effectively with the realities that will confront them in the twenty-first century? What kind of experiences have they been exposed to with people from other cultures? How well have they mastered understanding of their own culture? How much concern and sensitivity do they show for others? What understanding do they have of the relationships among the powerful and the less-advanced countries of the world? Do they understand the effect that their nation has on the actions of people around the world? These are questions to keep in mind as spaceship earth is introduced into the classroom, and the search for these answers should lead students toward a better understanding of international relations.

The best theme of spaceship earth can be presented in the form of a challenge and a simulation problem:

WHAT WOULD YOU DO?
Just for a moment, imagine that you are a first-class passenger on a huge spaceship traveling through space at a speed of 66,000 mph. You

discover that the craft's environmental system is faulty. Passengers in some sections are actually dying due to the emission of poisonous gases into their oxygen supply. Furthermore, you learn that there is a serious shortage of provisions—food supplies are rapidly diminishing and the water supply, thought previously to be more than adequate, is rapidly becoming polluted due to fouling from breakdowns in the craft's waste and propulsion systems.

To complicate matters even more, in the economy sections where passengers are crowded together under the most difficult of situations it is reported that many are seriously ill. The ship's medical officers are able to help only a fraction of the sick and medicines are in short supply.

Mutinies have been reported, and although some of the crew and passengers are engaged in serious conflict in one of the compartments, it is hoped that this conflict is being contained successfully; however, there is widespread fear as to what may happen if it cannot be contained or resolved within that compartment.

The spacecraft has been designed with an overall destruct system, the controls of which have been carefully guarded. Unfortunately the number of technologists who have gained access to the destruct system has increased, and all of the crew and passengers have become uneasy due to evidences of instability in some of those gaining such access.

We could go on, but the point is: what would you do, put in such a position? Now that you have "imagined" this situation, are you ready to face reality? You are on such a spaceship right now—Spaceship Earth!

What are you going to do about it?[6]

What kind of reactions did you have as you read the simulation? How do you think children would respond if this were presented to them? How much awareness of the earth as a spaceship and all that implies—interdependency, similarity, commonality, as well as understanding of cultural diversity—would the children be able to exhibit? You may want to role play different aspects of the simulation in the classroom. For example, the students could discuss the crisis that occurs when the captain has to ration the food and water for all people on the spaceship except certain crew members with critical job responsibilities. This will help children recognize the interdependence of people with each other and their environment and identify what is essential for survival.

GUIDELINES FOR
SELECTING CULTURES FOR STUDY

In studying about the globe as the home of man, it is important that children learn about other cultures. Obviously, it is impossible to study all cultures; therefore, it is important that the teacher wisely select topics for study. He should select the cultures that are most important for his group of children. Cultures that relate most closely to the lives of the children should be introduced first. Countries represented by the backgrounds of the children in the classroom are good examples. If a child has moved to this country from Japan, he brings with him a rich background of experiences that he can share with the other children. Also, this child will feel more a part of the group when the other children become involved in a study of his birthplace. Parents of these children are often willing to share their knowledge and realia of the country. If no children in the classroom have lived in another land, ancestral countries might be studied. The study of a country to be visited by any of the children would also be appropriate. A country that is highlighted in the news as a trouble spot, disaster area, or location of an interesting event also provides a good choice for study. Examples of such countries are Vietnam during the war, Turkey after an earthquake, and Germany at the time of the Olympics.

Neighboring countries of Canada and Mexico should be included for study to develop an understanding of how countries maintain friendly relationships. Children should realize that we have long stretches of unprotected borders between the U. S. and these countries, and they should be aware of the cooperative ventures we've undertaken such as the St. Lawrence Seaway. More of the children might have had the opportunity to visit these countries.

Cultures that are quite similar to our own as well as those that provide contrasts should be studied. Select one culture of each type to be included after the study of some aspect of our culture. These studies enable children to comprehend the reasons cultures develop as they do.

WHEN TO START

An experiment conducted in a fourth-grade class in 1949 deepened the suspicions of Loretta Klee, then director of social studies in the Ithaca (New York) Public Schools, that education about people in other parts of the world had been too long delayed. Miss Klee recognized that the whole world was as near to the child of 1949 as the radio, movie theater, and printed or picture material that he was able to use. The children in this fourth-grade class had spent about four weeks in a variety of learning experiences that had been planned to give them some insight into "Community Life in China." Activities carried out included an imaginary trip, observation and discussion of pictures and slidefilms, dramatizations, art and construction work. With this variety of activities there seemed reason to believe that the children had an understanding and appreciation of "our Chinese neighbors" adequate for their present needs. However, in order to provide them with one more experience that might help to give them a feeling for the people of China, Mr. Peter Sih from Shanghai, a student at Cornell University, was invited to visit and talk to the class about his homeland. What had been planned as merely "one more experience" for the unit, turned out to be an impetus for teachers to begin to examine the content of the entire social studies curriculum.

After Mr. Sih's visit, the teacher had the pupils write thank-you letters to him. In a review of the letters before she sent them to Mr. Sih, the teacher was puzzled by the type and frequency of several of the questions asked by the children. Most of the queries were related to topics which had been dealt with directly in the learning activities. For example, how could one account for: "Why don't you dress like the Chinese really do?" All of the reading materials and visual aids used in class had pointed out the "growing tendency for the Chinese, especially in the cities, to dress like Europeans and Americans." There were also questions about "gods or spirits." A stated objective of the unit of study, and one toward which the teacher had worked conscientiously, was to develop an appreciation of likenesses between the Chinese and Americans. No mention had been made of "idol worship" or superstition. In fact, she had mentioned to the children that many Chinese are Christians. Even more serious in their responses was the notion that the Chinese people were to be feared and that many of them were "robbers." Yet the teaching materials had presented the Chinese people as "hard-working, patient, brave, honest, and courteous."

Were the experiences of the four weeks spent on the unit merely an exercise in abstract learning which assumed reality only when the children made the acquaintance of a "real, live Chinese person"?[7] Clearly, powerful educational influences beyond those of the classroom were indicated in the children's letters. Some of the preconceived notions of the children could be traced to a popular radio program of the time called "Terry and the Pirates." Terry was a detective and lived in Shanghai.

This example supports the notion that children do form attitudes and opinions toward people in other parts of the country and world in early childhood and these may become fixed parts of the child's personality. Because this is true, instruction about other persons and places should not be held off until the fifth grade. Today, more than ever, with early exposure through personal association and the mass media, kindergarten is not too soon to begin teaching children about other cultures that are within their understanding.

The Anthropology Project at the University of Georgia, the Sadlier Social Science Program, and the Concepts and Inquiry Program by the Educational Research Council of America provide learning experiences about other cultures at beginning levels. The Georgia Project adheres to the philosophy of Jerome Bruner and selects a culture—the Arunta—that is relatively unknown to pupils and teacher. The philosophy underlying this selection is that neither teacher nor pupils will approach the study of the culture with any preconceived ideas.

The Sadlier Social Science Program includes in its first beginning unit: Who Am I? How Are We Alike? How Are We Different? Children of Other Lands. This last booklet in Unit I introduces children to cultures other than their own and the pictures in the booklet show children of other lands in their environments. Included are children of Africa, France, Iran, Japan, Mexico, and Peru. The Concepts and Inquiry Program includes in kindergarten: Children in other lands: Globe Study, Japan, Mexico, American Samoa, Lapland, Nigeria, Central Congo, and England.

Another program that carries the international theme throughout the entire primary level is the International Studies Program in Chelmsford, Massachusetts. The program is primarily based on the materials developed at the Project Social Studies Curriculum Center at the University of Minnesota, but the classroom teachers of Chelmsford have studied, tested, and revised the materials in an extensive program within their own local schools. The Chelmsford social studies program is also notable for its break with the traditional pattern of widening horizons and expanding environments based upon the questionable assumption that only things nearby are of interest to children in the primary level.

The kindergarten program first acquaints the child with his school and his local area but quickly places these in the context of the world as a whole—a world in which many children live, each in their own local areas, and about whom there is much of interest to know. The specific units studied at this level are: *The Earth as the Home of Man, A World of Many Peoples, Our Global Earth, A Home of Varied Resources,* and *Man Changes the Earth.* Although the local community is often used as a point of focus, it becomes an experiential reference with which to tie the child to the larger world around him.

Grades one and two offer a two-year sequence which focuses upon a variety of "Families Around the World." Specific unit topics in grade one are a Hopi family, an Indian family living nearest the local community, an urban Latin American family, and a Japanese family. Second grade continues the sequence with a colonial New England family, a Soviet family in Moscow, an Ashanti family of Ghana, and a kibbutz family of Israel.

Emphasis on the international dimension is continued throughout the third and fourth grades under the theme of "Communities Around the World." In the third grade, cultural concepts learned earlier are woven into the material, with the focus on comparing the social and political institutions of diverse communities, as in the study of the children's own and a neighboring rural or urban community, or the study of a Manus community of the Admiralty Islands and a Parisian urban community.

The fourth-grade program stresses economics and economic institutions. Starting with an examination of the economic system in their own community, Chelmsford pupils build on their earlier learning about the Soviet family and examine both rural and urban communities in Soviet Russia. Later units focus on the traditional or reciprocal exchange system of the Trobriand Islanders and a village community in India, which combines elements of market, command, and traditional economic systems.

This inquiry-oriented, multimedia, five-year program under the name of *The Family of Man, A Social Studies Program* is designed to bring pupils to where they can begin to look at their own culture and society from many different perspectives and apply and test a range of generalizations they have formulated on their own while so doing.[8]

Spaceship Earth themes also are incorporated into intermediate social studies programs such as the one in the Joint County School System in Iowa. Application of this theme in the fourth grade focuses on man and his relationship to his spaceship: Planet Earth—its environment and cultural diversity. Each unit begins with a problem. Units included in Grade four are: How can Planet Earth be described as a spaceship? What is the composition of Planet Earth? How was Planet Earth formed? What are the land forms of the planet and where are they located? Who lives on Planet Earth and why do animals live where they do on the planet? Where does man live on the planet? What is man's greatest advantage over the animals? What problems has man encountered living in an island environment? Why is the ocean a frontier for man?

In the fifth grade the specific environment of Iowa is the focus. View of Iowa in 1770, 1870, and 1970 provide the data for the development of the concept of change. The final study allows the students to speculate about changes that may occur in their lives or by 2070.

The sixth-grade focus is on man, the Latin American environment, and the culture that evolved as a result of this interaction.[9] The study of selected cultures throughout the elementary grades is extremely important. The method used for the study can be based on problem solving, unit development, or a combination of these approaches. An in-depth study of one culture—especially at the intermediate-grade level—is preferable to cursory studies of several cultures, which fail to develop any real understandings.

No one would deny that a thorough understanding of the United States, its institutions, heritage, and democratic procedures is important and vital to any social studies program. However, in our present world the exclusive study of our nation without learning about other cultures is unwise.

ATMOSPHERE OF THE CLASSROOM

The attitude of the teacher and the atmosphere that is established in the classroom are vital to the development of international understanding. A teacher who displays anything but complete acceptance of every child in the class regardless of race, religion, or national origin would most probably fail in an attempt to teach the children to accept others who are different. Even the casual comments a teacher makes about children in the classroom or about individuals of another culture have an effect upon children. It also is difficult to hide real feelings behind a facade, for children soon detect a lack of sincerity in a person.

A classroom where there is an attitude of mutual respect for and sensitivity toward the feelings of others provides the proper atmosphere for developing empathy with peoples of different cultures. Such an attitude does not just happen—activities must be planned to aid its growth. Children have a natural tendency to be concerned about themselves and their own problems; but they need to discover the pleasure that comes from assisting others. A classroom partner plan for helping one another with school work, committee assignments, assisting in the school library, and working in the safety patrol are examples of activities within the school that help children develop the ability to empathize with others. Projects initiated in the community such as cleaning up a local lot for playground, collecting toys for underprivileged children, singing or performing at a home for the elderly, and participating in fundraising drives are identified as representative of the type of activity needed. It is doubtful that children will be able to develop empathy for people of another culture with whom they have no contact if they have little feeling for those with whom they associate daily.

Involvement with People of Another Culture

To actively participate, whenever possible, with people of another culture is certainly more worthwhile than merely reading about them in a book or seeing a film. Activities that provide participation are:

1. Pen Pals—Children acquire names of those in other lands who wish to correspond with someone. These relationships may produce interesting sidelights as illustrated in the following excerpt. While visiting Expo '70 in Osaka, Japan, a conversation was started with a young Japanese girl working at one of the exhibits. Throughout the course of the conversation it was learned that Toyoko had been corresponding with a pen pal in Phoenix, Arizona, for the past seven years and that this pen pal had invited Toyoko to stay with her family for one year and attend the last year of college with her in the United States. It so happened that the college was located in a town in Pennsylvania only a few miles from where the author had recently finished his undergraduate work. Talk about a small world! Try this and see what experiences await your youngsters.

2. Exchange programs—Classes exchange samples of art work, scrapbooks, etc. with classes in another country. (Write: Art for World Friendship, Friendly Acres, Media, Pennsylvania.) Another illustration

will attest to the effectiveness of this activity. While teaching in a sixth-grade classroom at Eleele School, on the island of Kauai in Hawaii, this author began such a program with a friend who was teaching in a fourth-grade, rural school in Pennsylvania. The classes exchanged letters, pictures, and other odds and ends. Some excitement was created when the class in Hawaii elaborately decorated a coconut, signed all their names, dropped it in the mail, and surprised an unsuspecting Pennsylvania secretary who opened the mailbox to find the coconut staring her in the face! I'm sure the reaction it evoked from the class was just as stirring.

3. Visitors—Visitors from another culture are invited to the school for discussions of their country, demonstration of their language, and display of any realia they may have. The contact with a resident of another culture makes the culture appear more realistic to the children. Remember when Mr. Sih visited the classroom?

4. Adopting Children—There are several plans that permit financial assistance to children in countries where special help is needed. An example is the Christian Children's Fund, Box 511, Richmond, Virginia 23204. The agencies send a picture of the child with his background information and permit the exchange of letters.

5. Ship Adoption—Children become affiliated with one of the boats in the Merchant Marine for one year and exchange letters with sailors aboard ship, who write about the places they are visiting. They may even come to visit the class when they return to the area.[10] Information about the Adopt-A-Ship Plan in the United States may be obtained by writing to Peter H. Moreno, Director, Adopt-A-Ship-Plan, The Propellor Club of the United States, 17 Battery Place, New York, N. Y. 10004.

ACTIVITIES TOWARD INTERNATIONAL UNDERSTANDING

How does one facilitate the development of empathy and sensitivity to the real condition of human beings in the world today? Will descriptive statements, charts, tables, and maps showing population distribution, concentration of wealth, mineral resources, food production and the like suffice? How can we cause the child to become actively involved in learning about these conditions?

In a classroom of 30, one child could represent one-thirtieth of the population of the world—approximately 100 million persons. Whether teaching first graders or sixth graders, it is easier to conceptualize that part of the world that is American by having two pupils stand up in a class of 30. About 18 children would then represent the population of Asia and three, Africa. From such an exercise, the students might have a clearer idea of population distribution.

The relationship of population to land area could be illustrated by using both children and desks. Each desk might represent one-thirtieth of the world's land surface, and the desks could be moved so that they correspond to continents. The students could then be placed near the "continents" according to population. About the time 18 children tried to accommodate themselves at the group of desks representing the continent of Asia, while three students had access to a slightly larger number of desks representing Africa, the phenomenon of population density in this world would begin to become a reality.

By looking at the United Nations Statistical Yearbook, a teacher could use this same strategy for demonstrating the world conditions of hunger, poverty, and racial, ethnic, and religious distributions of population. For example, distribute lollipops to the various continents according to the amount of wealth in that part of the world and then check the reaction when the 18 children in Asia do not receive near sufficient number for even half their people and the two children in America representing 6 percent of the population account for 60 percent of the wealth and get 18 of the 30 lollipops to divide between them!

The cafeteria may provide the setting to demonstrate to children from relatively affluent families what it might be like to live in a part of the world where there is not enough for everyone to eat. The teachers and two-thirds of the class may go without lunch and watch the other one-third of the class eat their usual, plentiful meal. A follow up discussion should indicate some significant results.

Further sensitivity to the problem of hunger and food distribution might be developed—particularly in the upper elementary grades—by planning and preparing meals that corresponded to the diet of undernourished people, both in terms of the portion and the balance of basic food groups. An average, suburban child who sat down to a small portion of rice would gain more in empathy and sensitivity than he would lose in nutrition.

How do we help children understand their ethnocentric bias? One way is for children to see discrepancies between their own perception of a situation and that of others. Although there is little material available at the elementary level, teachers can get copies of history books printed in the United Kingdom, Canada, and other English-speaking areas of the world, and read to the class those portions that describe historical periods of interaction of these nations with the United States—for example, the Revolutionary War and the War of 1812. Such readings should be followed by accounts of how and why these historical accounts may differ significantly.

Another project would be to send for newspapers from English-speaking countries around the world and then compare the coverage given to the same topics in their local paper. Ethnocentrism can be observed not only in the way the "news" is dealt with, but also in the selection and relative space given to various news stories.

Another way to develop an awareness of ethnocentric bias is by an examination of the language used in describing our relations with other peoples and cultures—past and present. Why was it a "massacre" when the Indians killed white men, but a "battle" when Indians were slaughtered?"

Also, a primary teacher could point out the left-to-right pattern we use in reading and writing and call attention to the variety of ways people in other cultures read and write—both with vertical patterns as well as right-to-left. An example of the development of an awareness of one child to his own ethnocentric view is illustrated by this hypothetical response to a lesson: "They write backwards don't they? But I bet they think we write backwards."

A limited form of ethnocentrism can be exhibited by children with the blue eyes/brown eyes simulation activity. All the blue-eyed children in the classroom are told that they are "better" than the brown-eyed children and the way that they decide to do things that particular day is the "best" way. The teacher lets the blue-eyed group dictate the games to play, the way they are to proceed to the lunch room (blue-eyed children first, of course), and all other activities that the class participates in for that day. Afterwards, the experience should be discussed and roles exchanged on another day. It has been reported that those children who experience the position of being inferior first seem to exhibit a greater degree of empathy and do not display as much bias in their behavior as did the first group. [11]

Activities for Primary Grades

The young child is especially interested in learning about the aspects with another culture that are most important to him in his own daily activities. Questions he wants answered are:

1. What games do they play?
2. What is their school like?
3. What type of clothes do they wear?
4. What are their favorite foods?
5. Do they have toys?
6. What type of work do their fathers do?
7. What are the houses like?
8. How can I travel to the country and how long will it take?

Learning experiences that develop from these questions are numerous. Map and globe skills can be acquired by determining the country's location. A planned trip from the child's home to the other country aids in developing space relationships; and in planning the time required for the trip, the child acquires more knowledge of distances. Children can play games from the country and learn its simple folk dances. Singing the songs and listening to the music of a country also adds to the flavor of the study.

Children's books are excellent sources for children of any age, but they are especially helpful with young children. Generally, these books contain stories of children from other countries, and they describe their customs and cultures in terms that children can easily understand. It is important that the information in the book is accurate. Care in the selection of books should prevent the use of those that present only the differences between cultures and fail to show the similarities among all children no matter where they live. It is interesting to compare the folktales, fables, and myths of other lands with those of our own country.

A comparison study of the holidays and festivals around the world or in individual countries aids international understanding. A country's religious celebrations, in particular, reveal considerable information about the historical background of the country. Preparing food from different lands, discussing meals served in the school or home that originated in other countries, and visiting zoos to identify animals from other lands are additional activities that can be planned.

These activities should not be presented to children as a haphazard collection of things to do; rather, they should be regarded as the type of learning experiences that can be planned when studying other cultures. The teacher may emphasize pertinent activities when working with a particular culture. Of course, different aspects would be emphasized for different studies.

Activities for Intermediate Grades

The maturity level of the intermediate-grade child permits in depth studies of other cultures. These children should learn about the historical and geographical factors that influence the culture of a country. The social, political, and economic problems of the cultures under study also should be investigated, for most intermediate-grade children can understand these situations and propose alternate solutions.

Many of the activities discussed for primary grades also can be used in the intermediate grades; however, the older children's questions will be more penetrating, for example:

1. How are the people governed?
2. What are the important industries?
3. What are the agricultural products?
4. Who are some of the famous people of the country?
5. What freedoms do the people possess?
6. How did the country develop?

7. What are the people like?
8. What position does the country have in the world?

These questions require in depth study, and intermediate children are capable of doing more extensive research in order to obtain answers.

Children should learn of the activities of the United States government in its aid to other nations. Programs such as the Marshall Plan and AID have invested vast amounts of money for development projects in foreign nations. Critics of these projects, who portray the image of the "ugly American," also should be discussed, for some of the projects have failed to meet expectations. However, children should be aware of the many people who have benefited from them.

A thorough study of the United Nations should be initiated in the intermediate grades. It is important that children gain an understanding of its role in maintaining good international relationships. The different responsibilities of each of the organs of the United Nations is an important factor to stress. Countries that have major responsibilities at the time of the study such as the countries of the president of the United Nations and chairman of the Security Council may be investigated in greater depth.

In developing international understanding, it is significant to remember that this learning must be an on-going process, not a once-a-year activity. Every opportunity to relate daily activities with the world-mindedness should be used to advantage.[12]

SELECTED REFERENCES

Anderson, Lee. "An Examination of the Structure and Objectives of International Education." *Social Education* 32 (November 1968): 646.

Becker, James, ed. *An Examination of Objectives, Needs and Priorities in International Education in U. S. Secondary and Elementary Schools*, Final Report, Project No. 6–2908, Contract No. OEC 1–7–002908–2028. Washington, D. C.: U. S. Office of Education, Bureau of Research, July 1969, p. 29.

Brown, Lester R. "An Overview of World Trends." *Futurist*, December 1972, p. 225.

Douglass, Malcolm P. "Ship Adoption May Be Your International Thing." *Social Education* 34 (January 1970): 56.

Kenworthy, Leonard S. "The International Dimension of Education." *Association for Supervision and Curriculum Development*, NEA, 1970.

Klee, Loretta E. "Larger Horizons for the Child: A Fourth Grade Experiment." *Social Education* 13 (February 1949): 69.

Long, Harold M., and King, Robert N. *Improving the Teaching of World Affairs: The Glens Falls Story* (Washington, D. C.: National Council for the Social Studies, 1964).

Loving, Alvin D. "Men for Tomorrow: A Challenge for Education," in Alice Miel and Louise Berman, eds, *"Educating the Young People of the World."* Association for Supervision and Curriculum Development, NEA.

Morris, Donald N. "Developing Global Units for Elementary Schools." *International Education for Spaceship Earth*, David C. King, ed., Foreign Policy Association, 1970.

Morris, Donald N., and King, Edith W. "Bringing Spaceship Earth into Elementary School Classrooms." *Social Education* 32 (November 1968): 676–77.

Skeel, Dorothy J. *The Challenge of Teaching Social Studies in the Elementary School* 1st ed. Goodyear, 1970.

Tourney, Judith V., and Morris, Donald N. *Global Dimensions in U. S. Education: The Elementary School.* The Center for War/Peace Studies of the New York Friends Group, 1972.

Skill Development

Opportunities for skill development in the social studies are numerous. In addition to the specific skills needed in the social studies, the subject provides a real purpose for use of the skills introduced in other curriculum areas such as language arts, science, mathematics, art, music, and physical education. The 33rd Yearbook of the National Council for the Social Studies analyzes skills of shared responsibility and those pertaining specifically to the social studies.

I. Skills that are a definite but shared responsibility of the social studies:

1. locating information
2. organizing information
3. evaluating information
4. acquiring information through reading
5. acquiring information through listening and observing
6. communicating orally and in writing
7. interpreting pictures, charts, graphs, and tables
8. working with others

II. Skills that are a major responsibility of the social studies.

1. reading social studies materials

2. applying problem-solving and critical-thinking skills to social issues
3. interpreting maps and globes
4. understanding time and chronology[1]

The Council suggests that development should be based on the following principles of learning and teaching.

1. The skill should be taught functionally, in the concept of a topic of study, rather than as a separate exercise.
2. The learner must understand the meaning and purpose of the skill, and have motivation for developing it.
3. The learner should be carefully supervised in his first attempts to apply the skill, so that he will form correct habits from the beginning.
4. The learner needs repeated opportunities to practice the skill, with immediate evaluation so that he knows where he has succeeded or failed in his performance.
5. The learner needs individual help, through diagnostic measures and follow-up exercises, since not all members of any group learn at exactly the same rate or retain equal amounts of what they have learned.
6. Skill instruction should be presented at increasing levels of difficulty, moving from the simple to the more complex; the resulting growth in skills should be cumulative as the learner moves through school, with each level of instruction building on and reinforcing what has been taught previously.
7. Students should be helped, at each stage, to generalize the skills, by applying them in many and varied situations, in this way maximum transfer of learning can be achieved.
8. The program of instruction should be sufficiently flexible to allow skills to be taught as they are needed by the learner; many skills should be developed concurrently.[2]

[1]Helen McCracken Carpenter, ed., *Skill Development in Social Studies*, 33rd Yearbook (Washington, D. C.: National Council for the Social Studies, 1963), pp. 310-11.
[2]Carpenter, *Skill Development in Social Studies*, pp. 311-12.

Part four discusses (1) the skills of valuing, (2) committee work as the primary vehicle for developing intellectual, expressive, and social skills in social studies, and (3) map and globe skills with suggested activities.

Valuing is included in the skills section since it should be emphasized that the children are learning a process of valuing skills in evaluating and making judgments.

Committee work was selected because of the many opportunities for skill development it offers. Committee work in social studies is a representative activity that is effective in developing skills; of course, these skills can be developed in other ways. Because map and globe skills are of a particularly specialized nature and are frequently neglected by the teacher, they are given special emphasis.

CHAPTER 9

The Skills of Valuing

RATIONALE

Value issues confront children daily as they attempt to make decisions about their lives. Should I take the money in Sylvia's desk? Will I be a friend to Herby who is black? All the other kids are going to boycott Mr. Jim's market because he won't hire Puerto Ricans, should I? My mother wants me to be a doctor and make lots of money; I want to work with poor people in India. What should I do? How does the child make a decision? What values does he possess? Where and how did he acquire his values? Does his family influence his values more than does his peer group? Why don't people behave the way they say they should? Possibly now, more than at any other time in our history, children observe tremendous conflicts in the values that people say they possess and what they actually exhibit by their behaviors. Equality of opportunity for all is a phrase often heard, but children witness discrimination against minority groups and women particularly for jobs and schooling. Children find to be untrue advertising claims on television suggesting the virtues of certain products. Parents warn children against breaking laws, but serve as poor examples by exceeding speed limits when they are late. Everyone talks about how important it is to protect the environment, but litter is everywhere and the local strip mining company attempts to leave without reforesting the area. Government is supposed to operate for all people, but some officials can be bribed to grant special favors. In light of these conflicts, what values should a child possess? How does the school affect the child's value system? How should it?

Different subcultures and life-styles in our society possess varied value beliefs. Children from these homes come to school with different value structures. Often, the teacher does not possess the same values as those of the children. What set of values will be accepted? Hopefully, no one particular set of values will be indoctrinated, but rather the teacher will aid the children in acquiring the skills that will help them evaluate and clarify the values they possess.

Research findings by Kohlberg suggest that children achieve the ability to make value judgments dependent upon the stage of development in moral concepts they have reached. He indicates that there are six stages through which a child must go step by step. These are as follows:

Level I—Premoral
    Stage 1. Obedience and punishment orientation.
    Stage 2. Instrumentally satisfying the self's needs and occasionally others'.
Level II—Conventional Role conformity
    Stage 3. Good-boy orientation.
    Stage 4. Authority and social-order maintaining orientation.
Level III—Self-Accepted Moral Principles
    Stage 5. Recognition of an arbitrary element or starting point in rules or expectations for the sake of agreement.
    Stage 6. Orientation to conscience as a directing agent and to mutual respect and trust.[1]

This developmental view strengthens the position of the school to stimulate the individual child's moral judgment and character rather than teaching fixed values.[2] ". . . The sign of the child's moral maturity is his ability to make moral judgments and formulate moral principles of his own, rather than his ability to conform to moral judgments of the adults around him."[3] Therefore, it is the responsibility of the school to provide opportunities for the child to assess real and challenging conflict situations. These should be situations that do not have the obvious adult answer at hand to discourage the child's own moral thought.[4]

A similar approach to the classroom process of valuing is advanced by Raths, Harmin, and Simon, who suggest that teaching strategies should help children clarify their values. The process of valuing as posed by them is based on the following criteria:

1. choosing from alternatives
2. choosing after careful consideration of the consequences of each alternative
3. choosing freely
4. prizing, being glad of one's choice
5. prizing, being willing to publicly affirm one's choice
6. acting upon one's choice, incorporating choices into behavior
7. acting upon one's choice repeatedly, over time.[5]

This approach labeled values-clarification ". . . is based on the premise that none of us has the "right" set of values to pass on to other people's children."[6]

What effect does the classroom peer group have upon the child's value structure? Kohlberg found that children with extensive peer-group participation advance more quickly through the stages of moral judgment than those who are isolated from participation.[7] Once again, it is obvious that active participation with value issues in the classroom with peers will foster the development of valuing process.

How then should the teacher approach values in the classroom? The atmosphere of the classroom is a crucial factor that should take top priority in planning the valuing aspect of the social studies curriculum. If the atmosphere is to foster freedom of thought about values, then teachers should be cautious not to make statements that would suggest that the student's values should be the same as theirs. Comments that will quickly stifle any child's attempt to make his own decisions include, "How could you possibly believe that cheating is acceptable in certain situations?" "You're the only one who would think that was the best solution." "Why don't you think the situation over again and come up with a better answer?" This is not to suggest that teachers should not indicate their own value judgements, but it is important how and when they voice them. For instance, if a student asks your opinion you suggest that he is not obligated to agree with you. "If I had to make a choice, I would ⎯⎯⎯⎯⎯⎯⎯⎯⎯⎯⎯⎯⎯⎯⎯⎯⎯⎯⎯

for these reasons _____, but you make your choice based on your reasons" is a constructive response.

TEACHING STRATEGIES FOR VALUING

If the developmental stages of Kohlberg are to be followed, it is suggested that the teacher first determine the stage that the children have reached before deciding on the types of instructional materials to use.[8] Research indicates that posing value judgements that are one level above the children's present stage of development proves most effective.[9] Kohlberg uses examples of moral dilemmas to determine the levels of development. These can be used as instructional materials as well as those developed by the teacher.

An example of one of them follows:

In Europe a woman was near death from cancer. One drug might save her, a form of radium that a druggist in the same town had recently discovered. The druggist was charging $2,000, ten times what the drug cost him to make. The sick woman's husband, Heinz, went to everyone he knew to borrow the money, but he could only get together about half of what it cost. He told the druggist that his wife was dying and asked him to sell it cheaper or let him pay later. But the druggist said, "No." The husband got desperate and broke into the man's store to steal the drug for his wife. Should the husband have done that? Why?[10]

Newspaper Sources

Many valuing situations are provided by the reports in newspapers. For example, the following headlines are given to children and they are requested to rank them in order of importance to them.

Committee Upholds Ban On Phosphates

Rich Nations Must Pay for Earth's Cleanup

Indians, Police Clash in South Dakota

Sunday Drinking Bill Now Confronts Governor

President Has Implied Right to Impound Funds, Aide Says

IRA Rejects New Irish Peace Plan; 2 Soldiers Killed

Afterwards, children are requested to write and then to discuss the reasons behind their rankings. This gives children the opportunity to think about what things are important to them and why.

Frequently, newspaper articles will provide excellent situations for pursuing valuing issues. The teacher should use the following article in conjunction with the strategy presented in Figure 9.1.

The news article may present only one side of the issue and it will be necessary to search out factual information and possibly opinions from other sources. Children should not be forced to make their own value decisions until they are ready. It should be

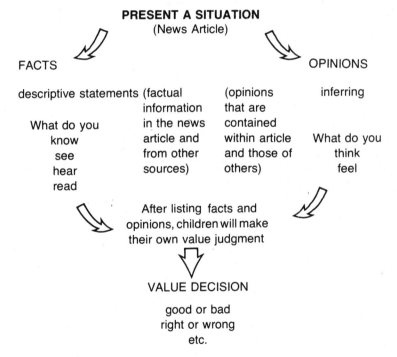

Figure 9.1 Situation for Valuing

SOURCE: The Courier-Journal, (Louisville), October 27, 1971.

'Deplorable conditions' cited

Migrants satisfied, state senator says

Special to The Courier-Journal

BEDFORD, Ind. — Migrant farm workers who come to Indiana each fall to harvest tomatoes live like animals because they want it that way in the opinion of state Sen. Earl Wilson of Bedford.

Wilson, chairman of the Indiana Legislative Council's Migrant Workers Interim Study Committee, and two other members of his committee, Rep. Wilma J. Fay, R-Indianapolis, and Rep. Glen R. Harden, D-Columbus, visited four migrant workers' camps early this month in Henry and Delaware counties.

Wilson said he came away with the feeling that conditions cannot be greatly improved for migrant workers, because they do not want them to. Efforts in the past to improve conditions have largely met with failure, he said.

What is needed, the senator said, is legislation to provide some standardized regulations, with inspections of the camps, preferably by local health authorities, to ascertain that the minimum standards are maintained.

"We have to be careful," he said, "not to impose more severe restrictions on Indiana farmers and packers than exist in other states, because that would put Hoosier farmers at a disadvantage competitively with farmers in other states."

"We probably need some federal legislation with which all employers of migrant workers would have to comply," he said.

Wilson said his committee found generally unsanitary conditions in the camps, and some conditions that could be classed as deplorable. "But generally speaking, the deplorable conditions were much of the workers' own doings," he said. "You can't make a silk purse of a sow's ear," he declared.

"They complained of cesspools stinking," he said, "but in some quarters the toilets had been used a dozen or more times without being flushed. I flushed them to see if they were working properly, and they were.

"We found screens deliberately torn from the windows. Maybe that was so there could be fast exit out windows if the wrong person came in the door. Management people said they could repair the screens, but the workers would promptly tear them out again.

"Garbage pails were outside some living units everywhere we went, but in some cases the cans were empty and garbage was strewn all over the floor inside. In a matter of five minutes, 75 per cent improvement could be brought about in this situation," the state senator said.

Wilson said it is his recommendation that there be daily inspection of the migrant worker camps, with supervision, to see that the recommendations and regulations are carried out. This, he said, should be done by the employer and local or state health authorities—preferably by local health boards if possible.

Wilson said many of the workers with whom he talked said they were perfectly satisfied and that conditions in Indiana were better than in some other states.

Despite the bad conditions under which the migrants live, Wilson said there didn't seem to be any illness to speak of.

Wilson said that one of the better camps which his committee visited was at Sulphur Springs in Henry County. There a new mobile home village was created two years ago for the migrant workers. The project cost $250,-000, he said, but the first year the migrant workers did $36,000 damage.

The migrant workers committee will meet again Nov. 4 at the Indianapolis State House and expects to come up with recommendations for stop-gap legislation for 1972. Wilson said the committee will work toward a more comprehensive bill for introduction in the 1973 legislature.

pointed out that with the addition of new information, new experiences, or hearing other opinions, their original decisions may change.

Another source for ranking values is the Values Survey developed by Rokeach. There are two lists, each containing 18 items—instrumental (preferred modes of behavior) and terminal (end states of existence). The individual is requested to rank these values in order of importance to him in guiding his daily life. Fifth- and sixth-grade children should be able to rank these and discuss why they are so ranked. Of equal importance is the teacher's ranking. Such ranking may indicate wide discrepancy between the teacher and the children's value beliefs.

One of the most effective strategies to use in the valuing process is the unfinished-story or "what-should-I-do-now" situation. It is outlined in Figure 9.2.

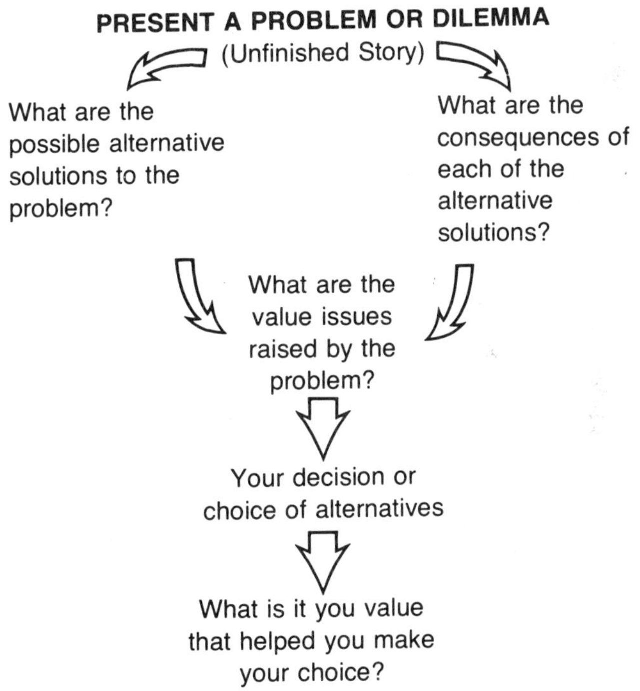

PRESENT A PROBLEM OR DILEMMA
(Unfinished Story)

What are the possible alternative solutions to the problem?

What are the consequences of each of the alternative solutions?

What are the value issues raised by the problem?

Your decision or choice of alternatives

What is it you value that helped you make your choice?

Figure 9.2 Unfinished Story for Valuing

The above strategy can be implemented in a variety of ways. The story can be presented to the children for discussion of the alternatives and consequences, or children can be requested to list their own alternatives and consequences to be discussed later with the class. Children should not be forced to express their solutions and value choices if they show any hesitation. The teacher should indicate that it is a free choice. The following is a sample unfinished story and the classroom dialogue that it initiated.

What Should David Do?

David had the reputation for being the "character" of the class. He enjoyed his success of being the "unpopular star" of the class. It was the only time he received any attention. If something happened, David was the first to be accused. One morning Susan discovered that her week's lunch tickets were missing. David was the first person to be mentioned as the culprit. However, David did not take the lunch tickets and he knew Sammy had done it. Sammy had told him that morning that his mother did not have any money for his lunches that week. What should David do?

TEACHER:	What are some ways in which David might solve the problem?
SARAH:	He could pretend he doesn't know anything about it.
JIM:	Tell the teacher what happened.
TEACHER:	What about Sammy?
JIM:	Let the teacher talk to Sammy.
KARA:	Go to Sammy and ask him what he's going to do.
NANCY:	Yes, and tell him that otherwise David will take the blame.
BILL:	That won't work. Sammy probably wouldn't care if David took the blame.
NANCY:	No, I think Sammy would feel bad about that.
BOB:	David should tell everyone that he isn't guilty, but that Sammy is.
SARAH:	No, he should give Sammy a chance to confess.
BOB:	If David tells everyone, it will hurt Sammy.

	Maybe it is the first time he has taken anything. Maybe he was hungry.
BOB:	You can't take things just because you are hungry.
SARAH:	Have you ever been hungry and not had any money?
NANCY:	It isn't that Sammy was right in what he did, but how to work things out so that neither David or Sammy will be hurt anymore than necessary.
TEACHER:	Do you have any more ideas about what David might do? No. Then let's look at the consequences of each possible solution.

ALTERNATIVE	CONSEQUENCES
Ignore the situation.	David will be blamed for taking the tickets. The kids won't trust David. Sammy would get away with it.
Tell the teacher	David would not be blamed. Sammy would be punished. Sammy would be angry at David.
Talk to Sammy	Sammy may not be willing to confess. Sammy may confess. David may lose Sammy as a friend.
Tell everyone that Sammy took the tickets.	Sammy will be hurt. David won't be blamed. The kids may not believe David.

TEACHER:	What are the value issues involved with the problem?
TRACEY:	I don't understand what you mean.
TEACHER:	What important things are a part of the problem? Is it a matter of money, trust, friendship?
TRACEY:	Oh! I see! It's trust. The kids don't trust David.
KIM:	Also, friendship. David's friendship with Sammy.
JASON:	How about the value of each person?

BILL:	Self-respect. When you are guilty and want to somehow make up for your mistake.
SKIP:	Honesty.
BOB:	If you tell everyone, then they will know you didn't do it.

The teacher then asked if any of the children were ready to role play their choice of solution. Role playing any of these value situations is most effective. Children can be asked to suddenly reverse roles to get the feel of another view. Bob quickly volunteered and opted to tell everyone what had happened. Several of the children argued with him and role played their own solutions. This did not change Bob's mind and the teacher remained out of the discussion. The children completed this activity by each child recording in his log his choice and the reasons for it.

The previous example is included to emphasize the point that the teacher should not attempt to tell Bob his position is "wrong," because it is his choice and he feels strongly about it. If the teacher moralizes with Bob, he may not be as open in future discussions and the teacher's position is not likely to change Bob's basic value beliefs. You may question whether the previous experience was worthwhile for him. The answer is "yes" because he is very much aware of what values are most important to him and it is possible that the other children's discussion with him may have quite an effect on similar future value decisions.

Sidney Simon[11] suggests the following activity to help children find out what they really want. He suggests that the teacher provide Western Union telegram blanks or have children write on paper headed "Telegram." Ask each child to think of someone in his own life to whom he would send a telegram that begins with these words *I urge you to.* These telegrams are used several times a year and kept by the children so that they may refer back to them and write "I learned statements" from the messages carried by the telegrams.

Frequently specific problem-solving situations or units of study will contain value issues that should be confronted instead of avoided. When a fifth-grade class studied the pollution problems of a local factory, the value issues of profit versus nonpolluted air were pursued. In playing the simulation game *Sunshine*, the children identified the value issue of equality versus inequality. The unit of study that focuses on India identified the religious value placed on the sacredness of animals, particularly the cow, versus the lack of food. Young children in their study of the community encountered the value of community pride versus encouraging more industry to settle there.

Discussions that give children the opportunity to express how they feel about important things in their lives are becoming increasingly more useful. Teachers have been learning that the things that they value are not always valued by others and that moralizing with a group of children has less effect on them than providing a forum where they can pursue these value issues with their peers. When some portion of the day is devoted to a "magic circle"[12] or to other valuing situations where children can talk (rather than be talked to) about their feelings, hopes, wants, and needs, they grow in their ability to understand what they value and are prepared to act upon those values.

SELECTED REFERENCES

Borton, Terry. *Reach Touch and Teach*. New York: McGraw-Hill, 1970.

Greer, Mary and Rubinstein, Bonnie. *Will the Real Teacher Please Stand Up?* Pacific Palisades, Calif.: Goodyear, 1972.

Kohlberg, Lawrence. "Moral Education in the Schools: A Developmental View." *School Review* 74 (Spring 1966): 1–30.

Mackey, James. "Moral Insight In the Classroom." *Elementary School Journal* 73 (February 1973): 233–38.

Metcalf, Lawrence E., ed. *Values Education*. Washington: National Council for Social Studies, 41st Yearbook, 1971.

Raths, Louis; Harmin, Merrill; and Simon, Sidney. *Values and Teaching*. Columbus, Ohio: Charles E. Merrill, 1966.

Rosen, Bernard C. "Family Structure and Value Transmission." *Merrill-Palmer Quarterly* 10 (January 1964): 59–76.

Simon, Sidney B. "Values-Clarification vs. Indoctrination." *Social Education* 35 (December 1971): 902.

Williams, Marianne E. T. A. Study of the Effectiveness of a Systematic Instructional Model on the Rational Decision Making Behavior of Sixth Grade Students. Unpublished doctoral dissertation, Indiana University, 1972.

CHAPTER *10*

Working In Committees

WHAT IS TO BE GAINED

Experience in working in committees for the attainment of specific goals develops skill in cooperative behavior. The ability to get along with others is a skill that should be acquired as early as possible. As he enters school, the young child is often self-centered and frequently unwilling to share materials with others. He learns the skills of cooperative behavior by sharing playthings, working on projects with other children, and participating in group activities such as singing, dancing, and listening to stories. At the kindergarten level, committees should be small, consisting of two or three children; and their task should be of a simple nature. Building a house with blocks, getting the milk, or cleaning up materials in the play areas are suggested as beginning activities for committee work. Later in kindergarten and in first grade, more formal tasks can be assigned such as preparing a story for creative dramatics, drawing a movie roll of a story, or finding answers to questions by looking at pictures. One first-grade class organized a pet show with committees of children responsible for invitations, judging, refreshments, prizes, and care of pets. Children soon learn that the success of such an activity is dependent upon each person cooperating and completing his share of the task.

Continual involvement in committee work throughout the elementary grades is necessary to maintain and refine skill in working together. As children mature, they are capable of working in larger groups (of perhaps five or six members) and of completing more difficult tasks. It is crucial that the teacher establish a definite purpose for committee work and that the children understand this purpose.

Organization

The method of selecting members for committees can vary depending upon the group of children and the purpose. Classes of children who have few discipline problems and get along well with one another generally can be permitted to select committee memberships of their choice, based on each individual's interest in a particular subject or task. However, classes of children who experience considerable difficulty in getting along, have discipline problems, or have too many leaders should be organized in committees by the teacher. At times, it is beneficial for the teacher to select particular students for a committee in order to meet individual differences. For example, the child who is exceptional in art may be placed on a committee in which he can use his talent. Or, the child not very adept in research skills should receive help when placed on a committee of children more capable. It is not necessarily good, however, to place outstanding children with the very slow, for too great a discrepancy in ability may result in frustration for all concerned.

The teacher who has never worked with committees before or a class that has not had experience in working in committees may wish to begin the activity one committee at a time. Using this method, the teacher organizes one committee to work on a task; and at the completion of its responsibility, she organizes another committee. This method allows the teacher more time to work with each group to guide its activities. After all members of the class have participated in this experience, the whole class can be organized into committees.

Teacher-Pupil Planning

Successful committee experiences depend considerably upon the routines established within the classroom. Children respond more favorably when they have the opportunity to aid in developing the guidelines for a project. The following is an example of the dialogue of a class planning for committee work. The children are fourth graders who have had previous but limited experience working in committees.

TEACHER:	What is the first thing a committee should do after the members have been selected?
GEORGE:	We should decide on someone to be a chairman.
TEACHER:	How do you make this decision?
JANE:	We can hold an election and nominate people and then vote.
BILL:	Yes, but that takes too long. You can have each person decide who he wants and write the name on a slip of paper.
TEACHER:	What type of person makes the best chairman?
SALLY:	Someone who isn't too bossy and always telling you what to do.
SAM:	Someone who will do his share, but also help you if you need it.
TEACHER:	Suppose we list the responsibilities of a chairman.

The children's completed list of responsibilities for the chairman follows:

The chairman should:
1. understand the responsibility of his committee
2. help each person understand his task
3. be sure each person completes his task
4. accept the opinions and suggestions of committee members
5. report the committee's progress and problems concerning materials to the class
6. be sure members share materials

TEACHER:	What responsibilities do the members of the committee have?
JIM:	We need to be sure that we do our share of the work and not wait to be told.
MISSY:	Don't forget that sharing materials is a committee member's responsibility too.

The completed list was placed on a chart for all to observe when needed. These are the points listed:

Committee members should:
1. share materials with others

2. listen to the committee members' and the chairman's suggestions
3. complete their tasks on time
4. do their share of the work
5. be willing to help others

TEACHER:	Are there certain things we should all remember when working in committees?
MARY:	Work quietly, so you won't disturb others.
RICK:	Clean up your materials at the end of the period.
BILL:	I think that the big thing is to get your work done on time so others won't have to wait for you.
SHELLY:	Also, stick to your topic and don't spoil someone else's report.

The type of responses listed here are typical of those most classes will offer. The crucial aspect is not the content of the response but rather the process involved, whereby the children take an active part in the decision making, which affects their behavior as they work in committees. With young children, a teacher may find it necessary to be more directive in her questioning. For example, the teacher might ask questions such as: When we play a game and choose a leader, how do we do this? What is the leader's job?

The guidelines that have been established by the class should be referred to daily before beginning the work. In addition, when a problem arises, the teacher should suggest that the children analyze the cause of the problem and check the guidelines for a solution. Children become more self-reliant and self-disciplined when they share in the process of making the rules.

INTELLECTUAL SKILLS

Within the framework of committee responsibility, intellectual skills of using reference materials, locating information, outlining and notetaking, critical thinking, and making oral and written reports are utilized. Each of these skills will be discussed in detail. The ease with which the social studies and the language arts can be interrelated through the development of these skills is easily recognizable.

Using Reference Materials

As children search for information pertaining to their assigned topics, they will need assistance in using a variety of resource materials.

1. Library—In preparing to use the library for committee assignments, the children should learn the arrangement of the card catalog, the placement of books on the shelves, and the procedure for checking out books. The topic under study may be used as an example to be located in the card catalog, etc.

2. Encyclopedia—One of the favorite sources of information for young children is the encyclopedia, because its organization makes it easy for them to locate topics. Frequently, children copy information from this book without any understanding. The vocabulary may be too difficult and the children do not look up words in the dictionary that they do not understand. Guidelines should be established for using the encyclopedia.

The child should ask himself these questions:

a. Do I understand the information given about the topic?

b. Are there any vocabulary words I do not know?

c. How can I best report this information to the class?

d. Will an outline of the information be enough or should I take notes?

e. Are there cross-references where I might secure additional information about the topic?

f. If I prepare a written report, can I complete it in my own words?

3. Textbook—The textbook can be used for background reading by the entire class prior to committee research, or individual committees can use the text to secure information about their aspect of the topic. The teacher should be sure that the children understand the organization of the text and that the reading level is suitable. When available, a variety of texts or multitexts provide the opportunity to compare viewpoints and information presented by different authors.

4. Primary sources—Work with primary source material (original source of information without some other person's interpretation) is valuable in helping children draw their own conclusions, interpret the

facts presented, and evaluate the validity of the material. G. P. Putnam and Sons have produced "Jackdaws," which are kits of primary source material. Each kit is organized around a topic such as "Columbus and the Discovery of America." They include reproductions of actual documents from this early historical period.

Another primary source of information is obtained by conducting interviews and surveys. Children should prepare their questions for the interview in advance. An example of an interview the children might conduct would be questioning an official about the building of a recreational park for the city :

a. Where will the park be located?
b. What type of equipment will it include?
c. How much will it cost the taxpayers?
d. When will it be completed?
e. Why is it being built?

After securing information from a primary source, the child should compare it, if possible, with its coverage in the newspaper. The children should try to answer these questions: Does the paper report the same information? Does it express a bias? If so, why? Is it possible that the reporters were given incorrect information?

5. Other sources—Newspapers, magazines, films, filmstrips, and recordings are sources children can use to secure information. They need to evaluate the sources to determine which are most valid.

Locating Information

Skills children need for locating information are:

1. knowledge of available resources (as discussed in the preceding section)
2. understanding of how the resource is organized—alphabetically, topically, etc.
3. ability to use the table of contents, which lists the major headings
4. ability to use the index, which cites a page number for each entry
5. knowledge of cross references, which indicate a related topic that may give additional information
6. ability to glean information from illustrations
7. ability to read maps, graphs, and charts

Outlining and Notetaking

Information is outlined to provide a skeleton of the important points. An outline is useful in helping a child to organize his information; however, useless outlining of page after page of material for practice is a waste of time. Because an outline presents important information in a shortened and simplified form, children should start with the short form. The main points about a topic are called the main topics or main headings and are designated by Roman numerals. Points about the topic that fall under the main headings are subtopics or subheadings and are designated by capital letters. Details about the subtopics follow them and are designated by numbers, as in the following example:

I. Africa

   A. Geography

      1. Mountains

      2. Rainforests

      3. Rivers

Notetaking necessitates a decision regarding the purpose of the information. Before they start to take notes, children should be encouraged to ask themselves: (1) Am I attempting to entertain someone with the information? (2) Am I selecting information that I think an audience would not know? and (3) Am I selecting information I think everyone should know about the topic? After they have answered these questions, they can begin to select the appropriate information.

Critical Thinking

Children are encouraged to use a variety of resource materials as they search for information to fulfill their committee tasks. The resource materials should stimulate critical thinking, initiating questions such as: Does the author of the material express a point of view? Does he use any methods of propaganda in his writing? Does the information vary from source to source? Is the author stating fact or opinion?

When the information has been collected and reported to the class, another opportunity for developing thinking skills arises. Analysis of this information is necessary. Did the committee look at all sides of the issue? Did they present the information accurately or did they express their own opinions? The teacher is responsible for directing these questions to the children so that each child will become accustomed to asking them of himself.

Oral and Written Reports

Skills needed for oral and written reports can be developed through the wide variety of activities involved in presenting committee reports to the class. These skills also can be identified as expressive skills, for the children express themselves in writing, speaking, or drawing. After research has been completed, the development of a method of sharing each committee's information with the group becomes necessary. Criteria for the success of this method are: (1) Did the children gain knowledge from the reports? (2) Did they exhibit an interest in the reports? The guidelines established for reporting include:

Present the information in such a way that others will be interested in the topic.

Be sure the information is accurate and easily understood. Don't obscure the information in gimmicks to develop interest.

The type of information that has been secured will determine, to a certain extent, the choice of presentation. Children should learn what type of presentation best communicates the information they have to report. The oral skills to be developed are:

1. to acquire poise and confidence in a group situation
2. to speak with expression

3. to acquire fluency in phrasing
4. to speak clearly and slowly
5. to express an idea so that it may be understood
6. to adjust volume of voice to size of group

Panel Discussions

Organizing information for a panel discussion generally is better accomplished by intermediate-grade children, but variations of the panel can be presented by young children. For example, first- or second-grade committee members can prepare their part of the presentation on charts, with or without pictures they have drawn. If a child has difficulty in writing, the teacher can prepare a chart from the child's dictation or the child can use pictures and give information in his own words. Questions to be asked back and forth by the panel members are only beneficial if they are prepared in advance so the children know what to expect.

Intermediate-grade children need to be cautioned against merely reading their reports rather than discussing them. A time limit of two to three minutes for each discussant helps the children to learn to be concise and to select only the most pertinent information. To increase interest in their discussion, children will benefit from visual aids such as illustrations, transparencies, charts, graphs, or a short filmstrip. The following are points children should remember for any oral presentation:

1. stick to the topic of your report
2. speak clearly and slowly enough to be heard by all
3. use inflections in your voice
4. maintain good eye contact with your audience

Debates

To be effective, debates should be utilized by intermediate-grade children. They are more capable of the extensive research needed to discover all the pros and cons of an issue. The issue selected for the debate should be one that provokes critical analysis and presents the possibility for taking a position. An example might be—Resolved: The United States Government should spend sufficient funds for research to continue its space probe to Mars; or Resolved: The United States Government should grant amnesty to those who left the country to avoid the draft during an undeclared war. Rules should be established for the debate, with time limits set for each presentation and rebuttal. The children should be cautioned about becoming too emotional over the debate. They should understand that a debate is won by presenting the most persuasive arguments for their side.

Role Playing

An historical incident or an attempted solution to a problem can be role played by a committee. In this activity, the children can use their own language and ideas, based on their research, to depict some incident. Role playing the signing of the Declaration of Independence or peace treaty talks will help children to understand and to remember these events. Role playing gives children the opportunity to express emotions and to attempt to involve themselves in a situation. Children at any grade level can participate in this activity.

TV or Radio Programs

Patterning an oral report after the format of a TV or radio program adds an element of interest. Some children may even add the commercials to make it realistic. Children who have difficulty with oral presentations are often less self-conscious when given the opportunity to pretend to be someone else or to hide behind a microphone.

Show formats such as "This Is Your Life" or "You Were There" are appropriate for historical incidents, while an interview type format like the "Today Show" is good for factual and opinion reports. The former "Huntley-Brinkley" news format is enjoyed by children for factual reporting.

Dramatic Presentations

Similar to role playing, but with more definite lines and costumes and props, skits and plays can be used by children to present their committee reports. Once again this activity increases the element of interest, and children can hide their self-consciousness behind a character in the play. An example of this type of activity might be a skit depicting a day in the life of a child in Mexico—showing his food, clothing, home, and customs. This information is much more easily remembered as a result of visual representation.

The lines for a dramatic presentation can be taped. Children can practice by taping and playing back the presentation until they are satisfied with the performance. Preparation of any oral report can be improved by use of the tape recorder. Each child has the opportunity to hear his mistakes and improve the quality of his voice.

WRITTEN REPORTS

Skills to be developed in the written reports are:

1. organize the information in a meaningful sequence
2. select the relevant information
3. use correct language, capitalization, and punctuation

The information gathered by a committee can be compiled into a written report when the teacher sees a need for increased skill in this area. The written report might be assembled in a scrapbook with illustrations or in a booklet form. Children can use a textbook format with a table of contents, chapter headings, glossary, etc. All members of the committee should agree on the same format. Reports such as these should be interesting, concise, written in the child's language, and available for all to read. A display of the reports can remain on the reading table until all have had the chance to read them. These reports also can be used for reference when possible.

GRAPHIC REPORTS

Committees can present their research information through graphic representations. For example, the preparation of a wall mural depicting methods of transportation may be more easily interpreted by children than verbal description. Or the building of a model village may relate more to children about life in Peru than a dozen written reports. The child who is more adept at painting than writing or speaking can meet with success in this type of activity.

SOCIAL SKILLS

Social skills, which are so necessary in any society, are developed through most learning experiences in school; however, committee membership provides many fine opportunities for their practice. Learning to get along with others, sharing materials, the giving and taking of opinions, and assuming responsibility are important skills to be acquired if the committees are to be successful. If these skills are acquired during committee work, the results should carry over into activities in other areas such as on the playground, during other classwork, and after school in the neighborhood.

The organization of a committee necessitates getting along with others. Each member must be willing to accept the guidance of the chairman. The membership of a committee may not consist of each person's best friends; therefore, the child must learn to cooperate with any classmate. If committee tasks are to be completed, members must be willing to share materials and readily respect the opinions of others. Each committee member has a responsibility that he must assume if success is to be achieved.

Frequently, classes that have failed to develop any real group feeling or "esprit de corps" will be more successful after the experience of working together in committees.

SELECTED REFERENCES

Bergeson, Clarence O. "Using Learning Resources in Social Studies Skill Development." *Social Education* 31 (March 1967): 227.

Carpenter, Helen McCracken. "The Role of Skills in Elementary Social Studies." *Social Education* 31 (March 1967): 219.

Carpenter, Helen McCracken, ed. *Skill Development in Social Studies.* 33rd Yearbook. Washington, D. C.: National Council for the Social Studies, 1963.

Davis, O. L., Jr. "Building Skills for Social Study in the Middle Grades." *Social Education* 31 (March 1967): 224.

Douglass, Malcolm P. *Social Studies From Theory to Practice in Elementary Education.* Philadelphia: J. B. Lippincott, 1967.

Dunfee, Maxine and Sagl, Helen. *Social Studies Through Problem Solving.* New York: Holt, Rinehart, and Winston, 1966.

Foster, Clifford D. "Skills in the Elementary School Social Studies Curriculum." *Social Education* 31 (March 1967): 230.

Groeschell, Robert. "Curriculum Provisions for Individual Differences." *Social Education* 31 (May 1967): 416.

Jarolimek, John. "Skills Teaching in the Primary Grades." *Social Education* 31 (March 1967): 222.

Joyce, Bruce. *New Strategies For Social Education.* Chicago: Science Research Associates, 1972.

O'Connor, John R. "Reading Skills in the Social Studies." *Social Education* 31 (February 1967): 104.

Ploghoft, Milton, and Shuster, Albert H. *Social Science Education in the Elementary School.* Columbus, Ohio: Charles E. Merrill, 1971.

Rogers, Vincent R. "The Individual and the Social Studies." *Social Education* 31 (May 1967): 405.

Shaftel, Fannie R., and Shaftel, George. *Role-Playing for Social Values: Decision Making in the Social Studies.* Englewood Cliffs, N. J.: Prentice-Hall, 1967.

Skeel, Dorothy J. *Developing Creative Ability.* South Holland, Ill.: H. Wilson, 1967.

Skeel, Dorothy J. *Developing Language Arts Skills.* South Holland, Ill.: H. Wilson, 1968.

Smith, James A. *Creative Teaching of the Social Studies.* Boston: Allyn & Bacon, 1967.

CHAPTER *11*

Map And Globe Skills

"WHERE DO YOU LIVE?" "WHAT IS IT NEAR?" "HOW CAN I GET THERE?" These are common questions asked by a person attempting to locate someone's house. Depending upon the location and the individual's ability in locational skills, he might answer by naming the place, expressing the distance from his present location to his home, expressing this distance in terms of the time required to go there, or he might designate the location by readings of latitude and longitude to be more exact. With the increased speed of today's travel, the time involved in reaching one's destination has changed; however, many of the skills required to locate a place remain the same. Mass media, which includes a great number of unfamiliar places in its reporting, and the increased mobility of people enhance the study of locational skills. Map reading requires the learning of a new language, which enables the individual to interpret map symbols. Six basic skills have been recognized as comprehensive for map reading and interpretation.

1. ability to orient the map and note directions
2. ability to recognize the scale of a map and compute distances
3. ability to locate places on maps and globes by means of grid systems
4. ability to express relative locations
5. ability to read map symbols
6. ability to compare maps and to make inferences[1]

Limited research has been completed to determine children's ability with map skills at varying grade levels. On the basis of child development studies, Bacon contends that young children learn to think geographically much sooner than they learn to think historically.[2] Rushdoony found that primary children were able to profit from instruction in map-reading skills recommended for fourth and fifth graders. He suggests that curriculums be revised to introduce map skills to children at an earlier level. He also found high positive correlation between map-reading achievement and intelligence, reading achievement, and arithmetic achievement.[3]

Most social studies educators agree that effective instruction in map and globe skills is accomplished through developmental tasks and that this instruction should be conducted in the context of the study of a topic. Thus, the six basic skills will be developed in the primary and intermediate grades in the context of a suggested topic. In the following discussion of methods for teaching map skills, the six basic skills (listed above) will be indicated by the number to which they correspond in the list. In mastering these map skills, children will need to build upon a progression of learning experiences. These suggested activities are representative and are not intended to be the only ones developed at each grade level.

SKILLS BY GRADE LEVELS

Kindergarten

As the children study the family and home, they develop a map of the community, using blocks placed on butcher paper to represent the school and their homes (5). A trip outside the school on a sunny day enables the children to note the location of the sun when they arrive at school and when they leave. With this knowledge, the children are able to place the sun on their map as a directional guide (1). The children place blocks on the map to locate the other outstanding buildings such as the fire station, library, and churches relative to their homes (4). Beginning at the school, they count the number of blocks (in a city) or miles (in a rural area) to their homes (2). The teacher draws the same map on a piece of paper representing their homes and other buildings with drawings (5). The children compare their block map with the teacher's map to locate their homes (6). The simple slate or physical-relief globe is then used to locate the placement of their homes in relation to the other areas of the world (3, 1, 5).

First Grade

Young children are fascinated by the study of a culture different from their own, especially one they think is quite far away. Japan is an example of a culture that might be used in first grade. The children first locate Japan on a simple globe and realize that it is a group of islands (1, 5). The teacher uses a tub of water and a cardboard representation of the islands to help develop this concept (6). The children note the direction of Japan from their homes (1). In an attempt to determine the distance of Japan from the children's homes, they compute the time in days it would take to reach the islands by plane or boat (2). By using a floor map of the world with land masses and water indicated, they place a toy plane and boat on the map, and move them at their approximate speed of travel—one day of school for the plane and five days of school for the boat (1, 2, 3, 4, 5). Using a globe that has an attachment showing the division of day and night they interpret the time differences (6, 5).

Second Grade

Wall maps can be introduced at this level, but transition from the floor map to the wall map should be provided. During a study of community helpers, children can make a large floor map using symbols to locate the buildings of the helpers such as the fire station and police station (1, 4, 5). The teacher should then draw to scale a smaller map of the area, hang it on the wall, and permit children to place buildings on the map (2, 3, 4, 5). Have the children locate their city or town on a simplified state map (1, 5, 6).

Then refer them to a map of the United States to see where their state is located (1, 2, 3, 4, 5, 6).

Third Grade

During a study of contrasting communities, children learn that people wear different clothes in different parts of the world. The relationship of this understanding to map interpretation is then presented. Pictures of people in typical dress for a particular time of year are placed on a map of the world that has a three-color key—water, lowlands, and mountains (1, 5). People are placed, for example, on the equator, on lowlands and mountains, on a desert area, near the North Pole, and in the children's own community. Climatic conditions are estimated from the type of clothes worn and the effect of location on the climate (2, 3, 5, 6). The effect of altitude on climate and the resulting type of clothing also is interpreted. A representative relief map of clay or flour and salt is made to relate water, lowland, and mountains to the three-color key (1, 5, 6).

Fourth Grade

Beginning a study of their state, the children use a large sand table to prepare a model representing the physical features of their state such as mountains, valleys, lakes, rivers, and lowlands (1, 2, 3, 5, 6). As the study progresses, the children can locate on the map major cities, their own city or town, recreational areas, and major products of the state (1, 2, 3, 4, 5, 6). The products and characteristics of an area located in the same latitude with approximately the same land formation should be compared (1, 3, 5, 6).

Fifth Grade

Fifth graders should use degrees of latitude and longitude for locating places. As children report daily news events from around the world, they should indicate the location of the event in degrees of latitude and longitude. The children can use individual desk maps to locate the places (1, 3, 4, 5). A world map with time zones designated is used to determine the time difference between the children's location and that of the event (1, 2, 3, 4, 5). The children interpret the map key representing physical features and relation of latitude to determine the land formation and climate of the news event's location (5, 6). The map key can also be used to interpret water formations or ocean currents that might be applicable to the event (5, 6).

Sixth Grade

During a study of United Nations, committees of children can select areas of the world where United Nations organizations are operating such as UNICEF, peace-keeping troops, and the economic advisory committee. Reproduce maps of these areas with the opaque projector to insure accuracy (1, 2, 3, 6). Reproduce physical features using a five- or seven-color key (5, 6). These maps can be done on transparencies using overlays to represent political divisions, cities, physical features, products, and population (1, 2, 3, 4, 5, 6).

OTHER SUGGESTED ACTIVITIES

Because children need many concrete experiences to help them understand the concepts of map reading and interpretation, activities that can be used with various topics are suggested for both the primary and intermediate grades.

Primary Grades

Study the land formation around the school observing any variations and vegetation. Build a model of the area using clay or the sand table. Children in the upper-primary grades can refer to a physical map of the state to understand how the color key represents the land formation.

Plan a field trip to study local geographic features such as a river basin, rock formation, canyon, plateau, plain, or mountain. Observe them at different times of the year to note the effects of nature—the changing seasons, rain, wind, and snow.

Construct a globe using a balloon as the base. Place strips of papier-mâché over the balloon. When it dries, the balloon can be broken, and the land formations and water can be painted on the papier-mâché.

Children who are planning trips should study road maps and physical relief maps to anticipate land formations before they start their journey. They can follow the road map during the trip and share their experiences with the other children after they return.

Obtain aerial photos of different land formations and compare them with the same location of a geophysical map.

Intermediate Grades

Children should work with map construction frequently, especially when they are studying different areas of the world. Various materials can be used including plasticene clay, sawdust mixture, flour and salt, and papier-mâché. Children should develop a color key to indicate elevations.

The teacher can make sure that his students understand geographical terms such as "bay," "isthmus," "peninsula," etc. by helping them to construct models of these physical features when they occur in the course of the study. Blank maps of the area under study are also helpful learning aids. As the study of an area progresses, each child can complete his map by drawing in the physical features, major cities, etc.

Children should be able to interpret many things from the information given on political and physical maps. When introducing a new area for study, before any preliminary reading or introduction has been made, the teacher should ask the children to suggest as much information about the area as possible from interpreting the map. In a study of cities, children should suggest geographic reasons for the locations of the cities.

PROBLEMS TO DETERMINE THE EXTENT OF CHILDREN'S SKILLS

As children begin to acquire skills in map reading and interpretation, they should be presented with problem situations that require them to use the skills they have learned. The following problem example might be presented to kindergarten or first-grade children after they have learned directions and know where the sun rises and sets. The following picture is placed on a transparency:

Question

If the sun is just rising, which way is the wind blowing?

This problem requires the children to think about the direction from which the sun rises and the resulting shadows. The bending of the tree indicates the direction of the wind.

As children learn to identify the types of products grown in different climatic and geographic regions, they should be able to describe conditions necessary for their growth. The teacher might present pictures of different types of vegetation and ask the children to name the type of climate and geographic conditions necessary for their growth.

The fact that the location rather than the physical appearance or natural resources of an area sometimes determines its importance offers an interesting problem for children to analyze. Some examples follow:

PLACE "A"

This is a chain of islands that covers in all an area of about 6,400 square miles. Some small shrubs and mosses grow here, but there are no trees. The climate is very cold and foggy. The population survives largely through fishing . . . .

PLACE "B"

This is a rocky peninsula, which is largely a limestone "mountain" rising 1,400 feet above the water. It covers an area of about two square miles . . . .

PLACE "C"

This is an island of volcanic origin. It is about 65 miles long and 2 to 18 miles wide. It has an area of about 463 square miles. Its climate is hot and humid, and it is subject to a large number of wind storms each. . . .[4]

After a discussion of possible reasons for the importance of these places, the teacher can reveal their names—the Aleutian Islands, Gibraltar, and Okinawa.

When older children have a good grasp of the color key on a map and knowledge of the various theories about building a city, the following problem can be presented:

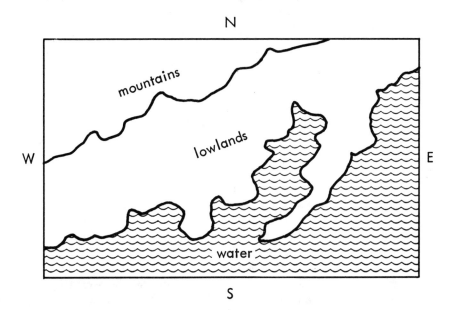

Questions

If you were to pick the site for a city in this area, where would you build it? Why?

This map should be presented on a transparency using a color key to distinguish the different physical features. The problem can be tackled individually or by the total class. The teacher may wish to add additional information about the natural resources, the winds, etc. It should be noted that this also can be used as an excellent inquiry activity to initiate a study of cities.

USING INTEREST CENTERS TO INCREASE SKILLS

There are numerous activities related to maps and globes that children can complete on their own without the aid of the teacher. By developing an interest center for them in one corner of the room, the children can participate in the activities during free time or while the teacher is working with other groups. There should be a globe and a variety of maps available in the area. The following are some examples of the type of activities to plan:

1. Clip out downtown street maps of two city areas such as Savannah, Georgia and Chattanooga, Tennessee. These two cities have quite different land-use patterns. Pose questions for the children to answer:
    What information can you find out about these cities?
    How are they alike? How are they different?
2. Clip from a map skill book the page which lists the geographic terms and the physical model that has examples of each type of land formation for them to match.
3. Find an enlarged physical features map of an area of the world such as Alaska and pose the question: How much information can you find about this area?
4. Supply a globe, a piece of string, and an air age map with questions about the "great circle routes."
5. Provide a map with the degrees of latitude and longitude plainly marked. Have children locate certain places in the world by their degrees of latitude and longitude.
6. Find a clipping of a news event that has occurred in some other area of the world. Ask questions relative to the geographic factors of the area. Example: Are there any bodies of water nearby? What type of land forms are found there? On what continent is it located?

Map skill workbooks and old textbooks provide good sources for these activities as well as travel books, newspapers, and magazines.

URBAN MAP SKILLS

Since there are increasing numbers of people living in urban areas and a corresponding increase in urban problems, it is important that children acquire an understanding of the urban concept. What is a city? How can it be described? The following presents an accurate conception:

1. a substantial number of people   (number)
2. living in close proximity   (density)
3. over an extended period of time   (stability)
4. engaging in a variety of economic activities   (occupational diversity)[5]

Activities introduced to acquire this concept include categorizing communities according to size, classifying occupations by community size, and working with aerial maps of cities.

Children can construct land-use maps of one part of the city (probably their own areas) or select a few functions such as industrial and reidential for mapping the entire city. Listed below is a land-use category system that may be used by the children for city land uses:

1. single family residences
2. multiple family dwellings or apartments
3. commercial or business: retail, wholesale, and service
4. industrial, manufacturing, and railroads
5. public: schools, government functions, parks, and churches.
6. streets
7. vacant and unused lands[6]

Problems that confront cities from the building of a new highway to urban renewal are presented in simulation materials Urban Planning and the MATCH kit, The City. The materials give children the opportunity to role play the solutions to these problems.

MAPS AND GLOBES

Every elementary classroom should contain a globe. In kindergarten and first grade, a simple globe of slate or one that shows only the outline of the continents should be used. The slate globe can be drawn on with tempera or chalk and then washed or erased. Children should be permitted to manipulate the globe and to locate places such as their home and the United States. Reference to the globe by the teacher whenever feasible is important, for the children should form the habit of seeking it when the need arises.

Older children can use a more detailed globe—for example, the three- or five-color key of physical features can be used for the middle grades and a seven-color key for the intermediate grades. Use of a globe showing political boundaries with each country a different color has sometimes led children to believe that a country actually is the color shown on the globe. A globe that uses green for lowlands, brown for mountains, and blue for water might better orient children to globe usage.

Care should be exercised in the transition from globes to maps. The comparative size of Greenland is a good indicator of how shapes and sizes change from a globe to a map. Some map projections increase its size considerably while others decrease the size. The teacher might have the children split a tennis ball or the peel of an orange and attempt to flatten it completely to help them to see what happens in the transition from a globe to a flat map.

Wall maps are generally not used before the end of second or third grade, depending upon the ability and background of the children. As indicated earlier, the first maps used should be home-made. Commercial maps should not contain too much detail to avoid confusing the children. They should be large enough to be read easily across the classroom. Every upper-grade classroom should have a physical-political map of the world, and, if money allows, physical-political maps of North America and other continents. Little use is made of separate physical and political maps, and the combination saves money.

A chart of geographical terms is a useful instructional tool for older children. This chart shows pictorially most of the geographic terms such as "isthmus," "harbor," "bay," and "plateau." These terms, however, should be taught as the need arises. They should not all be taught from the chart at one time.

The wall map of the world should be pulled down each day for ready reference. Games utilizing locational skills can be introduced during free play time—for example, a box with slips of paper containing places to be located might be kept by the map rack. Depending upon the grade level, various clues to the areas' locations can be added. Intermediate-grade children may use only the degrees of latitude and longitude for their reference.

To increase the children's understanding of the grid system, a simple demonstration can be completed. Place an "X" anywhere on the blackboard and have children tell exactly where it is located. Place several other "X's" on the board and give the same direction. Children soon realize that some additional reference points are needed. Draw horizontal lines several inches apart and number them. Problems still arise in determining the exact location until numbered vertical lines have been added. Children should readily associate this method with that used on maps and globes to increase accuracy in locating places.

Maps and globes can be purchased from a number of companies. The following list is representative of some of these companies. Catalogs can be secured upon request.

George F. Cram Co., Inc., 730 E. Washington Street, Indianapolis, Indiana 46206

Denoyer-Geppert Co., 5235 Ravenswood Avenue, Chicago, Illinois 60640

C. S. Hammond and Company, Inc., Maplewood, New Jersey 07040

Rand McNally and Company, P. O. Box 7800, Chicago, Illinois 60639

Map companies generally supply teachers with guides for instructional uses of their materials, and they also suggest lists of map and globe skills for each grade level.[7]

National Geographic Magazine supplies maps with each publication, but they usually contain too much detail for younger children. State chambers of commerce and embassies of foreign countries will provide maps of their areas. News magazines contain maps of areas where the news is happening. Weekly news maps with pictures of the events can be secured from *Time* magazine for a minimum charge.

SELECTED REFERENCES

Arnsdoff, Val. "Geographic Education: Principles and Practices in the Primary Grades." *Social Education* 31 (November 1967): 612–14.

Bacon, Phillip, ed. *Focus on Geography* 40th Yearbook. Washington, D. C.: National Council for the Social Studies, 1970.

Carpenter, Helen McCracken, ed. *Skill Development in Social Studies.* Washington, D. C.: National Council for the Social Studies, 1963.

Drummond, Dorothy W. "Developing Geography Concepts in the Intermediate Grades." *Social Education* 30 (December 1966): 628–31.

Hanna, Paul R.; Sabaroff, Rose; and Davies, Gordon F. *Geography in the Teaching of Social Studies: Concepts and Skills.* Boston: Houghton Mifflin, 1966.

James, Preston E., ed. *New Viewpoints in Geography.* Washington, D. C.: National Council for the Social Studies, 1959.

Kennamer, Lorin, Jr. "Geography in the Middle Grades." *Social Education* 31 (November 1967): 615–17.

Lee, John R., and Stampfer, Nathaniel. "Two Studies in Learning Geography: Implications for the Primary Grades." *Social Education* 30 (December 1966): 627–28.

McAulay, John D. "Geography Understandings of the Primary Child." *Journal of Geography* 55 (April 1966).

McAulay, John D. "What Understandings Do Second-Grade Children Have of Time Relationships?" *Journal of Educational Research* 54 (1961): 312–14.

Rushdoony, Haig A., "Achievement in Map-Reading: An Experimental Study." *The Elementary School Journal* 64 (November 1963): 70–75.

Wisniewski, Richard, ed. *Teaching About Life in the City,* 42nd Yearbook, Washington, D. C.: National Council for the Social Studies, 1972.

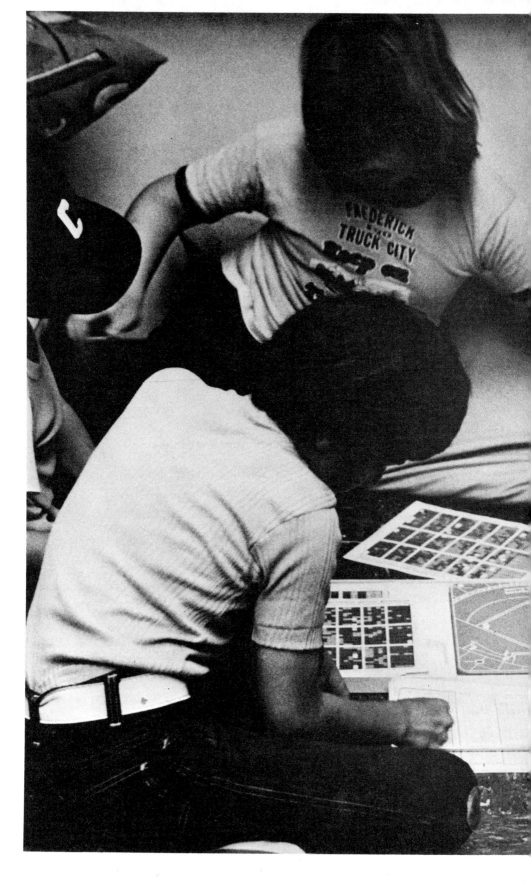

PART V

Utilization Of Materials

A rich and inviting supply of materials is available for use in social studies instruction. Fresh new materials enhance the social studies. The textbooks are colorful and appealing to children, films and filmstrips can be found to supplement almost any study, children's trade books add a spark of interest, realia kits present an opportunity to see the artifacts of a country, simulated games permit active involvement, and the vast amount of free and inexpensive materials provide extensive background information.

Part five discusses the selection and utilization of materials in elementary social studies with regard to, when feasible, the different methods of instruction.

CHAPTER *12*

Utilization of Materials
In the Social Studies

The following discussion of materials for use in the social studies includes children's trade books, games, programmed materials, cartoons, graphs and charts, textbooks, multimedia kits, films and filmstrips, and free and inexpensive materials. These materials are a representative but not exhaustive list of those available.

CHILDREN'S TRADE BOOKS

Two types of children's books can be incorporated with social studies—informational books that are primarily concerned with facts and fiction books that incorporate facts with hypothetical situations. May Hill Arbuthnot suggests that the following criteria be considered in selecting informational books:

1. *Scrupulous accuracy*—children have a tendency to accept what is in the book and therefore care should be exercised to check the accuracy of the information presented.
2. *Convenient presentation*—the information should be organized in such a way that children can easily find what they are looking for.
3. *Clarity*—little value will come from the information unless it is clearly stated for ease of understanding.
4. *Adequate treatment*—sufficient information should be included to insure understanding, but irrevelant details should not obscure the facts needed.

5. *Style*—an informational book should be interesting and as well written as possible.[1]

Informational books include titles such as Mabel Pyne's *The Little Geography of the United States*, which uses picture maps and colorful illustrations. *Landmark Books* is a series that is concerned with the various periods of development in the United States. Genevieve Foster's *George Washington's World*, *Abraham Lincoln's World*, and *Augustus Caesar's World* take a horizontal look at history to help children understand the events taking place in other parts of the world throughout the lifetime of each of these men. Both the *American Heritage Series* and *American Adventure Series* are written about the lives and events of famous people in American history. The *Childhood of Famous Americans Series* contains about one hundred selections dealing with people such as Abraham Lincoln, Booker T. Washington, and Babe Ruth. These stories begin with the individual's childhood and end during his adult life. The *We Were There Series* emphasizes dramatic events in our history. Any of these books can be used in research activities by individuals or committees. Role playing and dramatic presentations are easily adapted from books about historical events or famous people.

People and Places by Margaret Mead discusses anthropological concepts of the similarities and differences among peoples of the world and offers suggestions that might solve man's problems so all may live together peacefully. *Why We Live Where We Live* by Eva Knox Evans presents geographical information about the United States and the interdependence of people. Her final chapter "Your Own Home Town" encourages the reader to seek information about his own community.

For the child who has an aversion to geography and history, fiction books like Holling C. Holling's *Paddle-to-the-Sea* or *Tree in the Trail* should prove fascinating as well as educational. *Tree in the Trail* presents the history of our westward movement through the experiences of a cottonwood tree on the Santa Fe Trail. *Paddle-to-the-Sea* is the story of a small, carved canoe containing the figure of an Indian. The canoe is set afloat from the Upper Great Lakes to make its way to the sea. These books contain accurate geographical and historical material presented in a way that should interest children and motivate them to learn more about the topics under consideration.

Depicting the forces of change, Virginia Lee Burton's *The Little House* finds itself in a country setting until the growth of the surrounding area overwhelms it and a city grows up around it. Intended for young children, this book can be used in conjunction with a study of the local community.

Children who read Marguerite DeAngeli's *Bright April* are provided with a much better understanding of the need for improving race relations. Lois Lenski is another author who has described the lives of children in various parts of our country. *Strawberry Girl* and *Cotton in My Sack* were written about farm workers in Florida and Arkansas. Her *Prairie School* discusses the hard life of the plains states.

Books about minority groups include *Striped Ice Cream* by Joan Lexan; *The Contender* by Walter Lipsyte; *A Ride on High* by Candida Palmer; *Lillie of Watts: A Birthday Discovery* by Mildred Pitts Walter; *The Soul Brothers and Sister Lou* by Kristin Hunter. They are all stories about ghetto children's lives. *Candita's Choice* by Mina Lewiton is a book about the adjustment problems of a Puerto Rican child in New York City. *That Bad Carlos* and *The Spider Plant* discuss respectively a boy who is acquiring a bad reputation and family life. Stories about poverty are depicted in *My Name is Pablo, Maggie Rose, Her Birthday Christmas,* and *The Family Under the Bridge.*

Books about children from other lands such as May McNeer's *The Mexican Story,* which provides descriptions of accounts in the history of that country, or *Nine Days to Christmas,* which gives an account of the customs of a country, are useful when studying other cultures. Folktales of our own and other countries provide an excellent introduction to the study of other areas. Children are fascinated to learn why certain traditions have withstood the passing of time. Helen Huus' *Children's Books to Enrich the Social Studies* also is an excellent resource. These children's books add a touch of interest and uniqueness to social studies that cannot be found in any other resource. Many other fine books too numerous to mention can be used readily in social studies.

SIMULATIONS AND GAMES

New materials have been developed for the social studies classroom. They are labeled "simulation," "simulation games," or just "games." Herman, in the Encyclopedia of the Social Sciences, defines simulation as a situation having human players and rules and outcomes that are sufficiently elaborate to require the use of calculators or computers. Games are more simplistic, more manual, and less amenable to computer analysis. Simulated games are situations in which the less sophisticated may "assume the roles of decision-makers in a simulated (imitated) environment according to specified procedures or rules."[2]

No specific rules have been established for designing simulated games, but elements that might be involved in them are suggested:

1. Identification of objectives—what will be learned by the game?
2. Construction of a simplified model of the process or system that will best serve the objectives.
3. Identification of the various actors or teams so that the number would demonstrate the model effectively and also conform to classroom needs.
4. Provision of resources for the players to exchange in competition with other players.
5. Establishing rules or limits of permissible behavior during the game.
6. Identification of objectives or goals for the actors as they engage in trading resources.
7. Development of a scene or setting the stage for the beginning of play.[3]

The exciting aspect of simulation games is their involvement of the children, who actively participate in decision making, diplomatic maneuvers, or some other equally stimulating experience. Most children enjoy these simulation games and benefit educationally from their participation. Because there are no hard-and-fast rules for game design, teachers and students can produce their own games, utilizing the previously discussed elements. Four games that were developed for a sixth-grade classroom are:

Inflation—simulates the inflation of a money system; *Production Line*—"demonstrates the greater efficiency of the production line as compared to the output of individual craftsmen;"[4] *Landlocked Nations*—demonstrates "why nations through history have been willing to fight for control of narrow waterways;"[5] *Parent-Satellite Nations*—helps children gain insight into the developent of a nation from a satellite to a power in its own right.

There are several commercially produced games for elementary school classrooms, but more are available at junior, senior, and adult levels. *Caribou Hunting* and *Seal Hunting*, elementary school games, are both board games in which students simulate some of the difficulties Eskimos experience in acquiring an adequate food supply.[6] *Democracy*[7] presents the processes of our government while *Inter-Nation Simulation*[8] offers an international view. *Starpower*[9] distributes wealth in the form of chips, which emphasizes the low mobility of low-income members of society. *Pollution*[10] and *Water Pollution*[11] emphasize ecology problems and permit children to make decisions about their solutions. *Inner-City Planning*[12] provides the opportunity for making decisions about the planning of a city. *Sunshine*[13] specifically designed for junior high school children can be adapted for the upper-elementary grades. This game presents some of the situations that can occur in the course of race relations in a city. *Ghetto*[14] is another that relates the conditions and problems of living within an inner-city area. *Consumer*[15] is designed to teach something about the problems and economics of installment buying. *Market*[16] aids children in the acquisition of the concepts of supply, demand, and prices. *Sierra Leone* and the *Sumerian Game* are both computer-based games in economics.[17] "The child makes decisions and enters his answers at the computer terminal"[18] and immediately receives a progress report.

"Proponents of simulation and games in social studies education claim that intuitive thinking is developed, learning is made entertaining and relevant to student life experiences. Emphasis is placed on developing analytical approaches and organizing concepts transferable to other problems."[19] Certainly more research is needed in this area, but teachers can experiment in their own classrooms to determine the success of games with their students. Do the games improve intuitive thinking? Are children more interested in learning? Do they learn as much? A review of the research indicates that:

1. simulation games do not appear to have any clear advantage in teaching content to students,
2. games and simulations appear to have a positive influence on student attitudes,
3. games and simulations appear to be influential in encouraging students to become more active in the learning process.[20]

One area that particularly needs exploring is that of the lasting effect of game playing on children. Does it change values? Does it increase competitiveness? What effect does the power to manipulate the lives of others assumed in a game have upon children? These are questions that require answers before the total effectiveness of games can be determined.

PROGRAMMED MATERIAL

The objective of programmed material is to give the learner elements of a subject in sequential order. This material provides immediate feedback for the learner, who then knows whether his answer is correct. Many programmed materials require review before the learner can go on, if an incorrect answer is given. The success of achieving correct answers is expected to motivate the learner to continue the study.

Programmed materials are available in several forms—textbooks, teaching machines, and computers. In programmed textbooks, answers to questions appear either on another page or are covered by a flap on the same page. Teaching machines are found in a variety of forms such as the Cyclo Teacher of *Encyclopedia Britannica*, which hides the answer until the children move to the next question, or computer-based systems, which assess children's answers and present information for their next step.

The potential of programmed materials has not been realized, especially in the area of computerized instruction. The research completed to date has not determined what type of material is best presented by programming.

Few programmed materials have been produced for elementary school. Some examples of those in use are *Learning To Use A Globe Set I and II* by Ewing and Seibel, which is a scrambled text to teach global concepts. A programmed text for teaching about maps is *Geography of the United States* by MacGraw and Williams. *An Introduction To American Government* by Rosenhack illustrates the separation of powers in our federal government. The latter two texts are for use in the upper-elementary grades.

CARTOONS

Cartoons are best used to stimulate discussions, present a particular point of view, and provide an opportunity to interpret the opinion of others. Most cartoons use symbols that require previous experience to be understood. If children lack this experience, teachers should assist in the interpretation.

Criteria for selecting cartoons for instruction include:

Does the cartoon present an idea quickly and effectively?

Does it present an idea that would be difficult to introduce using a different approach?

Will it be understood by the majority of the students without too much assistance?

Cartoons that might embarrass children of a certain race, religion, or national origin should be avoided unless the discussion to be initiated concerns prejudice or a controversial issue. Frequently, a cartoon expresses a view of a controversial issue better than most methods.

To enable all of the children in a class to see a cartoon at the same time, the teacher should make a transparency for the overhead projector or mount it for the opaque projector. Children should be encouraged to collect cartoons that provoke thought. These cartoons can be used in school for committee presentations or individual reports. Children delight in developing their own cartoons. This activity aids them in understanding the subtle use of symbols.

The following cartoons are examples that should effectively provoke discussion.

"Filibuster or no filibuster, I don't want my secret recipes in the Congressional Record!"

SOURCE: *Gurney Williams, ed.,* Look on the light side *(Englewood Cliffs, N.J: Prentice-Hall, 1957), reprinted from* Look *magazine.*

Teacher: What idea is the first cartoon attempting to portray?

The next cartoon quickly presents an idea. The idea presented, however, is one that children might not readily perceive.

Teacher: What does this cartoon suggest happens during a filibuster in Congress?

Many cartoons are too sophisticated for young children, but occasionally an appropriate one can be found. Also, the reluctant

"Boon to mankind, ha! One of these days it'll get loose and burn up the whole world."

SOURCE: Gurney Williams, ed., Look on the light side *(Englewood Cliffs, N.J.: Prentice-Hall, 1957), reprinted from* Look *magazine.*

learner may be motivated about a topic by the use of cartoons where he otherwise would be disinterested.

GRAPHS AND CHARTS

Just as cartoons can present certain ideas more effectively, graphs and charts can often be used to illustrate an idea or present information more readily than other methods. Children who have difficulty with reading may interpret a graph or chart successfully and acquire the concept that others read.

It is necessary to assist children in learning to read and interpret graphs and charts. Young children should start with picture graphs that are related to something familiar to them. An example is Figure 12.1, which uses stick figures to indicate the lunch count for the day.

Figure 12.1   Room 10 Lunch Count

Each child can readily perceive how he is represented on the graph. Children may wish to label the graph with their names to be sure that all are represented. Later, the teacher can explain that it is possible to represent several people with one figure as shown in Figure 12.2.

Figure 12.2   Room 10 Lunch Count

Bar graphs in the classroom can be used to represent the daily temperatures as shown in Figure 12.3. After the children can interpret the bar graph, line graphs illustrated by Figure 12.4 can be introduced using the same information as the bar graph for comparison and ease of understanding. Circle graphs, illustrated by

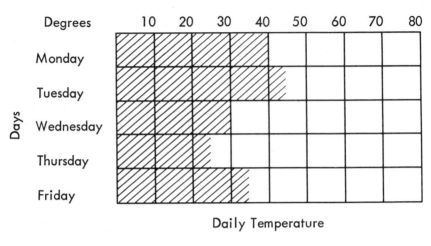

Figures 12.3   Daily Temperature

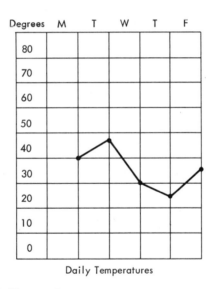

Figure 12.4   Daily Temperature

Figure 12.5 are easily understood when they are used to show how a pie might be divided among the children.

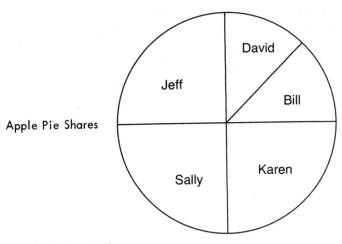

Figure 12.5 Apple Pie Shares

Preparation of graphs using information related to classroom experiences during early primary grades will provide children with the understanding necessary to tackle the more abstract statistics presented in the middle and upper grades. Correct labeling of the graphs is vital, and emphasis should be placed on reading them accurately.

A variety of charts are found in every elementary classroom. Most children are introduced to school activities through the use of experience charts. Here, a mutual class experience is recorded using the children's description for all to read. Charts also are developed to record the rules of a game, the directions for committee work, and the helpers for the week.

A chart with pictures (for example, one depicting the process of making paper from the cutting of a tree until the finished product) is called a flow chart. These charts aid in understanding the steps involved in a process. In the primary grades, children can be introduced to them by using the book *Pelle's New Suit*, which describes how Pelle obtains a new suit from the time he shears wool from the sheep until he picks up his suit at the tailor's shop. Young children can draw and interpret a flow chart of the process described in this book. More complicated processes such as drilling and refining oil can be understood by older children. Commercial flow charts are available on legislative processes such as "How a Bill Becomes a Law" or manufacturing processes such as "Milk from the Farm to You." Charts can be used for comparison—comparing the before and after, past and present, or another country's government with ours. A chart is described as a pictorial or line diagram of a topic.

PICTURES

Pictures are an extremely valuable resource in social studies. They can be used to develop numerous skills such as observing, classifying, grouping, comparing, and contrasting and to introduce inquiry and problem-solving situations. Also, concepts that otherwise might be difficult to present may be done through pictures. Sources for pictures are extensive—including newspapers, magazines, posters, and slides and photographs that individuals have acquired through travels.

Commercial companies are now producing picture series that are valuable in that they often provide resources that are difficult for the individual teacher to acquire. Many sets of pictures have guide books with suggestions for presentations and a series of questions intended to provoke inquiry. *Discussion Pictures for Beginning Social Studies* by Harper & Row is an example of such a series. *Interaction of Man and His Environment* by Rand McNally provides sets of pictures for contrast and comparison. A number of picture sets have been developed for the presentation of contrasting cultures and urban and rural life such as *Urban Series* by John Day Company. Pictures to promote role-playing situations are provided by *Words and Actions*.[21]

TEXTBOOKS

A prime source material for the social studies is the textbook. Frequently, it is the basis or guide for the organization of instruction in the classroom. For this reason, care should be exercised in selecting textbooks. The following criteria of selection are suggested:

1. Is the organization of the textbook easily followed?
2. Are the concepts presented in a manner that most students will be able to understand?
3. Are there sufficient illustrations, maps, charts, and graphs to increase the reader's understanding?
4. Does the text contain a table of contents, index, and sufficient appendices to aid the reader in locating information?
5. Are references listed where additional information can be secured such as films, books, records, etc.?
6. Is there a teacher's guide with suggestions concerning uses of the text in instruction?
7. Does the text contain a multiethnic presentation of topics?
8. Are the authors respected scholars from the social sciences and social studies education?

Utilization

For too long, the textbook has been used by too many teachers as a crutch in teaching social studies. This practice is exemplified by the teacher who, whether unprepared for the lesson or lacking an understanding of teaching principles, has each student read a text paragraph orally and then discusses the concepts. The underachieving reader does not benefit from the oral reading, and the more capable reader is bored. Several other techniques would better utilize the resources of the text. A sample lesson plan follows:

Topic: Mexico.
Objective: To understand the culture of Mexico by acquiring knowledge of its historical development.
Materials: Textbook study guide and visual aids.
Procedure: Group I, Underachievers—Use a textbook that contains a physical-political . map of Mexico, a historical map of early Spanish explorations, and a story of Cortez's capture of the Aztecs. Use realia of

Mexico including a record of Spanish and Mexican Indian language, dolls dressed in native Mexican dress, pottery, and musical instruments.

1. Using the maps in the textbook, discuss the location of Mexico in relation to the United States and its geographical areas. Using the historical map, trace the routes of the Spanish explorers to Mexico.

2. Read the story of Cortez's explorations and conquest of the Aztecs to the children. Observe the realia of the country and discuss how the Spanish conquest influenced its culture.

Group II, Average Achievers—Have the children read silently the chapter on Spanish exploration and conquest in Mexico. Establish a purpose for the reading with the following study guide questions.

1. Try to determine the reasons why Spanish explorers were interested in the New World, particularly Mexico.

2. Trace the route of Cortez in Mexico and discuss the type of problems the physical features and climate gave his men.

3. Why was Cortez able to defeat the Aztecs?

Group III, Above Average—Use the same study guide as above with these additional activities and questions.

1. Read another account of the Spanish conquest from a different resource and compare the two descriptions.

2. Are there any discrepancies in the accounts?

3. If so, why would this difference occur?

4. Discuss what you think Mexico would be like if the French or English had conquered the Aztecs.

In this sample lesson plan, all groups utilize the text, but each with a different level of abstraction.

The textbook can be used by committees for exploratory reading or research information. The suggested references included in the textbook provide excellent resources for extending research activities. The textbook also can be used for individual or group research in a problem-solving situation. Textbooks have been criticized because too many of the situations they present describe life in suburbia and fail to interest children who come from disadvantaged homes. Today, many textbook series are attempting to alleviate this problem.

Beginning teachers find the guide to the textbook invaluable for suggested teaching techniques, instructional activities, and additional resources. The danger in using the guide lies in the teacher's failure to adapt the use of the text and guide to the needs of the children in a particular classroom.

MULTIMEDIA KITS

Media materials organized around a major topic have been assembled into kits for use in social studies instruction.[22] These kits contain films, filmstrips, records, realia, written information, and a teacher's guide to instruction. International Communications Foundation has assembled these kits for the study of other cultures. Many kits are available for countries such as Pakistan, Afghanistan, and Turkey, for which it often is difficult to find sufficient information at the children's level.

Examples of the materials available for Mexico are films of the life of the people, filmstrips on aspects of the culture, records of the language and stories, and realia including dolls dressed in the native dress, pieces of clothing, and musical instruments. Also included is the teacher's guide with background information and suggested teaching techniques for use of the materials.

As previously mentioned, MATCH[23] kits provide multimedia materials organized around a specific topic. Currently available are these: *The City, A House of Ancient Greece,* and *Japanese Family.*

The advantage in using such kits is the accessibility of materials— many of the items included would be rather difficult for teachers to obtain elsewhere. Because some children will learn more from handling realia than from viewing a filmstrip about the items, use of the different media helps meet individual differences in the classroom.

These kits can be used with several teaching methods. Individual or committee research can be organized around the materials for unit teaching or problem solving. Because disadvantaged children benefit from concrete materials, the kits can be used successfully with them. The kits also can be presented to the entire class as introduction to a new study or for enrichment. More of these kits will soon be available.[24]

FILMS AND FILMSTRIPS

Films and filmstrips provide visual representations instead of the abstract representations provided by text descriptions. Both sources of information are important and must be carefully chosen. Criteria to be applied in the selection of every film or filmstrip include:

1. Is there continuity of content throughout the film or filmstrip?
2. Is the photography of good quality?
3. Is the sound of the film easily understood?
4. Will the presentation of the film or filmstrip contribute to the understanding of the topic under study?
5. Is the information presented accurate?
6. Can the information be understood by elementary school children?

Films and filmstrips should be selected on the basis of their best use. Does the film introduce a new topic effectively? Does it provide background information? Does it motivate interest in a topic? Would it be effective as a culmination to a study? Guides are available to aid teachers in selecting films and filmstrips.[25]

Effective presentation and follow-up of films and filmstrips is vital if they are to be worthwhile. An introduction to the film or filmstrip should establish some purpose for viewing them. Study-guide questions can be provided or oral discussions can be conducted to introduce the film or filmstrip. Follow-up after the viewing is necessary to clarify understanding and reinforce learning. Children can evaluate the effectiveness of the presentation.

FREE AND INEXPENSIVE MATERIALS

The teacher can obtain an abundance of free or inexpensive materials, which can aid considerably in social studies instruction. Travel agencies and transportation companies such as airlines, railways and trucking industries supply teachers with posters and charts of places to visit and with booklets that explain the transportation systems. These packets may also have background information for the teacher. Chambers of commerce in cities and states and embassies of countries provide extensive information about their areas. They often include maps and colorful posters and regulations for travel in their areas.

A variety of manufacturing, publishing, packing, and insurance companies have educational materials that they supply to teachers upon request. Agencies of the United States government provide materials at a small charge. Several guides are available with information about securing these materials.[26]

Pictures and information from magazines and newspapers often add resources for the study of a topic. Teachers should start a file of these resources for use when needed. For easy accessibility, the file should be divided into possible topics of study. Slides, photographs, and postcards collected from the teacher's own travels also should be added to the resources.

SELECTED REFERENCES

Boocock, Sarane S., ed. *Simulation Games in Learning*. Beverly Hills, Calif.: Sage, 1968.

Fraser, Dorothy M., ed. "Review of Curriculum Materials." *Social Education* 33 (April 1969): 575–91.

Free and Inexpensive Learning Materials, 14th ed. Nashville, Tenn.: George Peabody College for Teachers, 1968.

Gillespie, Judith. "Analyzing and Evaluating Classroom Games." *Social Education* 36 (January 1972): 33–42.

Hogan, Arthur J. "Simulation: An Annotated Bibliography." *Social Education*, 32 (March 1968): 242–44.

Ingraham, Leonard W. "Teachers, Computers, and Games: Innovations in the Social Studies." *Social Education* 31 (January 1967): 51–53.

Joyce, Bruce R. *New Strategies For Social Education*. Chicago: Science Research Associates, 1972.

Rader, William. "Yes—But What is Available?" *Social Education* 32 (January 1968): 57–59.

Rice, Marion. "Materials for Teaching Anthropology in the Elementary School." *Social Education* 32 (March 1968): 254–56.

Source Directory Single Concept Films, Technicolor Commercial and Educational Division, 1300 Frowley Drive, Costa Mesa, Calif. 92627.

Walsh, Huber M. "Learning Resources for Individualizing Instruction." *Social Education* 31 (May 1967): 413.

Wentworth, Donald R., and Lewis, Darrell R. "A Review of Research on Instructional Games and Simulations in Social Studies Education." *Social Education* 37 (May 1973): 432–40.

PART *VI*

Evaluation

Was the program of instruction in social studies successful? Were the teaching techniques effective? Have the objectives of the social studies program been achieved? Have the children acquired skill in intuitive thinking, problem solving, and developing human relationships? These are some of the questions that teachers ask themselves about the outcomes of their social studies instruction. How can they determine the answers to these questions? What evaluation techniques are effective for different aspects of the program? Will the method of instruction affect the evaluation techniques?

Part six discusses methods and techniques of evaluation used at the national, state, local, and classroom level.

CHAPTER *13*

Evaluation
of Social Studies Instruction

Evaluation of instruction at any level is accomplished by measuring the extent to which established objectives have been achieved. The objectives state the expected outcome of a learning experience. The technique of evaluation that best determines if the objectives have been reached must be selected. The primary purpose of evaluation is to determine the progress achieved, and when necessary, to initiate changes for the improvement of instruction.

The focus of emphasis of evaluation, however, might shift at the different levels—classroom, local, state, and national. The teacher in the classroom is concerned about Johnny and his success in getting along with the committee members, while local, state, and national concerns are more global—can all the Johnnys and Marys operate cooperatively in society? At each level, objectives are established on the basis of a philosophy of education. Then, utilizing various evaluation techniques, the success with which these objectives or goals have been met is determined. It is possible that different techniques of evaluation will be used at each level.

IN THE CLASSROOM

Evaluation of instruction in the classroom must be continuous and it must encompass all learning experiences. A teacher should ask himself these questions as he plans learning experiences. How will this experience benefit the children? What objective will this experience achieve? Too often teachers are not certain of what should be evaluated or of the standards of evaluation to be used. The teacher must establish goals for social studies instruction for the entire year, and he must attempt to select daily or weekly experiences that will lead to the attainment of these overall goals. Obviously, evaluation is necessary throughout the teaching/ learning process and it is particularly important at these points: (1) evaluation of a single learning experience; (2) evaluation of a group of experiences organized around a unit of study, a problem-solving situation, or the presentation of concepts from the social sciences; and (3) longitudinal evaluation of the progress achieved over a period of time whether a month, semester, or year.

At each point in the educational program, the teacher establishes objectives or goals, provides learning experiences for the children, and then evaluates the extent to which the objectives have been achieved. The evaluation involves several facets—the success of the teaching technique, the materials utilized, and the attainment of the objectives. Figure 13.1 illustrates this process.

The learning experience should be evaluated in terms of (1) the achievement of the goal or objective and (2) the effectiveness of the teaching/learning process and the materials utilized. It is important to determine how the goal was reached as well as whether or not it was reached.

If objectives have been stated in behavioral or performance terms, the teacher can evaluate the learning experience more easily. An example (given in Chapter One) of a cognitive objective stated in behavioral terms is:

Learning Experience

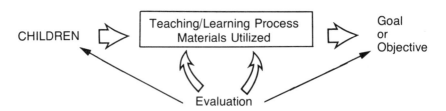

Figure 13.1   Process of Evaluation

To list at least one of the Mexican holidays that is different from those celebrated in the United States.

This knowledge can be evaluated by an objective test item or an essay question. The teacher knows exactly what he expects of the children.

An example of an affective objective in behavioral terms is:

To value the contributions the many subcultures have made to our heritage and express an appreciation for them.

Again, the teacher knows exactly what is to be evaluated. He can observe the children at work and at play and note their comments concerning other cultures or he can use a questionnaire to determine each child's attitudes.

Readily acknowledged is the difficulty of evaluating the affective domain (attitudes of children) versus the cognitive (thinking) domain. Obviously, a measurement of the knowledge or understanding gained through instruction can be more easily obtained (through objective or essay tests, discussions, and conferences) than can a measurement of the attitudes acquired or changed by the instruction. Successful evaluation, however, requires that multiple methods be used to complete the total picture of the achievement of the instruction. Observation, a checklist, and conferences may help the teacher to assess attitudes; an objective test reveals the amount of knowledge gained; and an essay test, group discussion, or conferences indicate the amount of understanding obtained. More difficult to assess may be the problem solving and valuing skills of the individual. Each method contributes its data to complete the complicated task of evaluation.

METHODS OF EVALUATION

Observation

In the classroom, the teacher uses the method of observation most frequently to evaluate learning experiences. As he conducts a discussion, the teacher observes the expressions on the children's faces. Are they interested? Which children are always ready with the answers? Are there shy children who never enter the discussion? Do the children appear to understand? Would another method of instruction be more effective? During committee participation, the teacher observes the children working together. Are they willing to share? Do all children participate in the decision making? Does the child understand what he values? Does he act upon his values? Does each child complete his work on time? Because it is often difficult to remember the answers to these questions for each child, teachers find it necessary to develop a record for reference. The most common method used is a checklist of the objectives of the learning experience on which the teacher records each child's success or failure in achieving the objectives. A sample checklist follows:

	Willing to Share	Listens to Others	Completes Work on Time	Expresses his Opinion	Posesses Creative Ideas	Identifies Value Issues	
1. Kay	U	U	O	O	O	O	
2. Bill	O	S	S	U	U	U	
3. Rita	S	S	S	S	S	O	
4. Gay	O	O	O	O	O	S	

O Outstanding
S Satisfactory
U Unsatisfactory

Another method of recording on a checklist involves keeping a separate sheet for each child, for example:

Name ___Gay___		Grade ___5___	
Map Skills		Social Skills	
Ability to interpret color key	✓	Gets along well with others	
Locates places readily		Accepts responsibility	✓
Ability to compute distances	✓	Shares materials	
		Supports his value beliefs	✓

Use of the checklist facilitates observation and makes it more systematic. The checklist provides the teacher with definite behaviors to observe and a valuable record for use in reporting the children's progress.

Rating Scales

Rating scales are more effective when the teacher is attempting to pinpoint a child's performance on a scale ranging from excellent to poor. Also, scores from rating scales are more easily translated to letter grades if such grades are required by the school's evaluation system. The following is a sample rating scale that a teacher might use during an observation period.

Objective: The child participates effectively in committee activities.

	Excellent 5	Good 4	Average 3	Fair 2	Poor 1
1. Contributes ideas to group goal.					
2. Does his share of the work.					
3. Listens to the opinions of others					
4. Works well with all types of children.					

Anecdotal Records

Some teachers prefer to make specific notations about children's behavior. With this procedure, they record statements about how each child reacts to learning situations or responds to statements from peers and the teacher.

An example:

Stewart was quite disturbed by Kim's reference to colored people. He corrected her, but also showed hostility toward her during game time.

Rita improves daily in her ability to understand the valuing process. She quickly identified the value issues in today's skit.

This type of record is particularly helpful when teachers are reporting pupil progress to parents through conferences or letters.

Conferences

The opportunity to converse with a child on a one-to-one basis is often a revealing form of evaluation. Attitudes, understandings, and interests may be assessed by this method. Certain guidelines should be followed while conducting an individual conference: (1) Identify the goal of the conference—for example, direct the conference toward learning about the child's attitude toward people of another culture. (2) Prepare questions and discuss them during the conference—for example, If you were to take a trip anywhere in the world, where would you go? Why? (3) Establish good rapport with the child as soon as possible—discuss some personal event, a game, an interest. (4) Listen carefully to what the child has to say and make notations about the child's answers after the completion of the conference. (5) Leave the conference with a word of encouragement to the child and a definite plan of action.

The child should be prepared for the conference and have his own goals and questions in mind. Before the conference, he might ask himself: Are there questions I want to ask? Do I understand what we are studying? Does the teacher have suggestions for the improvement of my work? Do I have any projects or research I want to complete? If children have a thorough understanding of the purpose of the conference, it will be more profitable for them and their teacher.

Individual conferences also can be used for oral testing. The child who has difficulty with reading or the child who has a mental block about tests can have the test administered in a conference situation.

Individual conferences are open to criticism, especially if the class is large, because of their time consuming nature. However, five or ten minutes spent with an individual child is well worth the time in terms of the results. In addition to obtaining the intended evaluation, the teacher also will get to know the child and he may be able to spot possible problem areas. Ten minutes in an individual conference could help solve a problem for a child that might otherwise go unnoticed. In the conference, the teacher also has the opportunity to guide the child toward self-evaluation with questions such as: Are you satisfied with your work? Do you think you could do better? What do you see as your problems? The number of individual conferences held will depend upon their success, their intended purpose, the children's reactions, and the teacher's schedule.

Group Discussion

The total class or small groups such as a committee can evaluate a mutual experience. This type of session permits a child to compare his or his group's performance with the performances of others and to assess his role in the total group process. In this situation, children should learn the role of constructive criticism. This example of a group discussion following the presentation of an oral report by a committee of sixth graders illustrates these values.

TEACHER:	As we look at the guidelines for presenting an oral report, how well do you think Kim's group followed them?
JERRY:	I didn't think the report was very good.
SANDY:	Me, neither.
TEACHER:	What is our first rule in evaluating someone else' work?
JERRY:	Look for something that was well done and comment on that.
TEACHER:	Yes, and if we criticize their work, what should we include?
SANDY:	We should tell what was wrong and how it might be improved.
TEACHER:	Right, shall we try again.
JUAN:	The group used pictures to illustrate their talk, which made it easier to understand.
KATHY:	Yes, and the art work was so beautiful.
MURPHY:	Some of the members of the group did not speak out so we all could hear and that spoiled their report.
SID:	If they had moved out in front of the table, it would have been easier to hear them.

In this example, the teacher quickly turned what might have been a useless evaluation session into positive constructive criticism.

In another group session, the children might evaluate the behavior and performance of the group on a field trip and the value of the trip. The teacher would ask for comments on general behavior and request that children refrain from pinpointing individual actions that might embarrass the children involved. In assessing the value of the field trip, the children compare what they learned with the goals that were previously established for the trip.

Group discussions can be conducted daily to evaluate topics such as groups working together, the effectiveness of materials utilized, or the children's understanding of a film, outside speaker, or a reading. Such discussion aids teachers in determining the effectiveness of a particular teaching technique. Through discussion and comparison of the work completed by individuals and groups, these sessions also lead the child toward introspection and evaluation of his own behavior and achievement.

Problem Solving and Valuing Skills

Different forms of evaluation are necessary with the introduction of the problem-solving-inquiry methods of teaching and the valuing process. The usual objectives or essay-type tests are not effective because the outcomes of the instruction are expected to be the process skills of identifying a problem, formulating hypotheses, testing hypotheses, drawing conclusions, forming generalizations, and applying generalizations to new situations. The valuing skills are choosing the value, prizing it, and acting upon it.

Problem situations can be presented to children in different forms. The following might be given to younger children and they would generate their own alternative solutions.

The children in a poor neighborhood of a community wanted a playground. There was a vacant lot on their street owned by one of the businessmen in town. How could they get their playground?

An example of the problem with alternate solutions provided is:

One of the boys in the second-grade class was poorly dressed and often came to school hungry. He would take food from the other children's lunch boxes. There was a cafeteria in the school, but the boy did not have enough money for lunch. What should the children do?

1. The children could take turns bringing lunch for the boy.
2. The children could tell the teacher the boy was taking the food.
3. The children could have their mothers put extra food in their lunch boxes for the boy to take and then not say anything to the teacher.
4. The boy could work in the cafeteria to earn his lunch.
5. Other solutions?

Older children can be confronted with more difficult problems such as these:

If a country is wealthy, has a high standard of living, sufficient natural resources, and a surplus of goods, should it help a country or countries that have starving people? If so, how can it help, and would there be any problems if it helped the country or countries? How much help should the wealthy country give the poorer country?

In addition to determining the extent of a child's problem-solving skills, it also is possible to assess the valuing process in the same manner. By asking the child to indicate what value issues are involved in the problem and what value is most important to him, depending on the solution he chooses, the teacher can determine to some extent whether the child can identify value issues and support his own value positions. Any of the above problems will give such an opportunity as well as the one that follows:

If a manufacturing company is seriously polluting a stream with its waste products and killing the fish that are usually caught by sportsmen, what should the local community do? The company has indicated it cannot withstand the cost of controlling the pollution and continue to operate at full capacity. Many of the people in the community work for the company and would lose their jobs if the company closed. On the other hand, the sportsmen bring tourist trade to the community. The community has discussed the possibility of forming an industrial park.

Here are some possible solutions for the community. Choose the one you think is best and give your reason for choosing it.

1. Share the expense for controlling the pollution with the manufacturing company.
2. Pass an ordinance that would force the company to control the pollution or close the factory.
3. Ignore the situation and lose the tourist trade.
4. Form a community corporation to develop an industrial park that would control polluting wastes for this company and encourage future companies to move into the area.
5. Suggest any other solutions you have.

Do you need further information before you can make a decision? If so, what information is needed?[1]

Analyzing Questions

The thought patterns of children can be assessed to a certain extent through the types of questions they ask. The following dialogue was taped during an activity where the teacher wrapped an article inside a package and the children were required to ask questions to find out what was in the box.

T: There is something in this box.

P: Can I feel it?

T: No. You have to try and figure out what is in this box by asking questions. You can't say is it this? Is it that? You have to ask questions that will help you figure out what is in the box. The only kind of question that you can ask me would be the kind that I can answer with yes or no. Now here is a sample of the kind of question that you could ask. You could say, Is it made of wood? And I would say yes or no.

P: Is that little girl in there?   (Remembering the first discussion)

T: No. Now remember that I said you have to ask the kind of questions that I can answer yes or no and you have to work toward finding out what is in the box.

P: It is made out of wood? Is it made out of steel?

T: No.

P: Is it made out of rubber?

T: I will have to take back what I said. It is partly made out of wood.

P: Is it plastic?

T: No.

P: Does it have legs?

T: No.

P: Does it have wheels?

T: No.

P: Does it have a face?

T: No.

P: It's a picture and it is made out of paper.

T: No.

P: Is it a box?

P: Is it made out of leather?

T: No.

P: Is it a piece of fish?

P: Is it a doll?

T: No.

P: Is it made out of glass?

P: Is it red, white, and blue?

T: Part of it is red.

P: Is it black, green, purple?

T: Part of it is purple.

P: Purple donkey.

P: Is it a little dress?

T: No.

P: Is it some animal?

T: Yes.

P: Is it different colors?

T: Yes.

P: Is it a painting she made for you?

P: We can't guess it.

T: Keep asking questions. You are asking is it this or is it that. Why don't you find out something about it?

P: How can we?

T: By asking questions.

P: Will you tell us one thing about it?

T: If you ask a couple of questions, I will let you shake the box.

P: Is it a house?

T: You are not asking questions about it. What do you know so far about it?

P: That it is a different color and that it is made of wood.

T: It is part wood. That is right.

P: Is it the face of her?

T: No, it doesn't have anything to do with the little girl.

P: Is it a pitcher?

P: Is it a little bucket?

T: No, it doesn't have anything to do with the little girl. What do you know so far about it?

P:	That it is different colors and it is part wood.
P:	Where did you get it from?
T:	It has to be a question that I can answer yes or no.
P:	Can we shake it?
T:	You can shake it but not too hard.
P:	Is it a block?
T:	No.
P:	Is it puzzles?
T:	No.
P:	Is it cookies?
T:	No.
P:	Is it hammers and things?
P:	Are you going to open it?
T:	You are going to try and find out without my opening it.
P:	Is it wooden blocks?
T:	Remember I said it was only partly wood. What other kinds of questions can you ask about it to try and find out?
P:	May I see what it is?
T:	No. Ask some questions about it. We said it wasn't steel.
P:	Is there any green in it?
P:	Is there yellow?
T:	Yes.
P:	Do you know what it is?
T:	Sure, I put it in there.
P:	She got it from her house.
T:	I said there was some red in it.
P:	Some play apples, play bananas, and play grapes.
P:	Different-colored rocks?
T:	No.
P:	What they eat out of.
P:	OK, open it then.
T:	You haven't asked good questions.
P:	It is a statue.
P:	You got it from home, what can it be?
T:	What are you doing? Instead of asking questions about it, you are guessing. So think of some questions you can ask about it.

267

P: I don't never know any.

T: Can't think of any questions?

P: Nope. Not a single one.

P: What can you use it for?

P: Can you make a house with it?

T: What are some questions you can ask about what you can do with it?

P: Is it big?

T: Now, Lonnie is getting to some good questions. No, Lonnie, it is not.

P: Is it little? Is it middle-sized?

T: It is a little larger . . . .

P: Is it large?

T: No.

P: Is it soft?

T: No. That is a good question. So if it isn't soft—

P: It is hard.

P: Is it hairy?

T: No. Your questions are very good.

P: What kind of wood is it made out of?

P: A wood that is different colors and not the kind of wood that we have.

T: No, it is not pretty wood necessarily. Kind of plain wood.

P: It is made out of skin?

T: Can you think of any more questions? Now what do you know about it so far?

P: It is different colors and it is hard.

P: It is middle-sized.

T: Very good. How can you find out what we do with it?

P: What they work with, what they eat on.

P: What their floor is made of.

T: I told you it didn't have anything to do with the little girl. You want to find out what you do with it. How would you find out what you do with it? What questions would you ask?

P: Does it take batteries—a motorcar?

P: Do they play with it?

T: Yes, you might call it that.
P: Is it round?
T: Yes.
P: Little round blocks?
T: The whole thing isn't round but part of it is round.
P: She said is it a scarecrow?
T: No. That is made out of part wood, isn't it? There is one thing that you haven't asked me about it.
P: Can you burn it?
T: No. The wood part of it you can burn but you wouldn't want to.
P: Could it be a clock? Is it striped?
T: There is one question you haven't asked me. You haven't asked me if you could eat it.
P: They are food.
P: Is it a sugarcane?
T: No, but it has sugar in it.
P: It is candy.
T: Yes, I'll give each one of you a piece.[2]

From the discussion it is apparent that some children have difficulty using the information that they have gathered and piecing it together. Their thought patterns are not well organized. Certain children can be identified as asking the better questions and interpreting the data acquired from the previous questions. It is obvious that these children need subsequent opportunities to ask questions to get information, as well as opportunities to interpret data that is already provided.

Teacher-made Objective Tests

The type of test a teacher devises depends upon: (1) what he is attempting to evaluate and (2) his method of instruction. For example, the teacher who has presented purely factual information would not give an essay test that evaluates understanding. It is advantageous for a teacher to prepare his own tests, for he can then base the test questions on the things he deems most valuable for evaluation.

Essay tests can present problem-solving situations, determine understanding, and assess attitudes. The reliability of scoring an essay test is questioned, however, and the time required to score such tests is listed as a disadvantage.

Objective tests can test a wider variety of topics and they are more easily scored, but they require more time in planning and writing than essay tests. The Educational Testing Service suggests the following steps in preparing an objective test:

Step 1. List the major topics covered in your particular teaching unit. This list should not exceed five.

Step 2. Indicate the number of items you want to devote to each topic.

Step 3. List under each topic the things you want students to know about, understand, or be able to do.

Step 4. Collect materials on which to base items. (Textual material—typed or read by teacher, pictorial material, music, or specimens to be examined).

Step 5. Begin writing of the items for your test.

Step 6. Submit the items for review by another individual.

Step 7. Rewrite or replace defective items.

Step 8. Arrange the items into a test. May be arranged from easy to hard or by common subject matter.

Step 9. Prepare directions for the test.

Step 10. Prepare an answer key.[4]

Different test elements that can be included are: (1) completion, (2) alternative response, (3) multiple choice, (4) matching, and (5) rearrangement.

Child Self-evaluation

One of the goals of instruction in any subject area is that of self-evaluation. The child who can look at his progress objectively and discuss his strengths and weaknesses has achieved a valuable goal. Checklists based on the objectives of social studies are helpful, for they allow children to record their achievement. The process of asking himself questions about his activities aids the child in self-evaluation. Examples of items for such checklists are:

1. Do I try to do my best work?
2. Do I look carefully at all sides of an issue?
3. Do I enjoy working with others?
4. Do I listen carefully to what others have to say?
5. Do I respect others who are different from me?

Another method of self-evaluation involves keeping a record of a series of experiences, for example, in a diary or log. As the child records a description of the activities, he should be encouraged to discuss his role and the degree to which he achieved the goal he had established for himself. Children, too, need to realize that there are limitations to their abilities and that they should not set unrealistic goals for themselves.

LOCAL

Evaluation of social studies instruction by the school district generally is accomplished through standardized achievement tests, evaluation by committees of teachers, and self-evaluation by individual teachers. Standardized tests are administered to determine the children's achievement as compared to the norm for selected groups across the nation. Care should be exercised in interpreting these tests, because children in a specific school may vary considerably in socioeconomic status, experiential background, and intelligence from the groups on which the norms are based. These test results should not be used to compare the teachers' competency nor the pupils' achievement from year to year. These tests do, however, indicate areas of instruction (for example, map-reading skills or sequential relationships) in which groups of children score low, and therefore, need additional instruction.

The *Sixth Mental Measurements Yearbook* provides information about the most recently published tests. This information includes a discussion of the test, price, and publisher. *Tests in Print* is another resource that briefly describes all tests available.

A selected list of standardized achievement tests for elementary school follows:

Sequential Tests of Educational Progress: Social Studies, 1063, Grades 4–6. Cooperative Test Division, Educational Testing Service, Princeton, N. J.

Stanford Achievement Test: Intermediate and Advanced Social Studies, Grades 5–9, 1954 (New York: Harcourt Brace Jovanovich, 1954).

Metropolitan Achievement Tests: Social Studies, Grades 5–6, 1964 (New York: Harcourt Brace Jovanovich, 1964).

Committees of teachers selected across school and grade levels are frequently assigned the task of evaluating the social studies program for the school district. On the basis of the established objectives, they may develop evaluation forms to be used in observing classrooms. The observation forms may be completed by administrators or teacher members of the committee during a visit in the classroom. The disadvantage of this method of evaluation is the limited time available for observation in each classroom.

There are formal models of evaluation that have been developed that provide guidelines for districts to use in the collection of evaluation data. One example is that by Robert Stake where he suggests a matrix of description and judgment with three main bodies of information: antecedents, transactions, and outcomes.[5]

Teacher self-evaluation forms also may be developed to be completed by individual teachers. This type of evaluation gives the teacher the opportunity to evaluate his program of instruction in terms of the standards established by the school district. If such a self-evaluation form is not a part of the school district evaluation, a teacher may devise his own checklist.

More recently, evaluation has been attempted through the use of videotaping, interaction analysis, and team-teaching observation. Use of a portable videotape machine permits television of a segment of the instruction conducted in the classroom. Preserving the experience on tape allows the teacher to view the lesson later by himself or with a supervisor to determine its effectiveness.

Interaction analysis has been researched by numerous educators including Marie Hughes, B. Othaniel Smith, Donald Medley and Harold Mitzel, John Withall, and Ned Flanders. Category systems have been developed to classify verbal interaction in the classroom. These systems consist of the establishment of basic categories for teacher talk, student talk, and silence to determine the amount and type of verbal interaction. Tape recordings of class sessions can be made for later categorization of the verbal interaction, or trained observers can use the category systems during live sessions. Most researchers emphasize that these systems are not directed toward evaluation per se, but rather toward the improvement of instruction. Their aim is to move away from teacher-talk-dominated instruction toward more verbal interaction from the students.

Team-teaching situations permit evaluation of instruction in group sessions by team members. As one member of the team is presenting a lesson, other team members can observe and analyze the results of the instruction. Close faculty cooperation is necessary to permit open discussion of the methods and techniques used during the teaching. Self-evaluation also can be accomplished by a team member as he observes another's teaching.

At the state level, the primary purpose for evaluation is to determine the extent of curriculum revision necessary, if any. As previously mentioned, the state of Oregon divided the state into ten regional districts for preevaluation before attempting any revision. California organized a Statewide Social Science Study Committee, which includes classroom teachers and social science educators, to analyze the social studies curriculum of the state. The most recent Progress Report of March, 1968, presents the abridgement of the new curriculum. Pennsylvania conducted an Educational Quality Assessment where ten broad goals were selected.[6]

NATIONAL

Evaluation of instructional programs has been undertaken at the national level in recent years. Different groups of teachers, scholars, and curriculum specialists from across the national have been engaged to develop instruments of evaluation. The National Assessment of Educational Progress, a study funded by the United States government, states as its purpose "to find out what Americans know, believe, and are able to do. It is an attempt to find out about such attainments in most fields of study considered important in American schools; for example, reading, language arts, science, mathematics, social studies, citizenship, fine arts, and vocational education."[7] Notice that social studies and citizenship education are to be assessed separately.

Before test items were written, the objectives of social studies education were developed. These objectives were formulated by a panel of scholars, teachers, and curriculum specialists and were submitted to a panel of citizens for approval. Five major objectives were established:

1. Within the limits of his maturity, a person competent in the area of social studies uses analytic, scientific procedures effectively.
2. A person competent in the area of social studies has knowledge relevant to the major ideas and concerns of social scientists.
3. He has a reasonable commitment to the values that sustain a free society.
4. He has curiosity about human affairs.
5. He is sensitive to creative-intuitive methods of explaining the condition.[8]

"On the basis of these objectives, a series of test items will be devised for varying age levels. Interviews, free response, and questionnaires will also be utilized. Data will be obtained for boys and girls, geographic regions, four age groups; 9, 13, 17 year-olds, and adults; urban, suburban, and rural, and two socioeconomic levels."[9] Concern has been expressed that this evaluation will be used to compare school districts, schools, and teachers. But because the data will be compiled in categories as stated above, there will be no way to compare different school districts, schools, teachers, or children.

A Center for the Study of Evaluation, a Research and Development Center funded by the U. S. Office of Education and located at the University of California at Los Angeles, has been developing a very complete model for the whole process of evaluation.[10]

Evaluation of an educational program—whether at the national, state, local, or classroom level—is an attempt to determine what the instruction has accomplished. It cannot be completed, however, without goals or objectives as guideposts. Research has indicated that: "evaluation is not really done well on any large scale; vague or ambiguous objectives contribute heavily to a lack of comprehensive evaluation; in most cases evaluation is regarded as being synonymous with grading and testing; and evaluation is not viewed as an integral part of instruction."[11] Thus, a teacher must identify that which is to be the result of his instruction, plan the learning experience, expose the children to it, and then evaluate to determine the success of his program.

SELECTED REFERENCES

Berg, Harry, ed. *Evaluation in Social Studies*, 35th Yearbook. Washington, D. C.: National Council for the Social Studies, 1965.

Bloom, Benjamin S., ed. *Taxonomy of Educational Objectives: Cognitive Domain*. New York: David McKay, 1956.

Campbell, Vincent N., and Nichols, Daryl G. "National Assessment of Citizenship Education." *Social Education* 32 (March 1968): 279.

Chase, W. Linwood, and John, Martha Tyler. *A Guide for the Elementary Social Studies Teacher*. 2d ed. Boston: Allyn & Bacon, 1972.

Dal Santo, John. "Guidelines for School Evaluation." *Clearing House* (November 1970), pp. 181–85.

Eulie, Joseph. "Meaningful Tests in Social Studies." *Clearing House* (February, 1971), pp. 333–36.

Gooler, Dennis D. "Evaluation and Change in the Social Studies." *Education Products Report* 3 (October 1969),pp. 6–13.

Jarolimek, John, and Walsh, Huber M., eds. *Readings for Social Studies in Elementary Education*. 2d ed. New York: Macmillan, 1969.

Krathwohl, David R.; Bloom, Benjamin S.; and Mesia, Bertram B. *Taxonomy of Educational Objectives: Affective Domain*. New York: David McKay, 1964.

Kurfman, Dana. "A National Assessment of Social Studies Education." *Social Education* 31 (March 1967): 209–11.

Michaelis, John U., ed. *Social Studies in Elementary Schools*. Washington, D. C.: National Council for the Social Studies, 1962.

Morrissett, Irving, "Accountability, Needs Assessment, and Social Studies." *Social Education* 38 (April 1973): 271–79.

Ploghoft, Milton, and Shuster, Albert H. *Social Science Education in the Elementary School*. Columbus, Ohio: Charles E. Merrill, 1971.

Ragan, William B., and McAulay, John D. *Social Studies for Today's Children*. New York: Appleton-Century-Crofts, 1964.

Notes

CHAPTER 1

[1]H. Millard Clements, William R. Fielder, and B. Robert Tabachnick, *Social Study: Inquiry in Elementary Classrooms* (Indianapolis: Bobbs-Merrill, © 1966), p. 13. Reprinted by permission of the publisher.

[2]H. Millard Clements, "Inquiry and Social Studies," *Elementary English*, March 1966, pp. 300–301.

[3]Peter B. Dow, "Man: A Course of Study Reexamined," *Teacher Guide, Trial Teaching Edition, Man: A Course of Study* (Cambridge, Mass.: Education Development Center, 1967). Reprinted by permission of Education Development Center, Inc.

[4]Robert F. Mager, *Preparing Instructional Objectives* (Palo Alto, Calif.: Fearon, 1962), p. 3.

[5]Mager, *Preparing Instructional Objectives*, p. 12.

[6]Robert M. Gagné and George F. Kneller, "Behavioral Objectives? Yes or No?" *Educational Leadership* 29 (February 1972): 394–400.

[7]Milton Rokeach, *Beliefs, Attitudes and Values* (San Francisco: Jossey-Bass, 1968), pp. 113–14.

[8]Rokeach, *Beliefs, Attitudes, Values*, p. 160.

[9]Ibid., p. 161.

[10]John U. Michaelis and A. Montgomery Johnston, eds., *The Social Sciences: Foundations of the Social Studies* (Boston: Allyn & Bacon, 1965), p. 28.

[11]Jan O. M. Broek, *Geography: Its Scope and Spirit* (Columbus, Ohio: Charles E. Merrill, 1965), p. 59.

[12]Broek, *Geography: Its Scope and Spirit*, p. 79.

[13]David Easton, "Introduction: The Current Meaning of Behavioralism in Political Science," in *The Limits of Behavioralsim in Political Science*, ed. James C. Charlesworth (Philadelphia: American Academy of Political Science, 1962), p. 7.

[14]Frank J. Sorauf, *Political Science: An Informal Overview* (Columbus, Ohio: Charles E. Merrill, 1965), p. 7.

[15]Richard S. Martin and Rueben G. Miller, *Economics and Its Significance* (Columbus, Ohio: Charles E. Merrill, 1965), p. 9.

[16]Michaelis et al., *Social Sciences*, p. 243.

CHAPTER 2

[1]Martin Deutsch and M. Brown, "Social Influence in Negro-White Intelligence Differences," *Journal of Social Issues* 20 (December 1964): 24–35.

[2]E. H. Hill and M. C. Giammatteo, "Socio-Economic Status and Its Relationship to School Achievement in the Elementary School," *Elementary English* 40 (March 1963): 265–70

[3]John S. Gibson, *New Frontiers in the Social Studies* (New York: Citation Press, 1967), p. 49.

[4]Gibson, *New Frontiers in the Social Studies*, p. 49.

[5]*A Conceptual Framework for the Social Studies in Wisconsin Schools*, rev. ed. (Madison: Wisconsin State Department of Education, 1967), p. 2.

[6]*Conceptual Framework for the Social Studies*, p. 3.

[7]*Knowledge Processes & Values in the New Social Studies*, pp. 45, 46.

[8]Gibson, *New Frontiers in the Social Studies*, p. 96.

[9]"Project Materials Analysis," *Social Education* 36 (November 1972): 769.

[10]*The Development of Man and His Culture*, No. 30 (Athens: University of Georgia, Anthropology Curriculum Project, 1966), p. 1–2.

[11]"Man: A Course of Study," *Social Education* 36 (November 1972): 743.

[12]*Teachers' Handbook for Elementary Social Studies* Introductory Edition by Hilda Taba, p. 1–3. Copyright © 1967 by Addison-Wesley Publishing Company, Inc. All rights reserved. Reprinted by permission.

[13]The Taba Program in Social Science: Teacher's Guide for *People in Communities* by Kim Ellis and Mary C. Durkin, p. 4–5. Copyright © 1972 by Addison-Wesley Publishing Company, Inc. All rights reserved. Reprinted by permission.

[14]The Taba Program in Social Science: Teacher's Guide for *People in Communities* by Kim Ellis and Mary C. Durkin. T3–T6. Copyright © 1972 by Addison-Wesley Publishing Company, Inc. All rights reserved. Reprinted by permission.

CHAPTER 3

[1]John Dewey, *How We Think* (Boston: D. C. Heath, 1933), p. 106.

[2]Joseph J. Schwab, *The Teaching of Science as Inquiry* (Cambridge: Harvard University Press, 1962), p. 14, cited in Charlotte Crabtree, "Supporting Reflective Thinking in the Classroom," in *Effective Thinking in the Social Studies*, eds. Jean Fair and Fannie Shaftel (Washington, D. C.: National Council for the Social Studies, 1967), p. 89.

[3]Fair and Shaftel, *Effective Thinking*, p. 89.

[4]Jerome Bruner, *On Knowing* (Cambridge: Belknap Press of H.U. Press, 1962), p. 82–83.

[5]Hilda Taba, *Teacher's Handbook for Elementary Social Studies* (Reading, Mass.: Addison-Wesley, 1967), p. 87.

[6]Taba, *Teacher's Handbook for Elementary Social Studies*, p. 88.

[7]Ibid.

[8]Ibid., p. 89.

[9]The writer acknowledges the use of Benjamin Bloom and David Krathwohl, *Taxonomy of Educational Objectives: Handbook I. The Cognitive Domain* (New York: David McKay, 1956).

[10]Maxine Dunfee and Helen Sagl, *Social Studies Through Problem Solving* (New York: Holt, Rinehart, and Winston, 1966), pp. 23-24.

[11]H. Millard Clements, William R. Fielder, and B. Robert Tabachnick, *Social Study: Inquiry in Elementary Classrooms* (Indianapolis: Bobbs-Merrill, 1966), p. 117.

[12]Clements, Fielder, and Tabachnick, *Social Study*, pp. 118-21.

[13]Ibid., p. 68.

[14]Robert Fox, Ronald Lippitt, and John Lohman, *Teaching of Social Science Material in the Elementary School*, USOE Cooperative Research Project E-011 (Ann Arbor, Michigan: University of Michigan, 1964), cited in Fair and Shaftel, *Effective Thinking in the Social Studies*, p. 156.

[15]Fair and Shaftel, *Effective Thinking in the Social Studies*, p. 157.

[16]Luman H. Long, ed., *The World Almanac* (New York: Newspaper Enterprise Association, Inc., 1974), p.585.

[17]Adapted from materials produced by the High School Geography Project, Association of American Geographers.

[18]Dialogue from classroom presentation by Ronald E. Sterling and a group of fifth and sixth graders.

[19]Bruner, *On Knowing*, p. 87.

[20]Ibid., p. 95.

[21]J. S. Allender, "Some Terminants of Inquiry Activity in Elementary School Children," *Journal of Educational Psychology* 61 (1970): 220-25.

[22]D. P. Ausubel, "A Teaching Strategy for Culturally Deprived Pupils: Cognitive and Motivational Considerations," *School Review* 71 (1963): 456.

[23]Bernard Z. Friedlander, "A Psychologist's Second Thoughts on Concepts, Curiosity, and Discovery in Learning," *Harvard Educational Review* 35 (1965): 25.

CHAPTER 4

[1]Carter V. Good, *Dictionary of Education* (New York: McGraw-Hill, 1945), p. 436.

[2]John U. Michaelis, *Social Studies in a Democracy* (Englewood Cliffs, N. J.: Prentice-Hall, 1968), p. 199.

[3]John Jarolimek, *Social Studies in Elementary Education* (New York: Macmillan, 1967), p. 56.

[4]Jarolimek, *Social Studies in Elementary Education*, pp. 44-45.

[5]William Ragan and John D. McAulay, *Social Studies for Today's Children* (New York: Appleton-Century-Crofts, 1964), pp. 201-202.

[6]Paul R. Hanna, "Revising the Social Studies: What is Needed?" *Social Education* 27 (April 1963): 190-96.

[7]*Social Studies Framework for the Public Schools of California* (Sacramento: California State Department of Education, 1962), pp. 90-109.

[8]Helen Huus, *Children's Books to Enrich the Social Studies* (Washington, D. C.: National Council for the Social Studies, 1966).

[9]Mary E. Greig, *How People Live in Africa* (Chicago: Benefic Press, 1963), p. 17.

[10]Ragan and McAulay, *Social Studies for Today's Children,* p. 217.

[11]Lavone A. Hanna, Gladys Potter, and Neva Hageman, *Unit Teaching in Elementary School* (New York: Holt, Rinehart, and Winston, 1963), pp. 233-34.

CHAPTER 5

[1]Virginia D. Moore, "Guidelines for the New Social Studies," *Instructor* 79 (February 1970): 112-13.

[2]Barry K. Beyer, *Inquiry in the Social Studies Classroom* (Columbus, Ohio: Charles E. Merrill, 1971), p. 111.

[3]Wisconsin State Department of Public Instruction, *Knowledge Processes and Values in the New Social Studies,* Bulletin No. 185, p. 6.

[4]Beyer, *Inquiry in the Social Studies Classroom,* p. 126.

[5]Jerome S. Bruner, *The Process of Education* (Cambridge: Harvard University Press, 1960), p. 7.

[6]Bruner, *The Process of Education,* p. 18.

[7]Ibid., p. 20.

[8]Bruce R. Joyce, *Strategies for Elementary Social Science Education* (Chicago: Science Research Associates, 1965), p. 25. Reprinted by permission of the publisher.

[9]Joyce, *Strategies for Elementary Social Science Education,* p. 29.

[10]Ibid., p. 37.

[11]Joseph J. Schwab, "The Concept of the Structure of a Discipline," *Educational Record* 43 (July 1962): 197-205.

[12]G. W. Ford and Lawrence Pugno, eds., *The Structure of Knowledge and the Curriculum* (Chicago: Rand McNally, 1964), p. 89.

[13]Ford and Pugno, *Structure of Knowledge and the Curriculum,* p. 89.

[14]Vincent Presno and Carol Presno, *Man in Action Series: People and Their Actions,* Teachers' Ed. (Englewood Cliffs, N. J.: Prentice-Hall, ©1967), p. ix.

[15]Presno, *Man in Action Series,* p. ix.

[16]Ford and Pugno, *Structure of Knowledge and the Curriculum,* p. 95.

[17]Joyce, *Strategies for Elementary Social Science Education,* p. 13.

[18]Agnes M. Inn, "Beginning Teacher's Problems in Developing Social Studies Concepts," *Social Education* 30 (November 1966): 540.

[19]*Regional Studies: Investigating Man's World* by Paul Hanna, Clyde Kohn and Clarence Ver Steeg. Copyright ©1970 by Scott, Foresman and Company. p. T-4.

[20]*Regional Studies: Investigating Man's World* by Paul Hanna, Clyde Kohn and Clarence Ver Steeg. Copyright ©1970 by Scott, Foresman and Company. p. T-5.

[21]Ibid., p. T-7.

[22]Educational Research Council of Greater Cleveland, *Teachers' Guide: Learning About Our Country* (Cleveland: GCSSP/1, I 1966), xi.

[23]*Teachers' Guide*, p. xiii.
[24]Ibid.
[25]Ibid., p. 90.
[26]Ibid., p. 116.

CHAPTER 6

[1]Susan S. Stodolsky and Gerald Lesser, "Learning Patterns in the Disadvantaged," *Challenging the Myths: The Schools, The Blacks, and the Poor, Harvard Educational Review* No. 5 (1971), p. 43.

[2]Stodolsky and Lesser, "Learning Patterns in the Disadvantaged," p. 43.

[3]Staten W. Webster, ed., *The Disadvantaged Learner: Knowing, Understanding, Educating* (San Francisco: Chandler, 1966), p. 491.

[4]Dorothy J. Skeel, "Determining the Compatibility of Student Teachers for Culturally Deprived Areas by Means of a Cultural Attitude Inventory" (Doctoral Dissertation, Pennsylvania State University, 1966).

[5]Patrick J. Groff, "Dissatisfaction in Teaching the CD Child," *Phi Delta Kappan* 45 (November 1963): 76.

[6]Skeel, "Determining the Compatibility of Student Teachers," p. 80.

[7]A. Harry Passow, ed., *Education in Depressed Areas* (New York: Teachers College Publications, 1963), p. 113.

[8]Frank Riessman, "The Culturally Deprived Child: A New View," *School Life* 45 (April, 1963): 57.

[9]Carl Bereiter and Siegfried Engelmann, *Teaching Disadvantaged Children in the Preschool* (Englewood Cliffs, N. J.: Prentice-Hall, © 1966), pp. 6-19.

[10]Bereiter and Engelmann, *Teaching Disadvantaged Children*, p. 42.

[11]Ibid., p. 31.

[12]Webster, *Disadvantaged Learner*, p. 477.

[13]Webster, *Disadvantaged Learner*, p. 586.

[14]Helen K. MacKintosh, Lillian Gore, and Gertrude Lewis, *Educating Children in the Middle Grades* (Washington, D. C.: U. S. Department of Health Education, and Welfare, Office of Education, 1965), p. 39.

[15]From Dorothy J. Skeel, *Children of the Street: Teaching in the Inner-City* (Pacific Palisades, Calif.: Goodyear, 1971), pp. 47-52.

[16]Webster, *Disadvantaged Learner*, p. 593.

[17]Fannie R. Shaftel and George Shaftel, *Role-Playing for Social Values: Decision Making in the Social Studies* (Englewood Cliffs, N. J.: Prentice-Hall, 1967), p. 149.

[18]W. A. Gill, "Innovative Social Studies in the Urban Elementary School," *School and Community* 58 (May 1972): 6; L. Rich, "Instead of Molotov Cocktails," *American Education* 33 (June 1970), pp. 11-15.

[19]Glenys G. Unruh, "Urban Relevance and the Social Studies Curriculum," *Social Education* 33 (October 1969): 710.

[20]Shaftel and Shaftel, *Role Playing for Social Values*.

[21]Josie Crystal, "Role Playing in a Troubled Class," *Elementary School Journal* 69 (January 1969): 169-79.

[22]Gill, *Innovative Social Studies*, p. 7.

CHAPTER 7

[1]John McHale, "Global Ecology: Toward the Planetary Society," a chapter in *It's Not Too Late*, edited by Fred Carvell and Max Tadlock (Beverly Hills, Calif.: Glencoe Press, 1971), p. 29.

[2]McHale, "Global Ecology," p. 39.

[3]Gordon J. F. MacDonald, "Caring For Our Planet," *Current*, January 1970, p. 21.

CHAPTER 8

[1]Leonard S. Kenworthy, "The International Dimension of Education," *Association for Supervision and Curriculum Development*, NEA, 1970, p. 115.

[2]James Becker, ed., *An Examination of Objectives, Needs and Priorities in International Education in U. S. Secondary and Elementary Schools*, Final Report, Project No. 6–2908, Contract No. OEC 1-7-002908-2028 (Washington, D. C.: U. S. Office of Education, Bureau of Research, July 1969), p. 29.

[3]Lee Anderson, "An Examination of the Structure and Objectives of International Education," *Social Education* 32 (November 1968):646.

[4]Lester R. Brown, "An Overview of World Trends," *Futurist*, December 1972, p. 225.

[5]Alvin D. Loving, "Men for Tomorrow: A Challenge for Education," in Alice Miel and Louise Berman, eds., "Educating the Young People of the World," Association for Supervision and Curriculum Development, NEA, 1970, p. 2.

[6]Donald N. Morris, "Developing Global Units for Elementary Schools," *International Education for Spaceship Earth*, David C. King, ed. (New York: Foreign Policy Association, 1970), p. 73.

[7]Loretta E. Klee, "Larger Horizons for the Child: A Fourth Grade Experiment," *Social Education*, 13 (February 1949): 69.

[8]Judith V. Tourney and Donald N. Morris, *Global Dimensions in U. S. Education: The Elementary School* (New York: The Center for War/Peace Studies of the New York Friends Group, 1972) p.34.

[9]Tourney and Morris, *Global Dimensions in U. S. Education*, p.28.

[10]Malcolm P. Douglass, "Ship Adoption May Be Your 'International Thing.'" *Social Education* 34 (January 1970): 56.

[11]These activities have been taken from Donald N. Morris and Edith W. King, "Bringing Spaceship Earth Into Elementary School Classrooms," *Social Education* 32 (November 1968): 676–77.

[12]Harold M. Long, and Robert N. King, *Improving the Teaching of World Affairs: The Glens Falls Story* (Washington, D. C.: National Council for the Social Studies, 1964).

CHAPTER 9

[1]Lawrence Kohlberg, "Moral Education in the Schools: A Developmental View," *School Review* 74 (Spring 1966): 7.

[2]Kohlberg, "Moral Education," p. 19.

[3]Ibid., p. 20.

[4]Ibid., p. 23.

[5]Louis E. Raths, Merrill Harmin, and Sidney B. Simon, *Values and Teaching* (Columbus, Ohio: Charles E. Merrill, 1966).

[6]Sidney B. Simon, "Values Clarification vs. Indoctrination," *Social Education* 35 (December 1971): 902.

[7]Kohlberg, "Moral Education," p. 17.

[8]James A. Mackey, "Moral Insight in the Classroom," *Elementary School Journal* 73 (February 1973): 235.

[9]Kohlberg, "Moral Education," p. 24.

[10]Lawrence Kohlberg, "Stage and Sequence: The Cognitive-Developmental Approach to Socialization," in David A. Goslin, ed., *Handbook of Socialization Theory and Research* (Chicago: Rand McNally, 1969), p. 347-480.

[11]"Values Clarification vs. Indoctrination," *Social Educaion* 35 (December 1971): 904.

[12]Activities organized for growth in the affective domain. A curriculum designed by Uvaldo Palomares and Harold Bessell, *Methods in Human Development* (San Diego, Calif.: Institute for Personal Effectiveness in Children).

CHAPTER 11

[1]*Skill Development in Social Studies*, 33rd Yearbook (Washington, D. C.: National Council for the Social Studies, 1963), p. 157.

[2]*New Viewpoints in Geography*, 29th Yearbook (Washington D. C.: National Council for the Social Studies, 1959), p. 150.

[3]Haig A. Rushdoony, "Achievement in Map-Reading: An Experimental Study," *Elementary School Journal,* 64 (November 1963): 74.

[4]Jan O. M. Broek, *Geography: Its Scope and Spirit* (Columbus, Ohio: Charles E. Merrill, 1965), p. 90.

[5]Gary Manson and Carol J. Price, "Introducing Cities to Elementary School Children," *Journal of Geography* (May 1969), p. 296.

[6]Fred A. Lampe and Orval C. Schaefer, Jr., "Land-Use Patterns in the City," *Journal of Geography* (May 1969), p. 302.

[7]Service Publication No. M44, Denoyer-Geppert Company, Chicago, Ill.

CHAPTER 12

[1]May Hill Arbuthnot, *Children and Books* (Chicago: Scott, Foresman, 1964), pp. 565–66.

[2]*Simulation Games for the Social Studies Classroom* (New York: Foreign Policy Association, 1968), p. 9.

[3]*Simulation Games for the Social Studies Classroom*, p. 114.

[4]Charles Christine and Dorothy Christine, "Four Simulation Games That Teach," *Grade Teacher*, October 1967, p. 112. ·Reprinted from *Grade Teacher*

Magazine by permission of the publishers. Copyright October 1967 by Teachers Publishing Corp.

[5]Christine and Christine, "Four Simulation Games That Teach," p. 114.

[6]Education Development Center, 15 Miflin Place, Cambridge, Mass. 02138.

[7]Western Publishing Co., New York, N. Y.

[8]Science Research Associates, Chicago, Ill.

[9]Western Behavioral Sciences Institute, 1150 Silverada, La Jolla, Calif.

[10]Educational Research Council of America, Houghton Mifflin Publishing Co., Boston, Mass.

[11]Urban Systems, Inc., 1033 Mass. Avenue, Cambridge, Mass.

[12]Macmillan Publishing Co., New York, N. Y.

[13]Interact, P. O. Box 262, Lakeside, Calif. 92040.

[14]Western Publishing Co., New York, N. Y.

[15]The Johns Hopkins University, Department of Social Relations, Baltimore, Md. 21218.

[16]Industrial Relations Center, University of Chicago, Chicago, Ill.

[17]Board of Cooperative Educational Services, Westchester Country, Yorktown Heights, N. Y. 10598.

[18]*Simulation Games for the Social Studies Classroom*, p. 21.

[19]Leonard W. Ingraham, "Teachers, Computers, and Games: Innovations in the Social Studies," *Social Education* 31 (January 1967):53.

[20]Donald R. Wentworth and Darrell R. Lewis, "A Review of Research on Instructional Games and Simulations in Social Studies Education," *Social Education* 37 (May 1973): 432–440.

[21]Fannie R. Shaftel and George Shaftel, *Words and Actions* (New York: Holt, Rinehart, and Winston).

[22]International Communications Foundation, 9033 Wilshire Boulevard, Beverly Hills, Calif.

[23]The Children's Museum, Boston, Mass.

[24]Educational Media Guide, The Educational Media Council, New York.

[25]*Education Film Guide* (H. W. Wilson, 950 University Avenue, New York City, New York 10052).

[26]*Educators' Progress Service* (Randolph, Wisconsin 53956) publishes *Educators' Guide to Free Films, Educators' Guide to Free Filmstrips, Educators' Guide to Free Social Studies Materials, Educators' Guide to Free Teaching Aids,* and *Educators' Index to Free Materials*.

CHAPTER 13

[1]From Dorothy J. Skeel and Owen Hagen, *The Process of Curriculum Change* (Pacific Palisades, Calif.: Goodyear, 1971), pp. 81–83.

[2]Dialogue from Dorothy J. Skeel, *Children of the Street: Teaching in the Inner City* (Pacific Palisades, Calif.: Goodyear, 1972), pp. 27–31.

[3]Educational Testing Service, Cooperative Test Division, Princeton, N. J. *Making Your Own Tests*, p. 15.

[4]ETS,*Making your Own Tests,* pp. 1–7.

[5]Dennis D. Gooler, "Evaluation and Change in the Social Studies," *Education Products Report* 3 (October 1969): 6–13.

[6]*Educational Quality Assessment.* Pennsylvania Department of Education, 1970.

[7]Dana Kurfman, "A National Assessment of Social Studies Education," *Social Education* 31 (March 1967): 210–11.

[8]"A National Assessment of Social Studies Education," pp. 210–11.

[9]Ibid., p. 209.

[10]Irving Morrisett, "Accountability, Needs Assessment, and Social Studies, " *Social Education* 37 (April 1973): 271.

[11]Joseph Decaroli, "What Research Says to the Classroom Teacher/ Evaluation," *Social Education* 36 (April 1972): 433.

Index

A

Activities:
  committee, 206
  culmination, 98
  current affairs, 152
  disadvantaged, 140–42
  group, 96, 97
  individual, 96, 97
  initiation, 66, 91
  integrating, 97
  map and globe, 218
Anderson, Lee, 168, 183
Anthropology:
  concepts, 20, 21
  definition, 18
  methods of inquiry, 18
  project, 42ff
Anthropology project, 42ff
Arbuthnot, May Hill, 234
Art, 98
Arranged environment, 92
Aspiration level, 28
Attitudes:
  definition, 9, 10
  evaluation, 257
  measurement, 10
Ausubel, D.P., 140

B

Bacon, Philip, 218, 230
Bailey, Wilfred, 42ff
Band-wagon technique, 156

Banks, James A., 49
Becker, James, 168, 183
Behavioral objectives:
  attitudes, 9, 10
  definition, 7
  knowledge and understanding, 8
  skills, 11–13
  value, 11
  writing, 7, 8
Bereiter, Carl, 128
Berg, Harry, 275
Beyer, Barry K., 80, 107, 108
Bloom, Benjamin, 64, 275
Broek, Jan O.M., 14, 224
Brubaker, Dale, L., 80
Bruner, Jerome, 25, 56, 79, 109

C

Carpenter, Helen, 187, 188, 230
Cartoons, 240
Charts, 242
Chase, Linwood, 50, 105
Checklist, 258
Children's books:
  criteria, 234
  fiction, 235
  informational, 235
Children's interests, 88, 89
Classroom atmosphere, 60, 87, 129, 176
Clements, H. Millard, 5, 65
Committees:
  organization, 204
  reporting activities, 203ff
  responsibilities:
    chairman, 205

Committees: responsibilities: (cont.)
  members, 205, 206
  teacher-pupil planning, 204
  what is to be gained, 203
Community environment, 27
Concept:
  definition, 107
Conceptual framework:
  definition, 36, 109
  methodology, 107
Conceptualization, 108
Conditions of change:
  cold war, 25
  mechanization, 26
  social and racial problems, 26
  Sputnik, 25
  technological advancement, 26
  transportation, ease of, 25
  underdeveloped nations, 25
  U.S. leadership, 25
  urbanization, 26
Controversial issues:
  economic, 160
  environmental, 162
  political, 161
  social, 158
Crabtree, Charlotte, 13
Criteria:
  cartoons, 240
  children's books, 234
  films and filmstrips, 250
  informational books, 235
  simulation games, 237
  textbooks, 247
Culminating activities, 98ff
Current affairs, 149ff
  economic, 160ff
  environmental, 162
  objectives, 150
  political, 161
  social, 158ff
  suggested activities, 152ff
  when to start, 150
Curriculum:
  disadvantaged, 123ff
  social studies, 23ff
Curriculum development:
  local, 26ff
  national, 40ff
  state, 35ff

D

Debate, 154, 211
Deutsch, Martin, 28

Disadvantaged:
  activities, 140
  benefits, 143
  characteristics, 124
  curriculum model, 131ff
  definition, 123
  environmental considerations, 127
  instructional considerations, 134
  learning conditions:
    classroom, 129
    role of the child, 142
    role of the teacher, 130
  materials, 142
  objectives, 126
  organizational patterns, 134
  selection of content, 130
Discipline, 108
Discovery, 56
Dow, Peter, 6
Dunfee, Maxine, 64

E

Easton, David, 15
Economics:
  concepts, 20, 21
  definition, 16
  method of inquiry, 16
  project, 41
Economic concepts, 20, 21
Economic issues, 160ff
Educational goals, 28
Educational Testing Service, 270
Emotionalized words, 154
Engleman, Siegfried, 128
Environmental factors, 27
Environmental issues, 162ff
Estvan, Frank, 22
Evaluation:
  classroom, 255
  local, 271
  methods, 255ff
    analyzing questions, 265
    anecdotal records, 260
    conferences, 260
    group discussion, 261
    observation, 257
    problem solving, 264
    rating scales, 259
    self-evaluation, 270
    standardized tests, 71–72
    teacher-made tests, 269
    unit, 99
    valuing, 264
  national, 273
  state, 273

Expanding environment, 24, 89
Experiential background, 27
Exploratory questioning, 92

F

Factors affecting curriculum
    development:
  aspirations, 28
  community environment, 27
  educational goals, 28
  experiential background, 27
  intelligence, 28
  other factors, 29
  socioeconomic background, 27
Fair, Jean, 65
Fielder, William, 5, 65
Fenton, Edwin, 80
Films, 93, 250
Filmstrips, 93, 250
Ford, G.W., 112, 113
Fox, Robert, 65
Fraenkel, Jack R., 50
Free and inexpensive materials, 250
Friedlander, Bernard, 80

G

Gagne, Robert, 8
Games, 228, 237
Generalizations, 21, 22
Geography:
  concepts, 20, 21
  definition, 14
Gibson, John, 22, 36, 41
Goldmark, Bernice, 80
Goodlad, John, 50
Grambs, Jean, 143
Graphs, 242ff
Greater Cleveland Social Science
    Program, 116–20
Group activities, 96

H

Hanna, Paul, 24, 89
History:
  concepts, 20, 21
  contribution, 14
  definition, 13
Huns, Helen, 93, 236

I

Individual activities, 96
Inductive reasoning, 55
Initiation:
  problem solving, 66ff
  unit, 91ff
Inn, Agnes, 113
Inquiry, 55ff
Inquiry model, 65
Integrating activities, 97
Intelligence, 28
Interaction analysis, 272
Interdisciplinary approach, 111,
    112, 116–20
Interest inventory, 88, 89
Intergroup Relations Curriculum, 42
International understanding:
  activities, 178ff
    intermediate grades, 182
    primary grades, 181
  atmosphere of the classroom, 176
  involvement with another
    culture, 177
  objectives, 168
  spaceship earth, 167ff
  when to start, 172
Introduction, 3–50
Investigating Man's World, 114–16

J

Jarolimek, John, 83, 88, 215
Johnston, A. Montgomery, 22
Joint Council in Economic
    Education, 40
Joyce, Bruce, 109, 112

K

Kennamer, Lorin, Jr., 230
Kenworthy, Leonard, 168, 184
Knowledge:
  definition, 8
  evaluation, 257
Kohlberg, Lawrence, 192, 193, 194
Kozol, Jonathan, 143
Kurfman, Dana, 274

L

Language arts, 97
Lippitt, Ronald, 65

Lohman, John, 65
Long, Harold M., 166, 184

M

Mackey, James, 194, 201
McAulay, John D., 22, 88, 104, 230
Mager, Robert, 7
Man: A Course of Study, 44
Manson, Gary, 227
Map and globe skills:
  basic, 227ff
  fifth grade, 220
  first grade, 219
  fourth grade, 220
  interest centers, 226
  intermediate-grade activities, 222
  kindergarten, 218
  primary-grade activities, 221
  problem situations, 223
  second grade, 219
  sixth grade, 221
  third grade, 220
  urban map skills, 226
Massialas, Byron, 80
MATCH, 248
  The City, 43, 227
  House of Ancient Greece, 43
  The Japanese Family, 43
Materials:
  cartoons, 240
  children's books, 234
  disadvantaged, 142
  films and filmstrips, 250
  free and inexpensive, 250
  games, 237
  graphs and charts, 242
  multi-media kits, 249
  pictures, 246
  programmed, 239
  simulation, 237
  textbooks, 247ff
Methodology:
  derived from structure of social
      sciences, 107–22
  for disadvantaged, 123ff, 135ff
  problem solving, 55–80
  unit development, 83–105
Michaelis, John U., 13, 19, 83
Miller, Rueben G., 16
Morris, Donald N., 170, 178ff, 184
Morrissett, Irving, 122, 274
Muessig, Raymond, 22
Multidisciplinary approach:
  definition, 111, 112
  sample program, 114–16

Multi-media kits, 249
Music, 98

N

Name calling, 156, 157
National assessment, 273
National Council for Geographic
    Education, 40
National Council for Social Studies, 40
National Geographic, 229
Newspaper:
  class, 153
  reading, 154
Nongraded classes, 134

O

Objectives:
  behavioral, 7–13
  current affairs, 150
  disadvantaged, 126
  international understanding, 168
  problem-solving method, 62ff
  specified, 8
  unit method, 84
Oregon Council for Curriculum
    and Instruction, 36

P

Panel discussions, 211
Passow, Harry, 128, 143
Pen pals, 177
Philosophy:
  definition, 18
Physical education, 98
Pictures, 246
Plain-folks technique, 156, 157
Political science:
  concepts, 20, 21
  definition, 15
  method of inquiry, 15
Political issues, 161ff
Price, Roy, 122
Problem solving:
  advantages and disadvantages, 79
  conditions for learning 60–62
    classroom, 60
    role of the teacher, 60–62
  discrepant data, 71
  initiation, 66
  objectives, 62–64
  presentation of facts, 67

Problem solving: (cont.)
  problem selection, 64
  questioning, 57ff
  responsibility of child, 78
  role playing, 71
  tape presentation, 73
  waste basket technique, 70
Programmed material, 239
Project Social Studies, 25, 41
Propaganda techniques:
  band wagon, 156, 157
  emotionalized words, 154, 157
  name calling, 157
  plain folks, 157
  testimonial, 156, 157
  vague general statements, 157
Psychology:
  definition, 18

Q

Questioning, 57ff

R

Racial problems, 158ff
Ragan, William, 88, 104
Raths, Louis, 193
Reflective thinking, 55
Reissman, Frank, 128, 143
Resource unit, 83
Rice, Marion, 42ff
Rogers, Vincent, 22, 215
Rokeach, Milton, 10, 197
Role-playing:
  committee reports, 212
  current affairs, 153
  disadvantaged, 140
  valuing, 200
Ryan, Frank, 22

S

Sagl, Helen, 64
Schwab, Joseph, 109, 122
Self-evaluation:
  pupil, 270
  teacher, 272
Servey, Richard, 81
Shaftel, Fannie, 65, 140, 141, 245
Simon, Sidney B., 193, 200
Simulation, 141, 142, 237
Skeel, Dorothy J., 81, 125, 135
        144, 215

Skill development, 187ff
  committee, 203ff
  critical thinking, 209
  intellectual, 12, 206
  locating information, 208
  map and globe, 217ff
  motor, 12
  note taking, 209
  oral reporting, 210
  outlining, 209
  social, 12, 214, 215
  using reference materials, 207
    encyclopedia, 207
    library, 207
    primary sources, 207
    textbook, 207
  valuing, 192ff
  written reports, 210, 213
Skills:
  definition, 11–13
  intellectual, 12
  motor, 12
  social, 12
Smith, James A., 215
Social issues, 158ff
Social sciences:
  anthropology:
    concepts, 20, 21
    definition, 18
    method of inquiry, 18
    project, 42ff
  contribution, 13–20
  economics:
    concepts, 20, 21
    definition, 16
    method of inquiry, 16
    project, 41
  geography:
    concepts, 20, 21
    definition, 14
    method of inquiry, 14
  history:
    concepts, 20, 21
    definition, 13
    method of inquiry, 13
  philosophy:
    definition, 18
  political science:
    concepts, 20, 21
    definition, 15
    method of inquiry, 15
  psychology:
    definition, 18
  sociology:
    concepts, 20
    definition, 16
    method of inquiry, 17

Social skills, 12, 214
Social studies:
    definition, 3
    objectives, 4–6
Social Science Laboratory Units, 41
Social Studies Framework for the
        Public Schools of California, 90
Socioeconomic level, 27
Sociology:
    concepts, 20, 21
    definition, 16
    method of inquiry, 17
Sorauf, Frank, 15
Standardized tests, 272
Sterling, Ronald E., 73ff, 167ff
Structure:
    advantages and disadvantages, 121
    definition, 107ff
    interdisciplinary, 111, 112, 116–120
    multidisciplinary, 111, 112, 114–116
    philosophy, 113ff
    role of teacher, 113
    sample programs, 111ff

T

Taba, Hilda, 44, 56, 144
    levels of questioning, 57
Taba Program in Social Science:
    concepts, 47–49
    objectives, 46
    rationale, 44
Tabachnick, B. Robert, 5, 65
Teacher-made tests, 269ff
Teacher-pupil planning, 93ff, 204ff
Teaching unit, 83
Team teaching, 134, 273
Testimonial, 156
Textbooks:
    criteria, 247
    utilization, 247ff
TV programs, 152, 212

U

Understandings:
    definition, 9
    measurement, 26J
Unit Development:
    advantages and
        disadvantages, 104–105
    conditions of classroom, 87
    culminating, 98
    directing children's interests, 89
    individual and group activities, 96
    initiation, 91ff
    integrating activities, 97
    objectives, 84

Union development: (cont.)
    resource, 100ff
    role of the children, 86
    role of the teacher, 86
    selection, 87
    topics, 90
    teaching unit, 83
    teacher-pupil planning, 93ff
Units:
    advantages and
        disadvantages, 104–105
    children's interests, 88
    conditions of learning, 87
        classroom, 87
        role of children, 86
        role of teacher, 86
    definition, 83
    evaluation, 99
    objectives, 84
    organization, 84
    resource, 83
    selection, 87
    teaching, 83
University of Georgia, 42ff, 173
Urbanization, 26
Using reference material, 207ff
Utilization of materials, 234ff

V

Vague general statements, 156, 157
Values:
    clarifying, 38, 193
    classroom activities, 194ff
    definition, 11
Valuing:
    atmosphere of classroom, 193
    classroom dialogue, 198ff
    evaluation, 263, 264
    process of valuing, 193
    rationale, 191
    stages of moral development, 192
    teaching strategies, 194ff

W

Ward, Barbara, 166
Warner, Sylvia Ashton, 144
Webster, Staten, 124, 129, 130, 144
Williams, Marianne. E.T., 201
Wisconsin Social Studies
        Committee, 36ff, 107
Wisniewski, Richard, 230

Z

Zacharias, Jerrold, 25